'At a time when pessimistic analyses of the failur[e of democracy are] ubiquitous, *Saving Democracy* provides a refreshing[ly constructive] approach.' – **Matthew Flinders, Vice President of the Political Studies [Association] of the United Kingdom and Founding Director of the Sir Bernard Crick Centre, University of Sheffield, UK**

'Evans and Stoker have brought together all the most innovative thinking on how to reform democracy into one book, offering a root-to-branch review of our political systems to unlock democracy's full potential. Brimming with insight and data, and written in a clear and accessible style, *Saving Democracy* will be at the centre of debates surrounding how to reform democracy in the years to come.' – **Hugo Drochon, Assistant Professor in Political Theory, University of Nottingham, UK**

'Democracy can be saved! Adopting a systematic perspective that captures exciting developments in participatory and deliberative democracy, alongside potential reforms to long-established institutions and practices of democracy such as parliaments, public bureaucracies and political parties, Evans and Stoker offer a much-needed recipe for democratic renewal. Whether or not you agree with all their proposals, you will admire their audacity in weaving together these disparate ingredients for systems change.' – **Graham Smith, Professor of Politics, University of Westminster, UK**

'*Saving Democracy* offers a unique integration of sub disciplines in and around democratic studies that are rarely combined in such a comprehensive manner. Behaviour studies, Democratic Theory studies, Democratic Innovation studies, Public Policy studies and Transparency studies, just to cite the main ones, are all integrated, creating a systemic theory of change for democracy. The book is a perfect companion for modules in public policy analysing democratic innovation.' – **Paolo Spada, Lecturer in Comparative Politics and Methodology, University of Southampton, UK**

SAVING DEMOCRACY

Mark Evans and Gerry Stoker

BLOOMSBURY ACADEMIC
LONDON • NEW YORK • OXFORD • NEW DELHI • SYDNEY

BLOOMSBURY ACADEMIC
Bloomsbury Publishing Plc
50 Bedford Square, London, WC1B 3DP, UK
1385 Broadway, New York, NY 10018, USA
29 Earlsfort Terrace, Dublin 2, Ireland

BLOOMSBURY, BLOOMSBURY ACADEMIC and the Diana logo are trademarks of Bloomsbury Publishing Plc

First published in Great Britain, 2022

Copyright © Mark Evans and Gerry Stoker, 2022

The authors have asserted their right under the Copyright, Designs and Patents Act, 1988, to be identified as Author of this work.

For legal purposes the Acknowledgements on p. xi constitute an extension of this copyright page.

Cover image © Andriy Onufriyenko/Getty

All rights reserved. No part of this publication may be reproduced or transmitted in any form or by any means, electronic or mechanical, including photocopying, recording, or any information storage or retrieval system, without prior permission in writing from the publishers.

Bloomsbury Publishing Plc does not have any control over, or responsibility for, any third-party websites referred to or in this book. All internet addresses given in this book were correct at the time of going to press. The author and publisher regret any inconvenience caused if addresses have changed or sites have ceased to exist, but can accept no responsibility for any such changes.

A catalogue record for this book is available from the British Library.

A catalog record for this book is available from the Library of Congress.

ISBN:	HB:	978-1-3503-2825-9
	PB:	978-1-3503-2824-2
	ePDF:	978-1-3503-2826-6
	eBook:	978-1-3503-2827-3

Typeset by Integra Software Services Pvt. Ltd.
Printed and bound in Great Britain

To find out more about our authors and books visit www.bloomsbury.com and sign up for our newsletters.

CONTENTS

List of Boxes, Figures and Tables　vii
Preface　ix
Acknowledgements　xi

1　Why 'saving' democracy?　1

2　Can democracy be saved?　17

Part 1: Interventions at the input stage to enable critical citizenship　33

3　Building participatory governance systems　35

4　Direct democracy　45

5　Deliberative democracy　59

6　Design-led digital democracy　71

Part 2: Interventions at the throughput stage to improve the quality and integrity of politics　89

7　Reforming elected assemblies　91

8　Cleaning up politics　105

9　Embedding experts and evidence in democratic governance　117

10　Old and new media: power with responsibility　133

Part 3: Interventions at the output stage to improve the capacity of politics to deliver quality services and policy outcomes　145

11　Improving the public service experience: the search for public value　147

12　Representative democracy and crisis management　163

Contents

13 Future proofing democracy — 179

14 In conclusion – restoring and strengthening the 'protective power' of democracy — 193

Postscript — 205
Notes — 207
Index — 239

LIST OF BOXES, FIGURES AND TABLES

Boxes

3.1	Creating a constitution for Mexico City through a participatory governance system	41
5.1	Participatory governance system informing deliberation on the termination of pregnancy	60
5.2	The 2007 European Citizen's Consultation	62
5.3	University of Michigan consensus dialogue on autonomous vehicles	65
5.4	How sortition or a civic lottery works: the case of Climate Assembly UK	67
5.5	The democracy in Geelong Citizen's Jury Project	68
6.1	Digital vision – the case of eGov2015 Singapore	78
6.2	Robotic process automation and artificial intelligence – the case of NADIA	80
6.3	Examples of the use of gamification for enhancing the quality of public participation	83
6.4	The City Council of Madrid's 'Decide Madrid'	85
7.1	Outreach and the National Assembly for Wales	100
7.2	e-Petitions	101
7.3	Outreach and the Scottish parliament	102
7.4	The UK Parliament's citizens' assembly on the future of social care	103
8.1	The Nolan principles	115
9.1	The Wiltshire criteria	125
9.2	What does a strategic, innovative, evidence-based policy system look like?	131
10.1	The Edward Snowden Leaks	135
10.2	Cambridge Analytica and the Facebook data breach	136
10.3	Criteria for evaluating the democratic performance of the media	144
11.1	Criteria for evaluating the democratic performance of public services	161
12.1	Criteria for evaluating democratic performance during and after crisis	177
13.1	Criteria for evaluating whether governments have achieved a long-term decision culture	190

Figures

2.1	What would you like Australian democracy post-Covid-19 to look like?	31
6.1	Service co-design	75
8.1	Building an integrity culture	113

List of Boxes, Figures and Tables

9.1	Covid-19 governance in Australia	120
9.2	Best practice collaborative governance	128
11.1	The scope of public involvement in public value decision-making	152
11.2	Why outcomes? Being strategic in government	157
12.1	The rise and fall of support for British Prime Minister Boris Johnson during Covid-19	172
12.2	Perceptions of political leadership during the Covid-19 crisis	174

Tables

1.1	The political system – challenges confronting representative democracies	9
1.2	The key features of allegiant and assertive civic cultures	12
3.1	Participatory governance systems	39
4.1	Three strategies of localism	49
4.2	Examples of participatory budgeting (PB) processes around the world	54
6.1	Four models of bureaucracy and the role of IT and digital technology	73
6.2	Most frequently mentioned government exemplars of digital innovation	77
7.1	Non-legislative roles for elected assemblies and citizen engagement	99
7.2	Putting the health of democracy first – the reform of elected assemblies	104
8.1	Behavioural insights for integrity reform	114
9.1	Key features of the Westminster advisory system in Australia, New Zealand and the UK	123
9.2	What are the major barriers to getting evidence into policy-making?	124
10.1	Media business models	138
11.1	The new public management toolkit	148
11.2	Approaches to public management	154
13.1	Reforms to improve long-term policy-making within democracies	186
14.1	Saving democracy	195

PREFACE

This book owes its existence to the establishment of the *Democracy 2025 – strengthening democratic practice* initiative, a collaboration between the Museum of Australian Democracy (MoAD) at Old Parliament House and the Institute for Governance and Policy Analysis at the University of Canberra which we founded with the Director of MoAD, Daryl Karp AM, in 2019 (see: democracy2025.gov.au). We launched the initiative in the context of the lowest level recording of public trust and satisfaction with Australia's democratic arrangements set against a global democratic malaise, the rise of debased semi-democracies and the Brexit debacle in the UK. The purpose of *Democracy 2025* is to ignite a national conversation on how we can bridge the trust divide between government and citizen, strengthen democratic practice and restore the confidence of Australians in the performance of their political institutions.

Our ambitions for this book stretch beyond the Australian context to Western democracies more generally and seek to address concern about democratic practice across the globe. Above all, we want to give hope to those who share our belief that democracy can be saved and that there are plenty of initiatives and reforms out there from which we can draw inspiration. This imperative has led us to tread into a range of territories where we are aware that there are other scholars with greater expertise and deeper knowledge. Our rationale for this approach is underwritten by two ideas. The first is that the way to improve democracy will vary from country context to country context and we hope that our broad agenda of reforms will give scope to that process of selection. The second is that if we have any criticism of the current debate around democratic renewal it is that it has been over-focused on generating new deliberative inputs from citizens. We are not opposed to such initiatives (indeed we support them) but we advocate instead for a more systematic approach that goes beyond inputs to the political system and looks also at how to reform throughputs and outputs. Boldly put we think that simply asking citizens to do more to save democracy lets elected and non-elected officials, political parties, parliaments, integrity agencies and other political institutions off the hook. A better democracy requires the establishment of common ground on whole of system change and not just the provision of new opportunities for citizens to exercise influence.

Unsurprisingly Covid-19 compelled us to rethink how we approached the book. In our view, the intrinsic value of democracy has not diminished but how it is practised began to transform in a range of different ways as we wrote. The emergence of the virtual Parliament in the UK and the National Cabinet in Australia were just two institutional examples in this regard. We also witnessed a renaissance in public faith in science and evidence informed policy-making and the media enjoyed renewed confidence in its

Preface

reporting, particularly public broadcasters. After a decade of disappointment with digital democratic innovation, governments and citizens around the world began to embrace opportunities for digital participation. More and more citizens appeared to be up for digital citizenship than ever before.

In short, how we understand and practise democratic renewal in the context of the 'new normal' has come into sharp focus and forms an important backdrop to the discussion that follows.

Mark Evans and Gerry Stoker

ACKNOWLEDGEMENTS

Books like this one are inevitably shaped by insightful conversations and productive collaborations with colleagues and friends. We would therefore like to begin by acknowledging a great debt of gratitude to Daryl Karp AM, Director of the Museum of Australian Democracy, as both a fountain of ideas and host to our stay at the salubrious and historic surroundings of Old Parliament House which has provided such an inspiration to our work.

The book draws on a broad range of collaborative work conducted in Australia and the UK over the past decade with several kind and generous colleagues. In Australia, we have benefitted enormously from our collaborations with Michelle Grattan AO, who continues to astonish and inspire her readers, Max Halupka for his important work on the Democracy 2025 initiative and Nicole Moore for her insightful thinking on co-design. At the University of Canberra we also benefitted from the insights gained and the challenge we wanted to provide to John Dryzek and his amazing group of deliberation scholars. In the UK, the ideas in this book have been influenced by our collaborators in the University of Southampton-based Trustgov project (see: https://trustgov.net/) funded by the UK's Economic and Social Research Council (ES/S009809/1) – Will Jennings, Hannah Bunting, Dan Devine, Jen Gaskell, Lawrence McKay and Viktor Valgardsson. Pippa Norris (Kennedy School of Government, Harvard University) as a co-investigator on the Trustgov project inevitably impacted on our understanding given her outstanding work in this area. Graham Smith (University of Westminster) provided a range of important insights for the manuscript as a whole. Matt Ryan and David Owen (both from the University of Southampton) were also very helpful in persuading Gerry to abandon some of his dafter ideas.

We are also grateful to the support of the Bloomsbury team led by Milly Weaver, and Lorna Evans for her general assistance with the book.

Finally, we would also like to thank the eighty-three champions of democracy who gave us such rich feedback on each chapter as the book developed through our open Facebook group discussion. We discuss the impact of this deliberative engagement on the contents of the book in the postscript. As always, however, the responsibility for shortcomings in this work rests entirely with us.

Mark Evans and Gerry Stoker

CHAPTER 1
WHY 'SAVING' DEMOCRACY?

To write a book that includes in its title the idea of saving democracy edges towards melodrama. Yet there is widespread concern among scholars and in popular commentary that citizens have grown more distrustful of politicians, sceptical about democratic institutions and disillusioned with democratic processes or even principles.[1] As Antonio Guterres, Secretary-General of the United Nations, observes: 'Trust is at a breaking point. Trust in national institutions. Trust among states. Trust in the rules-based global order. Within countries, people are losing faith in political establishments, polarization is on the rise and populism is on the march.'[2] There is evidence from many countries of a loss of confidence in the executive, legislative and judicial branches of national governments, as well as political parties, the news media and interest groups, some of the core institutions linking citizens and the state. These decaying institutions provide the connection to our understanding of how democracies end, as they are no longer as effective at connecting governors and the governed.[3] The risks of democratic backsliding and authoritarian resurgence are such that many observers see democracy in 'retreat', 'recession' or in a 'reverse wave' around the world, losing the war of ideas compared to the Chinese governance model or a newly assertive Russia.[4] Some fear that weak commitment to the democratic norms and rules of the game by political leaders means we are entering an era in which 'democracies die'.[5]

The world is at a crossroads, with tyranny a more likely path forward than the renewal of democracy. Larry Diamond, who has spent his career defending and promoting democracy, captures the mood with his usual insight:

> *In every region of the world, autocrats are seizing the initiative, democrats on the defensive, and the space for competitive politics and free expression is shrinking. Established democracies are becoming more polarized, intolerant, and dysfunctional. Emerging democracies are facing relentless scandal, sweeping citizen disaffection, and existential threats to their survival.*[6]

There are significant challenges, according to Diamond, in saving democracy from the threat of Russian aggression, Chinese power and the failings of the leader of democracy, the United States.

Democracies confront a diverse range of problems. *The Global Satisfaction with Democracy Report 2020* found that the share of people who express dissatisfaction with the performance of democracy had risen by 10 percentage points to 57.5 per cent, from 1995 to 2019.[7] In the past, most citizens in countries in North America, Latin

Saving Democracy

America, Europe, Africa, the Middle East, Asia and Australasia were satisfied with the performance of democracy but this is now no longer the case. The picture is undeniably mixed. Some smaller countries are reaching all-time highs in satisfaction such as the Netherlands, Switzerland and Norway. But some of the most populous countries in world have seen the steepest decline in satisfaction as in the United States, Brazil, Mexico and Nigeria. In the older democracies, the symptoms of decline are seen in the growing polarization of politics where social and political divisions appear deep-seated, cultural and antagonistic, matched by the rise of populism and associated social movements and political parties and a wider sense of frustration with the capacity of politics to deal with the problems confronting society. In the newer democracies, after the enthusiasm that greeted the arrival of democracy, there has followed a less glorious period of politics, with governance mired by corruption, inter- and intra-group conflict, and other failings that undermine democracy's appeal. The report concludes that 'across the globe, democracy is in a state of deep malaise'.[8]

The experience of the Covid-19 pandemic has added to the sense of democracy being at a crossroads which could lead to further decline or spark a renewal. The challenges created by the pandemic have been immense and many predict it will be followed by years of economic dislocation and potentially a recession that dwarfs in scale the Great Depression or Global Financial Crisis.[9] As we write, fears are growing that the downturn could be far more punishing and longer lasting than initially feared largely due to the distinctive nature of the pandemic and its impacts. The fear of the spread of the virus has reconceptualized how we understand public space, stagnating consumer-led business activity and economic growth. The consequent abrupt halt in commercial activity and dramatic increases in unemployment will impose economic pain so profound in every region of the world that recovery could take years.[10] And yet at the same time many governments around the world are rising to the challenge and rediscovering their raison d'etre – collective problem-solving in the national interest.

We have witnessed a renaissance in public faith in science and evidence informed policy-making. Even the media has enjoyed renewed confidence in its reporting, particularly public broadcasters. Most significantly, after a decade of disappointment with digital democratic innovation, governments and citizens around the world are beginning to embrace opportunities for digital participation.[11] More and more citizens appear to be up for digital citizenship than ever before. And governments are slowly recognizing the need to institutionalize citizen voice in pandemic recovery processes. We might also add that citizen volunteering and good neighbourliness have helped provide support and comfort to millions during the pandemic. Civil society has shown its capacities and provided both practical help and social care and psychological support especially in long periods of lockdown.[12]

Covid-19 has reminded voters that national governments are necessary and that with systemic renovation they can be made to work. Political leaders around the world have begun to talk about new thinking on the other side of the pandemic. Earlier references to a 'snap-back' have given way to a realization that what is needed is a much more root-and-branch approach, to taxation, transfer payments, industry policy, regulation, and across all these areas, the relative roles of governments and markets. Moreover, the argument in support of driving national conversations on democratic renewal when public trust is strong and before austerity bites is a compelling one. Of course, a note of caution is appropriate here. Old politics is not dead and will make a concerted attempt to survive for a further encore. But could we be entering a golden era for democratic renewal? And how can we imagine this process of recovery and renewal?

A golden age for democratic renewal?

We take the arguments of doomsayers about democracy seriously, but our approach is focused less on lamenting the problem or the international context and much more at looking at how people in democracies are searching for solutions. Our commitment to this approach is driven by recognition that both the idea and practice of democracy are not exclusively a product of geo-politics or good political leadership; it is strongly influenced by a social base of citizens with the resources to engage politically and committed to emancipatory values.[13] What sustains democracy is citizens with the capacity to organize and act politically with the necessary skills, cognitive ability and networks and an embedded commitment to the freedoms and rights of all citizens. That capacity to act and commitment to the values of freedom is not evenly spread across all regions – it is largely but not exclusively to be found in the established and some newer democracies. But from our perspective it provides the seedbed for the renewal of democracy. The future of democracies as much of its past depends on people finding ways to make it work for them.

Rather than add to the litany of woe and anxiety, our objective in choosing the phrase 'saving democracy' to adorn our book is to indicate a sense of optimism and hope. Our argument is that democracy is always in a process of remaking itself and it can create positive trends as much as negative ones. Reformers, however, need to not get fixated on one type of reform – for example, citizens' assemblies – and look at the issue in the round. Democracy is best understood as a system which has inputs, throughputs and outputs, and if you want to transform the system then you must address all the components of the system.

Systems of democratic governance have three broad tasks: to discover the best interests of the governed, to decide and make choices among those interests and then to act to support those interests. To save democracy political systems need to get better at all three tasks. There are other books that deal with the issue of democratic innovation.[14] These works have many qualities, but they focus rather narrowly on the input side of politics: about how to get citizens more involved in making decisions about what should be done. But we need to consider innovations that are not just about setting the agenda of politics but also transform the way governments decide and then act.

Our argument is premised on the idea that there is a need to look at reforms across the whole of the political system. With the emergence of the systematic turn in deliberation theory some attention has been paid to the various institutional arrangements driving decisions in political systems (e.g. parliaments, media and experts) but we would still consider what is on offer as a half turn rather than a full turn.[15] Developing a system understanding should focus on how the throughputs of politics are managed and how the practices of delivery are experienced. Both of which are as important, arguably, to citizens' experience of democratic politics as the input side of politics.

A second theme is about connecting old and new power.[16] Linking politicians and the political system back to citizens is at the heart of our strategy to 'save' democracy. Old power is what is familiar in a democracy: elected politicians, law-making assemblies, courts ensuring the rule of law, and governments trying to deliver services and get things done. New power is about citizens taking up a role beyond their traditional role of voting in elections. Why do many democracies appear to be facing pressures to make change in that direction? There is a lot of evidence to indicate that citizens are turning away from an allegiant towards a more assertive approach to politics. In doing so they have become more distrustful of politicians and governments and willing to confront them and make demands. The argument points to a trend rather than an achieved transformation but given the scale of developments it is implausible to imagine the genie being put back in the bottle. More positively by linking the dynamic and flexible new power of citizens to political systems, old power can be enabled to deliver public goods and services more effectively.

A third theme for this book is that exemplars and archetypes matter. Our book will be full of examples of practice as part of our aim is to show that changing democracy is happening and not a utopian hope. Our goal is to identify where there is a track record of practice and identify prospects for progress. Practice also matters because formal rules about democracy can provide guidance but good experiences and evidence of change on the ground provide an additional motivation for change but also a stronger understanding of how to do it. Bad practice can undermine a good idea. Public participation has rightly been seen as a way of improving democracy, but research shows that one of the biggest deterrents for participation is citizens' perception of the lack of response from official consultation schemes when they do engage.[17] Officially sponsored consultation has too often been blighted by asking for public engagement when decisions have already been made, or where there is no commitment to respond to the ideas that are generated.

What are democracies?

The scope of the book is focused on all countries struggling to make democracy a reality. It is helpful when talking about 'saving democracy' to recognize that 'every system purporting to be democratic is vulnerable to the charge that it is not democratic enough, or not "really" or "fully" democratic. The charge is bound to be correct since no polity has ever been fully democratized'.[18] Democracy is a practice not a utopian ideal, and it will always fall short of achieving all that people might want it to accomplish.

We deploy the characterization of democracy used by the *Varieties of Democracy Institute* that recognizes that democracies are made from a mix of components and different countries may have more or less of each of these elements in practice.[19] The first of these features is the 'electoral component' which measures a country on how consistent, open, fair, free and contested its elections are. The 'participatory component' asks how many legal channels of participation a country offers its citizens, from the local to the national level, and how easy it is for the citizens to use these channels. Finally, the 'liberal component' judges the extent of civil rights, including minority rights, as well as the extent that power is spread within the systems and that there are checks and balances to limit the power of any one actor.

If all three of these components are present in sufficient quality, then that country can be defined as a liberal democracy and comes within the scope of this book.[20] There were in the second decade of the twenty-first century about forty countries that met these criteria sufficiently, according to the Varieties project. But in addition, the Varieties project also identifies a larger number of electoral democracies (over fifty countries) that are substantially democratic but fall short in some way of meeting the third test, based on the liberal component. These countries also form part of our study; indeed, several examples of democratic innovation can be observed in these electoral democracies. Combining liberal and electoral democracies gives us coverage of about half the countries in the world. The other half of countries fall into the category where rulers are not accountable to citizens to any great degree. The Varieties project draws a broad distinction between 'open' and 'closed' autocracies. In the former, elections take place and leaders and other representatives are elected but limits to levels of party competition, media freedom and the rule of law take away much of the power of the electoral process. In 'closed' democracies, open elections are not part of the governing process. While these countries are not a central focus for our work they may, nevertheless, offer insights on how to improve democracy, especially as there are often forces from civil society (campaigners, human rights activists and community-based groups) trying to make the case for democracy or develop democratic practices.

No system of categorization is without problems and limitations. The allocation of specific countries to a category within the Varieties project might be justifiably questioned or debated. But given our theme is about 'saving democracy' it does imply that our focus is on those countries that have something to save rather than something to establish. Therefore, for the purposes of our argument, the societies we are primarily concerned with are liberal and electoral democracies. When we refer to democracies in this book, we mean to capture both types.

Why are democracies worth saving?

Democracy, it is often argued, is an exclusively Western concept. While it is true that some politicians in the West tend to claim democracy as their own, such claims should be disputed. Some institutions dominated by powerful Western countries – such as the World Bank – have pushed Western-style democracy as part of a package of good governance from the 1980s onwards, but it would be a mistake to assume that democracy is just another export of the West. Democracy is better understood as a universal value. As Nobel Prize-winning economist and philosopher Amartya Sen points out:

> *In any age and social climate, there are some sweeping beliefs that seem to command respect as a kind of general rule – like a 'default' setting in a computer program; they are considered right unless their claim is somehow negated. While democracy is not yet universally practiced, nor indeed uniformly accepted, in the general climate of world opinion, democratic governance has now achieved the status of being taken as generally right.*[21]

Democracy is attractive to a great many people for three fundamental reasons. Again, following Amartya Sen, we can view democracy as having intrinsic, instrumental and constructive features that make it desirable. There are powerful intrinsic arguments for democracy. Christian Welzel argues that 'democracy as a tool of human empowerment whose primary purpose is to entitle people to master their own lives and to give them a voice and vote'.[22] Elizabeth Anderson extends this understanding by noting that beyond its instrumental virtues democracy 'is a culture or way of life of a community defined by equality of membership, reciprocal cooperation, and mutual respect and sympathy and located in civic society'.[23] Democracy expresses the sense that each citizen is of equal worth and deserves to have their voice heard and their freedoms respected. Beyond that it enables people to engage in the noble art of finding mutually agreeable solutions to shared problems. Democracy both expresses the human desire to protect and promote your values and interests and demands empathy and engagement with others, making you a better person in doing so.

The instrumental argument comes in a variety of forms. Democracy can be defended as an effective and legitimate mechanism for reconciling people who hold different interests and values, without resorting to violence.[24] Given that the world is always likely to be full of disagreements and conflicts then having a way of resolving those disagreements without people killing each other is of value. More positively, it can be argued that democracy helps focus the minds of rulers on the welfare of citizens, as they require their votes. The marketing of what democracy can do needs to be cautious. Democracy cannot guarantee you a happy life, but it can make some disasters of human life less likely to be imposed on you. One study suggests tentatively 'there is a robust correlation between democratic institutions and health, resulting in greater life expectancy in democracies'.[25] Amartya Sen, in part, won his Nobel Prize for showing that major famines generally do not occur in democracies; recent famines in Ethiopia and Somalia occurred under dictatorships, and great historical famines such as those in the Soviet Union in the 1930s or China between 1958 and 1961 took place in authoritarian regimes. The explanation he offers is convincing:

> *Famines are easy to prevent if there is a serious effort to do so, and a democratic government facing elections and criticisms from opposition parties and independent newspapers, cannot help but make such an effort.*[26]

Why 'Saving' Democracy?

The experience of Covid-19 and the need for rapid decision-making and unusual levels of control over the behaviour of citizens has led some to wonder if democracies could cope. There is perhaps good reason to wonder if democracies are ill equipped to deal with a major crisis such as that provided by Covid-19.

> *In a context of high uncertainty, where decisions must be made quickly and often at the expense of political debate, one might be tempted to argue that authoritarian regimes would be better equipped to provide immediate and operational response.*[27]

However, there is also limited evidence that regime type determines outcomes. Some democracies did well in managing the pandemic at least in terms of avoiding large numbers of deaths (Australia and New Zealand). Others fared less well (Brazil, UK, United States). But similar mixed patterns could be observed in more authoritarian regimes, with arguably China managing Covid-19 effectively (if autocratically) after an initial failure and others such as Iran and Russia doing less well.

Finally, democracy can help in the search for solutions to intractable problems and challenges. This is the constructive value of democracy. Open dialogue can be the key to resolving many of the most challenging issues we confront; it enables the sharing of ideas, learning and the thinking through of problems. It is that public airing of issues that can make all the difference. Sometimes, however, contrary to the view of some theorists of deliberative democracy, politics does its work through smoke and mirrors. By enabling people who fundamentally disagree to find a way forward by sometimes giving different meanings to the same words, politics does much valuable work. Democracy – more often than we care to admit – relies on 'weasel phrases', hidden compromises or delayed gratification and various other forms of ambiguous construction that enable all sides to claim victory, or at least emerge defeated but with their honour intact. Democracy does its work in a variety of ways and with a considerable degree of messiness and compromise. It is constrained and limited. There are a range of intrinsic, instrumental and constructive arguments that can be made for the value of democracy, even if it is a rather imperfect and often disappointing process.

The value of a system approach – challenges facing representative democracy

We were partly inspired to write this book by a sense that reform advocates for democracy have focused most of their efforts on improving the inputs to democracy. We agree fully with their desire to improve the responsiveness of government to citizens through enhancing their participation and engagement, but we think that reformers should also ask questions about improving the outputs of democracy. Participation without delivery is a frustrating prospect. Equally delivery is unlikely to be viewed as either legitimate or attuned to effectiveness unless the throughput processes of democracy are working better. Throughput is about what is sometimes referred to as the 'black box' of governance where political actors, officials and experts and institutions work up preferences and ideas into policy measures that can be enacted and then implemented. Maybe citizen participation can tell you what people want but it cannot always tell you in detail how to deliver it and that is where the throughput part of governance comes to the fore. Getting throughput dynamics wrong can be seriously damaging to the legitimacy of governance, if either corruption or incompetence undermines the capacity to translate citizens' wishes into effective action.

The terms 'input', 'throughput' and 'output' all come from systems theory. The idea of thinking about politics as a system has a long pedigree. Gabriel Almond in 1956, for example, argued that the term 'system' 'satisfies the need for an inclusive concept which covers all of the patterned actions relevant to the making of political decisions'.[28] But it was David Easton that developed in 1965 one of the strongest statements for a systems perspective.[29] We do not need to embrace all the features of Easton's perspective to still use some of the concepts he advanced. Political systems have inputs which in a broader sense is everything in the environment that goes into making a political choice. Inputs provide both demands on the system and support for either specific proposals or more generally diffuse or generalized trust, indicating that the system is deemed legitimate. The legitimacy of a political system depends on how much citizens feel that their voices are heard and if there are opportunities for them to have access to influence. But as Vivien Schmidt argues legitimacy is also determined by the throughput part of the political system.[30] Throughput refers to those actors (politicians, bureaucrats, experts and stakeholders) who are tasked with making governing decisions and 'encompasses the myriad ways in which the policy-making processes work both institutionally and constructively to ensure' efficacy, accountability and transparency in the making of those decisions.[31] The final element in our system take on politics is the concept of *outputs*, broadly what the system produces. Outputs are about the effectiveness of delivery, the responsiveness of services and performance to societal need and the values of what is delivered, whether, for example, people are treated with respect and fairness. Bo Rothstein has argued about the importance of not forgetting 'the public administration side of the equation … what goes on at the "output" side of the political system has empirically been shown to be most important for creating political legitimacy'.[32]

We argue that the challenges facing democracies can be reflected in the problems in establishing legitimacy across the system: inputs, throughputs and outputs. Although there is an inevitable overlap between categories in how these challenges are treated, Table 1.1 captures our sense of some of the major challenges posed to democratic governance in recent decades that have potentially become more acute because of the impacts of Covid-19. It also identifies where the challenge is addressed in the book.

On the input side of politics there are several major issues to consider. Social inequality and lack of access to decision-making remain a challenge for many democracies and have arguably become greater in a digital world. A second input concern is about how best to organize citizen participation so that it avoids 'consultation fatigue', 'knee-jerk' responses and 'authenticity' and 'legitimacy' concerns. We explore the role that participatory governance systems can play in enabling critical citizenship through

Table 1.1 The political system – challenges confronting representative democracies

Inputs: responsiveness to citizen concerns and the framing of political demands to enable critical citizenship

Challenge	Issues
An unequal political community reflects and reproduces social inequality.	Democracy tacked on to an unequal society with structural disadvantages limiting the full engagement of several groups, including most women, many ethnic and indigenous minorities and other groups in society who lack the resources to believe that they can engage effectively. **See Chapters 3–6**
Lack of citizen voice and opportunity to engage effectively in politics.	Public consultation schemes are now an everyday practice, but they suffer from a sense of pointlessness and fatigue. The challenge is to find ways for critical citizens to take engagement further or deeper. **See Chapters 3–7, 10, 11 and 13**

Throughputs: the accountability, transparency and efficiency of decision-making processes

Challenge	Issues
Representative assemblies do their politics in ways that many citizens find alienating or pointless.	Out-of-date procedures, rules and culture; need to be better at holding the executive branch of government and more broadly politicians to account; lack of capacity for long-term policy-making; more engagement with the public and less grand-standing. **See Chapters 7 and 8**
The public distrusts parties and politicians and yet they remain pillars of mainstream democratic practice.	Parties and politicians are the mechanisms that feed representative democratic institutions but are struggling to match the growing divisions in society, declining membership in parties and public participation suggest they are not functioning effectively or sustaining public trust. **See Chapters 7 and 8**
Decisions made with lack of evidence, forward thinking and public purpose have legitimacy costs.	Policies need to be desirable but also feasible and that requires open exchange between politicians and administrative and technical experts, but too often evidence-based policymaking is undermined by lack of trust, pressures of short-termism and lack of communication. **See Chapters 9, 12 and 13**

Cross-boundary and multi-level problems do not fit easily within the confines of democracies designed around nation states.	Many key issues (climate change, tackling pandemics or obesity) require action at many levels of government both within nation states and beyond. But the practices of multi-level government remain fraught with difficulty. Mixing decentralization and devolution of power with the pooling of sovereignty with other nation states is not straightforward. In federal and unitary systems institutional forms designed in one era are not necessarily the right ones for a new era. **See Chapter 11**
Weak basis for shared political community due to polarization and 'truth decay'.	Politics involves competition and conflict but the emerging polarized and post-truth context for politics threatens the shared ground that is needed for dialogue and compromise. Competition driving the search for controversy by mainstream media and the weaponization of social media and the use of artificial intelligence are adding to negativity and division. **See Chapters 6 and 10**

Outputs: the capacity of politics to deliver quality services and policy outcomes

Challenge	Issues
Policy and interventions are failing at the design level without engagement from citizens, experts and stakeholders.	Designing the implementation of policies without the engagement of users or co-producers can limit effectiveness. The challenge is to develop citizen-centred design techniques that are suitable. **See Chapters 4, 5 and 11**
Making everyday bureaucracy better matters in times of crisis which means improving effectiveness, avoiding corruption and delivering a service that is fair and respectful.	There is evidence that problems in implementation undermine trust and discourage citizen to expect much from government. Yet there are good reasons why a bureaucracy that is both efficient and effective and fair and responsive is difficult to deliver. **See Chapters 11 and 12**
Developing long-term governance capacity matters so that major issues such as climate change and other major crises can be addressed.	Better governance requires working across sectors, boundaries and beyond the short term. **See Chapters 9–13**

the institutionalization of citizen voice via a mix of direct democracy, deliberative democracy and digital democracy and seek to identify the conditions underpinning quality participation.

When it comes to throughputs there are several challenges that need to be addressed by reformers. There are three we think are particularly worthy of attention. The first is the

Why 'Saving' Democracy?

way that politics is conducted in assemblies and parliaments and its wider relationship to the system of governing. There is something odd about the culture of parliamentary politics and there are substantial concerns around the representativeness and integrity of elected politicians. Are they drawn from a wide enough base? Do they reflect the nature of the community they claim to speak for? Do they work in a way that promotes public engagement and understanding? Do political parties need to do their job better?

A second challenge is at the heart of the machine where policy decisions are forged and framed. Is the policy process getting access to the right ideas, experts and evidence? And a third challenge is the issue of the media environment and the way that a sense of shared political community is difficult to maintain if citizens talk past one another or are diverted by fake news. And then of course, in terms of outputs it is all very well to have good policies, but they make no difference unless they can be delivered effectively. Here too democracies face challenges and demands for reform.

The practices of programme and service delivery design need to be improved. State institutions and bureaucracies need to be better at treating citizens with fairness and respect. Coping with crises also seems to have become a 'new normal' in democratic politics. How can we better prepare democracy for the reality of the regular experience of crisis? And what forms of democratic governance work best in crisis? Most significantly, to combat most of these crises, long-term thinking is required but governing bodies also need to be able to win citizen trust to govern for the long term. These four challenges demand major reform commitments and are united in their concern with how governing processes can be made to work across national and regional boundaries. Policy problems have a habit of never being entirely located at local, regional, national or global levels and mostly require intervention at all levels, but are governing arrangements capable of delivering that kind of flexibility, collaboration and partnership?

These challenges also give us ways to save democracy and provide the focus for the bulk of the chapters in the remainder of this book. We will explore various reform options that respond to the challenges outlined in Table 1.1 and ask what it is about them that can make a difference and contribute to an underlying theory of change. We will draw on evidence from practices across a range of countries and locations, and we will ask of each reform: what are the prospects for generalized and sustained roll-out? These questions will provide a shared analytical framework for our examination of ways to save democracy.

Merging old power and new power

One reason why democracy needs to change is that people and the way they engage with each other have changed from the founding decades of mass democracy over a hundred years ago. Citizens are now better educated and more critical. We live in a world that is more globally connected and intertwined challenging one of the building blocks for modern democracy, the nation state. Societies, whether they like it or not, are more strongly impacted by global events and globally driven rules and oversight. We have access to information, news and opinion in a way that is speedier and more multifaceted than was imaginable even a few decades ago. The main institutions of politics have not fared well in this changed context, and political leaders have in their adaptions to the new environment made politics more a focus of disdain and distrust. We will explore these issues further in Chapter 2 when considering what has gone wrong with democracy in practice. But for now, the rise of 'critical' citizens in part drives our sense of optimism about the prospects for positive change and we should develop that idea a little further.

A way of capturing the issue is our recognition that we are experiencing, using Welzel and Dalton's terms, a shift from an allegiant to an assertive democratic culture.[33] Table 1.2 expresses some of the key features of this dynamic of change. The development of easier access to education and wider social change has led to 'cognitive mobilization', a process by which education levels and political skills drive both lower trust in government and the emergence of new, less elite-directed forms of political action.[34] Pippa Norris argues that citizens across much of the world – and especially younger citizens – continue to support regime principles (democracy as an ideal form of government) but have withdrawn support from regime institutions (the performance of parties, parliaments, governments).[35]

These processes are combined with the impact of partisan dealignment so that citizens are less tied to a mainstream party and more likely to display volatility in their voting preferences. These disconnecting forces create a political landscape where political parties can rely less on loyalty and must attract voters by claims of competence or as in the case of populists by exploiting resentment.

But let us immediately add some caveats. It is possible that the extent of deference that existed in the past to those in authority from democratic citizens could be over-emphasized. In a study with colleagues published in 2018 we found that in the UK at least

no golden age of political support existed. Even in the immediate post-war period, substantial proportions of the population disapproved of governments and prime ministers (whatever their political persuasion). They thought politicians to be out for themselves and their party (as opposed to their country). They associated political campaigning with vote-catching stunts, mud-slinging, and a focus on personalities over policies. They imagined politicians to be self-seeking 'gasbags'.[36]

Table 1.2 The key features of allegiant and assertive civic cultures

Allegiant Civic Culture	Assertive Civic Culture
Emphasis on order and security	Emphasis on voice and participation due to rising inequalities
Deference to authority	Distance from authority
Trust in institutions	Scepticism of institutions
Limited liberal view of democracy	Expanded democratic expectations
Limited protest/protest potential	Direct, elite challenging action
Traditional forms of participation	Mixture of traditional and new forms of participation

Yet notwithstanding the idea that citizens have always been critical of politicians, the shift in focus among citizens has been towards a concern with their rights and their voice. The default position in democracies is trending towards being sceptical rather than trusting.

Citizens are better educated and less deferential, on average, and they have access to a wider range of sources of information and media. They expect to have a say in matters that affect them and are more open to using a range of participatory tools to get their message across. These trends may all help to deliver democratic empowerment. On the demand side of the equation, the capacity of citizens to act democratically is present to an unprecedented degree, although significant issues of inequality in access to resources and capacity to mobilize can still be observed. Nonetheless, as Russell J. Dalton and Christian Welzel contend, the 'erosion of allegiant cultures and the parallel emergence of assertive cultures should not be worrisome developments as regards the societies' governance performance. Instead, in terms of both accountable and effective governance, the cultural change has positive consequences'.[37]

More citizens are up for a role as critical citizens and more equipped than in the past to assume the responsibility. The demand for a more empowering politics is strengthening and better fuelled. The conditions for effective democracy could in this light be a positive trend. There are, however, some important qualifications to this claim (not least over levels of inequality in access to politics) that will be explored later in the book. In many democracies the sense of belonging to a successful 'national' project is being questioned as income inequality widens. There are increasing numbers of people who are either completely economically marginalized or feeling economically insecure and fearful for their jobs in an age of continual restructuring, cost containment and casualization.[38] In short, not only can old power structures no longer deliver on the promise of social inclusion, but they also function to fuel what John Kenneth Galbraith has termed the 'culture of contentment'.[39] Galbraith shows how a contented class – 'not the privileged few but the socially and economically advantaged majority – defend their comfortable status at all costs'. Middle-class voting against regulation and increased taxation that would remedy pressing social and environmental problems has created a culture of immediate gratification, leading to complacency and hindering long-term progress. For Galbraith, 'only economic or military disaster, or the eruption of an angry underclass who have been left behind by globalization, seem capable of changing the status quo'.

But for now, let's focus on a positive outlook. Although we agree with Galbraith's analysis, we are more optimistic about the way forward. As we shall see later in the book, effective democracy is shown to be most firmly embedded in creating empowering political and socio-economic conditions that make people both capable and willing to engage in democratic practice. This requires system reform to remove barriers to social, economic and political participation and ensure that governmental resources are fairly distributed. We also know that citizens are becoming more assertive. That provides an opportunity. The irony is, as Cas Mudde comments, that

> ... in many ways, only now the population is what democratic theorists have long prescribed: a collection of critical and independent citizens. This means that they have to be convinced of political programs and only give their support conditionally and temporarily. They hold politicians accountable, punishing them if they don't do (everything) they promised.[40]

The negative outlook is that the supply side of politics – mainstream politicians, political parties and political institutions – has not reacted well to this shift. The political system has failed to provide the opportunity structures for participation demanded by a newly assertive democratic culture.

Does this failure of the traditional political class point to the end of politicians and parties as we know them? Versions of this argument are advocated in less brutal and more intelligent ways by some. One proposal that is gaining traction is for democracy without elections or politicians. Instead of voting to select representatives, democracies would use random selection or sortition across the population to choose rotating groups of deciders. The co-founder of the Sortition Institute Brett Hennig comments, 'if you think democracy is broken, here's an idea: let's replace politicians with randomly selected people'.[41] We think there is something of real value in getting citizens more involved in this way but do not think that democracies would solve their problems by getting rid of politicians. Instead, we want to reconnect politicians with their publics.

One question that sortition advocates struggle to convincingly answer is who will oversee the delivery of public services and programmes once random selections of citizens have made their decisions about what they want. Who will make sure the military, the police, bureaucracy, regulators, government agencies, private contractors and non-profits deliver what was promised? It is difficult to deny that a relatively stable group of citizens with experience and administrative and expert support would be best placed to do that job. In a traditional political system, they are, of course, the elected politicians. These holders of old power have not always been great at doing the job of detailed direction and oversight to ensure delivery, but it cannot be denied that they are attempting to perform important roles.

Political systems, including those in democracies, rely on old power. Old power is based on *controlling* structures, specialism and oversight. Old power is especially pertinent in the operation of the throughput and output arenas of the system. The governing practice (that delivers concrete policy and implementation) in most democracies runs through the application of old power. Yet with control ultimately and indirectly resting in the hands of citizens. At any election, citizens choose politicians, and the politicians in turn oversee public officials, bureaucracies and government agencies with all their multiple branches, experts and specialisms. The politicians decide the detail of policy with the advice of officials and officials make it happen. If citizens are not happy with the outcomes, if they think that politicians have not done their job well, then citizens remove them from office at the next election. That in a nutshell is the main story we tell ourselves about how representative democracy is supposed to work. Democracy has been premised to a large degree on this old power understanding but in practice delivering control for citizens has proved to be illusive.

Indeed, we would go further and argue that the idea of control by citizens of governing processes in complex societies is illusory. Given 'take back control' was a theme in the Brexit vote in the UK and is a mantra shared by many populist movements, some might argue that reforms that give control to citizens should be the leitmotif of reform. Populism today finds its most common expression inside democracies and has in most cases forged a relationship with democratic institutions. These modern forms of populism do not propose to abolish free elections or install dictatorship: on the contrary, their demand is for a democracy that 'delivers what the people want'. One objection to 'putting the people in control' is that it is not deliverable. In a world that has become more globalized, inter-connected and subject to rapid technological change, control is no longer a tenable option. Yet many politicians still make promises of control but in doing so they ultimately stoke public disappointment with democratic politics. Another objection crystallizes around 'who the people are', which is not so clear cut in societies that have become more fragmented by geographical mobility, patterns of immigration and greater respect and support for diversity.

If democracy cannot deliver control as much as the old power framework promises, what can citizens expect? Our answer is influence through new power and our focus is on reforms that promise to citizens not control but the capacity for creativity. If old power is based on control through formal structures, new power is based on making connections of influence through systems that are relatively short-lived, informal and open. In terms of democracies, some of the leading new power developments include the rise of rapid sharing internet-based campaigns that make a call for action (e.g. petitions that attract millions of signatures within hours), political parties that lack formal memberships but offer a platform where citizens can join and engage on the issues they care about, and the use of the internet to spread and deliver messages by political leaders (e.g. former President Trump's use of Twitter).

But new power is not restricted to developments in digital politics. New power can be associated with any mechanism that provides an opportunity for an engagement with politics that is based on making a connection with others, agreeing to engagement but based on conditional affiliation and developing an intervention that is time-specific and limited. Many of the reforms we examine in this book have these qualities. New power is a way of doing politics that matches some of the development towards a more assertive political culture. Citizens are looking for opportunities to get things done, to find their own solutions, individually and collectively. New power provides a framework for doing as it is driven by greater connectivity and enabling activity and characterized by open sharing, conditional affiliation and more overall participation.

Old power has not been dissolved, nor has it disappeared. We therefore want to focus on reforms that either work with the grain of new power or are hybrids that combine elements of old and new power, for example, the democratization of the parliamentary committee system to include lay public representation.[42] This is a hybrid intervention that seeks to revitalize an old power institution of representative democracy by connecting up old and new power through public participation. The argument here is the need to move beyond old binaries that recognize the role that participation can play in bolstering the legitimacy and dynamism of representative democracy. Our goal is to work with the logic of new power to connect to old power.

In conclusion – why representative democracy can and should be saved

Reformers need vision and belief but matched by careful and critical analysis of what is and what could be. This is probably the thought shared by the Italian revolutionary Gramsci in his claim to be 'a pessimist because of intelligence, but an optimist because of will'.[43] We argue that democracy can and should be saved. But the task involves more than simply demanding that citizens have a greater say. It means exploring how to reform not only the inputs of democracy but the way the throughputs of governing work and how to achieve more effective and responsive outputs. It also demands that the institutionalized practices of old power find a new accommodation with the challenges of new power driven by a better educated, dynamic and diverse citizenry.

CHAPTER 2
CAN DEMOCRACY BE SAVED?

There is no doubt that democracy needs to change. But what is required to deliver the best democracy? Even a basic list of conditions presents a daunting picture. Citizens would need effective opportunities to get issues on the agenda for public discussion and decision. They would need to see themselves and their interests represented in political institutions. Their judgement, with equal weight, would count at each stage of the process of deciding. Their decision-making would reflect opportunities to access evidence and the chance to deliberate and detect fake news and information. Political institutions and elected officials would need to be responsive to decisions and competent and respectful in the implementation of those decisions. They would be driven by evidence and act to get things done with integrity, openness and with the best interests of citizens at the heart of their engagement. The media system would support free speech and a free flow of ideas. Long-term commitments would need to be legitimized and sustained to tackle major societal challenges.

Moreover, democracy works through human beings and institutions, with all the flaws and failings regularly associated with these carriers of its creed. It operates in the context of social and economic inequalities that undermine its operation and powerful threats from the forces of globalization. It confronts, daily, hostile nation-based political forces that threaten it, and its powers can appear fragile when faced with the challenges of, for example, climate change or Covid-19. But there remains hope. Citizens and politicians do fall short in practice, but they are not irredeemably condemned to fail. Democracy can be improved and made healthier. The challenge is to learn by creating, hence the celebration in this book of international examples of attempts to do just that. The malaise facing democracy is real but so too is the prospect of positive change.

This chapter examines how far citizens and politicians fall short of the democratic ideal but how much they can still contribute to democracy. The arguments against democracy premised on the limits of citizenship are not without force but they can be countered. It is arguable that it is the political elite (politicians and other elites at the top of the system) who are the greater threat to democracy and democratic reform. But even here, amongst the isolated political elite, we can find signs of hope. It is also important to recognize that institutions do exactly what they are designed to do – support certain norms, values and patterns of behaviour – so changing the institutional structure of politics is not an easy task but again it is possible.

We conclude our discussion by outlining our preferred reform strategy. There are some who start with philosophy or theory and move on to recommend sweeping changes to the practice of democracy. As noted in Chapter 1, one of the more radical suggestions that have gained traction is the idea that democracy could be based not on the selection of representatives but through random selection. Others argue that the secret is to get more deliberation into the process of decision-making. We need rational thought and shared reflection to drive decision-making rather than narrow self-interest or short-term preferences. Some who follow the democratic innovation debate might think that the only real reform on offer appears to be a deliberative assembly, citizens' jury or some mechanism that gets a group of citizens advised by experts to decide key policy issues. We do not deny the value of all of these ideas but we want to promote an approach that starts with where people are in their understanding of democracy and how it should work.

Can citizens play their part in delivering democracy?

There would be little point in saving democracy if the main agents of democracy – citizens – were not up to the task. This is a vital consideration given we are proposing a greater role for citizens in the democratic process in some of the reform options we consider later in the volume. It has been suggested that the majority of citizens are so far from the ideal of the challenging, engaged, reflective actor that democracy demands that they should not have a leading role. Joseph Schumpeter expresses the argument in colourful terms:

> *The typical citizen drops down to a lower level of mental performance as soon as he enters the political field. He argues and analyzes in a way which he would readily recognize as infantile within the sphere of his real interests. He becomes primitive again.*[1]

Yet there is robust evidence to suggest that citizens do find ways of making political choices that are good enough. Citizens, in short, are up to their role we shall argue.

There is a long-standing school of thought that can be given the generic title of 'competitive elitism' that in a broad sense argues that the complexity of modern civilization and the failings of citizens mean that little scope can be given for direct citizen participation.[2] Rather the role of citizens should be largely confined to choosing between competing leaders, with the democratic dynamic provided by the competition between these elites to win support. Max Weber in the early part of the twentieth century reflected on the impracticality of large-scale participation, as well as making a more general argument for caution in how much should be expected of citizens given the complexity of the policy choices they face.[3] In the aftermath of the rise of Hitler in Germany in the 1930s and 1940s, there was a shift in emphasis in the argument towards expressing fear about the implications of mass involvement in politics. Giving citizens too much of a say will lead to them choosing despots or populists.

There are twenty-first-century versions of these arguments. Bryan Caplan, for example, suggests that citizens indulge in fantasy and prejudice when engaging with politics.[4] It is not irrational to do so because it carries few individual costs, compared to decision-making in other parts of their lives, where not considering confounding evidence or the value of trade-offs can be personally damaging. Voting, by contrast, is a trivial act because the probability of any one vote influencing an election outcome is low and the costs for an election outcome are not obviously apparent. There is some truth to these arguments, although the costs of many decisions (not just voting in elections) are not easily known, or the trade-offs understood. There are other major decisions (e.g. saving for retirement or buying a house) where the evidence is not overwhelming that citizens act primarily as rational, calculating actors.[5]

Jason Brennan observes that there are many citizens who are relatively unreasoning in their approach to politics.[6] Like 'hobbits' citizens can be apathetic and ignorant. The problem is that those who are more engaged tend to be highly partisan and with fixed world views. Brennan describes them as 'hooligans' and his solution is a variation of that offered in earlier versions of competitive elitism, a call for rule by the knowledgeable and expert.

Beyond these broad swipes at the role of citizens in democracy, there are others who bring a range of evidence to the fore. Drawing on a range of experimental work, James Kuklinski and Paul Quirk conclude that on many occasions the political decision-making of citizens suffers from significant flaws.[7] One might expect a citizen to weigh policy-relevant information in a balanced way, but in practice they use stereotypes and are prone to misjudgements in their thinking. One might expect citizens to be knowledgeable about what they do not know, but in practice they are often wildly over-confident about their opinions. When new information becomes available a reflective thinker could be expected to take it on board and if appropriate change their view; however, citizens tend to be very resistant to new insights.

When citizens engage in political debate, 'hard' arguments that demand time to absorb and some mental effort often lose out to 'easy' arguments that are emotive and simple and make strong claims without providing evidence. Citizens listen to political debates but make biased interpretations of the messages they receive. Finally, citizens are often poor at following through on the logical implications of their own reasoning. These negative perspectives are supported by the research of Christopher Achen and Larry Bartels who make a compelling observation about how American citizens lack the capacity for retrospective judgement regarding government performance:[8]

> *We find that voters punish incumbent politicians for changes in their welfare that are clearly acts of God or nature. That suggests that their ability (or their inclination) to make sensible judgments regarding credit and blame is highly circumscribed. In that case, retrospection will be blind, and political accountability will be greatly attenuated.*

Their overall assessment is damning, when they claim that election results are 'mostly just erratic reflections of the current balance of partisan loyalties in a given political system. In a two-party system with competitive elections, that means that the choice between the candidates is essentially a coin toss.'

There is little point in trying to argue that citizens are always attentive to politics. Equally, it would seem obviously the case that when they are, they can miscalculate or be driven by broad partisan or ideological prejudices when making their judgements. Such is the problem of being human. We are fallible. So, what is the response of those who say that citizens can still do their job for democracy? The first rejoinder is that the way citizens make decisions is good enough. The second is to argue that when they want to, or more precisely, when they are given the opportunity, they can decide effectively by consuming and analysing more information.

Politics is carried out by humans and undertaken in a human way not according to some ideal model of the reflective, calibrating and committed citizen. Humans behave with respect to politics the way they do in most of the rest of their lives, as flexible thinkers responsive to their environment. Gerd Gigerenzer and colleagues have developed the concept of ecological rationality to capture the idea that human reasoning is adaptive rather than logical in its motivation.[9] Humans think to adapt, act and survive in complex environments. The best type of reasoning is the one that is most suited to the environment or task with which they are faced. Complexities in the environment and shortage of time have led to the human capacity for using fast and frugal heuristics that rarely follow the rules of formal logic, but which are nevertheless relatively successful. Moreover, the use of heuristics is not a second-best strategy; it is most often the best solution. Humans are not hopelessly prone to flaws in their decision-making, but rather adaptable thinkers, and the success of their strategies revolves around matching heuristics to the task environment.

With only modest cognitive effort, citizens can use cues from political elites to make reasoned choices that are a reliable guide to what they might choose if they had more information or put more cognitive effort into making the judgement. Elite actors provide the public with enough clues to make up their minds. But it is the voters who decide as they use endorsements from sources they trust to help them decide between options.[10] They are not just passive recipients of messages from elites; they can choose to learn from neighbours, friends or family. They can also seek help from a range of other sources.[11] Political parties that capture the broad views and loyalty of voters can provide a cue to a voter that is enough for them to decide. If a political party is backing a preferred policy option, then the voter can feel comfortable with backing them. Partisanship or knowing you share a world view with others can help rather than hinder in the process of deciding.[12] Equally, if a lobby group or association of which they are a supporter or member is campaigning on an issue (even backing an option in a referendum), then the supporter or member will take that as a cue about how to decide. Citizens need relatively modest amounts of knowledge to make reasoned choices and the cues they adopt can provide a substitute for more detailed information.

Citizens can also be moved to make more cognitive effort. Affective or emotional experiences may focus people's attention on an issue or provide them with the appropriate cues to decide and can therefore be a functional asset in imperfect information contexts requiring modest cognitive effort.[13] Cindy Kam's research shows that simply reminding citizens of their duty to reflect during campaigns can encourage citizens to think more about candidates and search more openly about issues: '[h]ow citizens think about politics is flexible, rather than fixed, and can be shaped in consequential ways by the nature of elite appeals during election campaigns'.[14]

Alongside the cognitive capacities of citizens there is value in looking at how choices are framed and offered to citizens. Herbert Simon, a foundational thinker for so much work in this area, argues that human behaviour is 'shaped by a scissors whose two blades are the structure of task environments and the computational capabilities of the actor'.[15] Cues and increasing attention can help overcome cognitive imitations but what could be done to improve the task environment, the way that choices are framed? There is less work on this issue but an initial study looking at the conduct of a plebiscite over same-sex marriage in Australia came up with the following insights:

Getting the task environment right might be a better route to greater and more confident citizen engagement. Our evidence suggests that carefully presented choices help, as does a focus on choices that are not too technical (more focused on values rather than consequences). Enabling citizens to access horizontal cues from their own experience or chosen contacts and peers provides a sense of efficacy and the creating a feeling of accountability to fellow citizens and a duty to engage can support the undertaking of inevitable cognitive effort involved in making a public choice. Starting where citizens are and assuming (given their hectic and busy lives) that is likely to be where they will stay is our reform mantra.[16]

In summary, the message of this research is that if you ask a question that demands a lot of technical judgement or a capacity to predict the future, then citizens feel uncomfortable in making those types of decisions. The case of the Brexit decision in the context of the 2016 referendum held in the UK fell into that category. People commented that they lacked the necessary information to make that choice using their own reflections and insights and instead relied on making their vote choice not so much on which camp they trusted but more by voting opposite to which camp did they most distrusted.[17] Decisions that require less technical knowledge or consequential prediction appear to be comfortable for citizens to make and increase their sense that they have the capacity to decide and decide well.

By understanding better how citizens make decisions and what helps them be more confident in their everyday capacity to make political judgements, it is possible to see that citizens are up for a greater say in democracy. Furthermore, more radical changes in institutional practice and the strengthening of existing practices open up further options. In Chapter 4, we will describe various forms of deliberative assemblies where citizens are randomly selected to participate just as they would be in the case of a criminal jury. Expert evidence, insight and analysis are provided to the citizens. In addition, they are given the time and opportunity to reflect, reason about and challenge that input. The evidence from a range of these initiatives shows that the public can 'given the right circumstances, discuss with respect the views of others, change their minds in the light of evidence and argument, and reach judicious conclusions that take into account the public interest'.[18] In short, many citizens could perform at least as well as existing politicians. Perhaps it is with the political class rather than citizens where the problem lies.

Are politicians able to deliver democracy?

Isobel Hardman asks a question that has, we suspect, occurred to many citizens: why do we get the wrong politicians?[19] It is common to imagine politicians as a group who live in a bubble, out of touch with the world and lacking understanding of the people they claim to represent. There was probably not a time when politicians were universally admired. Even during the heyday of the triumph of democracy over fascist totalitarianism in the aftermath of the Second World War many citizens were quite cynical about politicians and their motivations. Who is attracted to become a politician? The short answer is not many of us. In a study which combines survey data with detailed interviews, Jennifer Lawless and Richard Fox show how for most young citizens in the United States asking them if they want to become a politician is a question which encourages responses drenched in derision and disdain.[20] Their evidence leads them to conclude:

> *Today's high school and college students have grown up knowing nothing other than a politics characterized by nasty campaigns, partisan posturing, a media establishment focused on conflict and scandal, and political pundits who perpetually stoke the flames of public anger and dismay. This is not the kind of environment conducive to fostering or nurturing thoughts of a political candidacy later in life.*

There is, in this light, little in the way of a 'pull' factor towards politics. There is also limited evidence of push factors at work either. Most parents hold that politics is too often about lying and cheating and do not welcome the idea that their children might enter an arena where the main actors lack honesty and ethics. In most families, politics is not discussed to any great degree. In addition, in most households, politics is rarely discussed. There is no great encouragement perceived from the children from their parents to go down that career route and few children have strong political experiences to draw on. Broadly the view of both parents and children is that they would rather do anything else other than go into formal politics. If they are going to change the world, they do not see politics as a viable route to do so.

The pool from which elected politicians are drawn is small, primarily because many citizens and future citizens rule out a career in politics as an option for them. From that small pool of citizens who think that politics might be for them, a range of other biases come into play when it comes to getting into politics. Politics seems increasingly the preserve of those with specific professional backgrounds who can devote time and effort to becoming a career politician. As Pippa Norris observes, 'in many countries amateurs who live for politics have been increasingly replaced by professionals who live from politics'.[21] This transformation reflects wider societal change:

The state has been expanded and modernised. Occupations have been professionalised. Financial rewards for politicians – pensions, allowances, salaries – have been introduced and improved. Career opportunities for politicians have been expanded.[22]

There are also declining numbers of people coming into politics from other careers (whether business, professional or the manual working class) and increasing numbers of career politicians. The classic broker occupations that are still associated with politics such as lawyers, teachers and managers have been joined by a more directly connected cadre of party workers, assistants, aides to elected representatives, think tank researchers and special advisors:

There has emerged a 'political class' comprised of politicians but also political consultants, advisers, researchers, and lobbyists, that is relatively homogeneous and well-connected internally, but relatively detached from citizens in wider society.[23]

One other blatant bias is worth mentioning. In most democracies there are more men than women in the role of elected representatives. Why? There are a few possible explanations. Is it the toxic nature of political culture and the way that men and the media in politics do not value the contribution of women? Is it the persistence of negative stereotypes about what women can do? Is it that the measures to create greater gender balance are just not working? Do political parties do enough to help women get elected? Or is it that somehow women choose not to engage or give priority to other forms of public service? It could be that there is something in each of these explanations, and that appears to be the view of citizens themselves. When asked 'what is to blame for the under representation of women?' responses from citizens in twenty-seven European Union countries reveal some interesting insights.[24] Political culture is the top factor identified and the third ranked factor is negative stereotypes, suggesting that structural factors beyond the control of women are to blame. But a significant amount of support is given to ideas about how the underrepresentation of women is their choice. A key difference is that women tend to focus on the structural factors more than men. What this potentially means for addressing issues of underrepresentation will be addressed further in the next chapter.

There is also some detailed evidence emerging on who political leaders are that confirms the sense that they are not representative of wider society. As part of a new leadership project John Gerring and colleagues have collected global evidence about who makes up the political elite in countries across the globe.[25] They include in their census members of the executive branch of government, the legislature, the judiciary and other who hold some form of formal power. They discovered in 2019 that 81 per cent of the political elite are men, around a third speak English and around half were educated in the West. Only 2 per cent come from blue-collar occupational backgrounds or what might be called working-class backgrounds.

What do we know about the character make-up of politicians? It is interesting to start with what we know about the kind of people that would even consider the role. Political scientists have wondered in the past about whether there is a type or character of person that has the motivation to seek political power.[26] Standing for office is likely to require a mixture of ambition and outlook combined with the opportunities to stand and get elected.[27] Numbers of seats, chances of winning and selection procedures determine the nature of the opportunity structure for potential candidates. But to 'fully understand the decision dynamics involved in moving from "eligible potential candidate" to "actual office holder" it is necessary to step back and assess what Richard L. Fox and Jennifer L. Lawless term *nascent ambition*—or the inclination to consider a candidacy'.[28]

Broadly, there are six factors at play. You must be confident that you have the skills to be in public life. There is usually a specific issue or a general concern that is driving you towards politics as a vehicle for change. It helps if you have experience of politics through your upbringing or that there are strong role models that suggest that people like you could have a future in politics. You are more likely to engage if a move into politics will help with career ambitions and if the opportunity comes at the right stage in your life cycle when other concerns are not overwhelmingly present. Studies in the United States and UK have found that these factors mean that men are far more likely than women to consider running for office, as too are the highly educated and those who have higher incomes. In sum, politicians tend to have more ambition, confidence and a sense that they could make a difference.

A political type is likely to be confident in their own abilities, feel they could belong in the world of politics, have concerns that make them want to engage and a life situation that makes it possible to do so. These are arguably judicious and admirable factors to drive political ambition but already they hint at what Fox and Lawless refer to as a substantial 'winnowing process' that speaks 'to fundamental questions of political representation and democratic legitimacy'. If democracy relies on a diversity of representation then it appears that many citizens, women and ethnic minorities, those without professional education and those without a sense of political entitlement may be reluctant to put themselves forward, let alone experience the possibility of being rejected by selection procedures.

Does that 'winnowing process' produce politicians who are psychologically different to most citizens? The honest answer is that the quality and range of research available make it difficult to tell. One tentative study of the values of successful and unsuccessful UK parliamentary candidates found that they had both stronger emancipatory and power values than most members of the public, which means they support the freedoms associated with democracy but also, more than others, like directing and controlling others.[29] That politicians are not a perfect match with the range of fellow citizens in terms of their character and personalities is not surprising given that the pool of people who would even consider standing for election is small and that the job has very particular requirements. But equally there is a paucity of compelling evidence to match politicians to their often-expressed public image as individuals who are self-seeking, immoral and greedy.

In Chapter 1 we argued against the idea of replacing politicians as a group. We noted how strong advocates of sortition want to do away with politicians and replace them with randomly selected citizens to oversee political decision-making. We are not proposing to change our minds. But the evidence presented in this chapter that politicians come from a narrow pool and can form an isolated political class divorced from citizens gives pause for thought. Political elites are constructed in a way that leads to the underrepresentation of half the population (women), and the near absence of those with blue-collar jobs suggests that something is clearly wrong with the social representativeness of politics. Our view is that politicians remain a vital part of delivering politics but the range and diversity of who becomes an elected politician have got to change if democracy is going to be saved. We shall return to all of these issues later in the book.

So, when it comes to politicians, is there hope? We think there is a case for optimism for three reasons. First it must be recognized that no political system is going to be perfectly representative of all parts of society. This is partly due to the imperfect nature of electoral systems and partly down to the distinctive skill sets involved in the representative's role and function in a complex environment. To argue that politicians are not representative fits with the idea that representation is about someone being present to represent someone else, the elected member or trustee who represents her constituents. But another way of thinking about the idea is that the task of representing involves more than being present and it has to be based on a claim to speak for others, that must be demonstrated and accepted, rather than a fact achieved by either being elected or reflective of a specific social group.[30] The challenge then becomes not to match politicians with the make-up of society but rather to ask: are they able to represent the diverse interests of different groups in society? Achieving equity in this second sense is by no means an easy task but it might be possible through the innovations presented in this book to make some progress.

A second reason why there is cause for hope is that we agree with Isabel Hardman in her book *Why We Get the Wrong Politicians*,[31] that most politicians are not terrible people. Indeed, she goes further and comments that many politicians are 'decent human beings'.[32] Our own dealings with elected politicians would support the observation. Indeed, we too might go further and argue that putting yourself up for an election, dealing with voters' concerns on a regular basis and facing the potential for both being thrown out of your job by voters or abused by some to your face or online for doing it mark out a group of people who could claim to be more civic-minded than the average citizen.

Politicians are often talented individuals who want to make a difference, undertaking an extraordinarily difficult job. There are probably more larger egos amongst a group of politicians than in other social groups; such is the performative nature of key aspects of the role. But many engage in politics to do something that in their opinion helps others. In most democracies, doing the job of the elected representative can involve long working hours and engagement in that activity can involve law-making, scrutiny of government, dealing with constituent concerns, meeting lobbyists and those who want their opinions to be heard, and media engagement. All that work is done in the context of intensive interest and sometimes commentary on their public and often private behaviour through both mainstream and increasingly social media. Government in a goldfish bowl takes place in a manner that is way beyond the experience of most of us.

Insofar that there are behavioural issues with politicians, the issues are not about their character, in that they are as good or as bad as the rest of us. Not many of them are like TV's Frank Underwood from *House of Cards* and few come close to the politicians seen in *West Wing* or *Madam Secretary*. If we end up with bad politicians, as Hardman argues, it is in large part due to the institutions of politics, how they are selected, their behavioural norms and how their behaviour is rewarded. We can change the way those elements of the system of politics work, and again some of the innovations we cover in this book address these issues.

A third reason for hope is that citizens know what would make a good politician. This issue was addressed by one of the authors in a survey conducted in 2017 in Britain.[33] Let us focus on the characteristics that most view as 'very important' (these capture a shared understanding). It appears that the image of a good politician boils down to someone you can trust (trustworthy, honesty, means what they say), who is competent (wise, strong, level-headed, works hard), someone who has integrity (sincere, genuine, principled) and someone who is in touch with the world around them (understands everyday life, in touch with ordinary people and comfortable mixing with them). It helps if you have personality, are inspiring, dress well and have had another job outside politics. But a good politician above all needs to be trustworthy, have integrity, be in touch and be able to get things done. That is of course a rather daunting list of characteristics for any individual to possess. But as a combined group, politicians should be able to deliver. It is possible to believe that we might be able to design a politics better suited to delivering on that ambition.

The task will not be an easy one as being a good politician is not straightforward. Firstly, Politicians exercise control over collective resources and face the temptation of turning that power to provide personal rather than societal advantage. From blatant embezzlement, to favours for supporters, to exploiting network opportunities provided in their post-political careers, politicians appear as regular passengers on the gravy train of public life. The second set of circumstances that drive poor behaviour are reflected in the competing demands and complex tasks that we ask politicians to navigate. People disagree about what to do because they have different values and interests. Often the problems nations face in their economy and society have no obvious or clear-cut solutions to match them. In short politicians can face often radically competing demands, with little idea about what is a workable solution. Expectations inevitably outstrip the capacity to deliver. No wonder politicians who need to garner or sustain support might be prone to lacking candour, or over-claiming or seeking credit where it is far from justified or hiding behind a degree of ambiguity. Third, politicians are making decisions as governors where the stakes are higher, the consequences of failure more damaging and the degree of coercion stronger than in most exchanges between private individuals. This context may require from them hard-headed calculation, sacrificing some interests or reneging on promises, in order to secure an acceptable societal outcome. Hard choices are part of the everyday process of politics and yet there are few politicians who are completely comfortable about having an honest debate, devoid of wishful thinking, with their voters.

Can we design better politics?

To change politics, we do not need to change human nature but rather change political institutions and systems. That is no easy task, but it is a more plausible ambition than changing human nature. Yet some argue that designing better political institutions is a 'mission impossible' because it is not feasible to establish any clear understanding of cause and effect between intervention and outcome to guide our judgements. Lacking a complete model of causality does not however stop a commitment to reform in other areas of society and economy. Indeed, the way of working we would like to borrow from (admittedly more symbolically than substantially) comes from one of the frontiers of modern science – nanotechnology.[34] Scientists in that field are combining insights from physics, biology and chemistry to bring about a revolution in medical treatments. They are doing so through 'learning by creating or making' by drawing on broad understandings of how things work but testing them with interventions that are in turn monitored and evaluated.

Ultimately their goal is to design within medicine not the best average treatment for the average patient but instead to design medical interventions that are designed for an individual, matching their needs, DNA and circumstances. We want to draw on that spirit of learning through creating, and we have many examples to draw on over the last two decades as different countries and places have introduced successful interventions to improve the way politics works. Equally we do not think that all interventions are going to be the right ones for all democracies, but it might be possible, as in modern medicine, to begin to tailor solutions to countries or places.

We understand that all reforms are likely to face opposition. Albert Hirschman comments that opponents of change tend to frame their arguments along three lines.[35] Sometimes they claim that any change will jeopardize key valued elements of existing arrangements. At other times they argue that the reforms will be futile; they will not achieve their stated purposes. Finally, they argue that the reforms will have perverse, unintended consequences. None of these concerns are without substance. The first argument is a useful prompt to remember that any process of institutional design for democracy is unlikely to start with a blank sheet and must meet the challenge of being better than the existing system. We can perhaps be confident that reform, if done well, will preserve what is good in the current system and move us on to a better level of democratic practice. Hirschman's last two arguments are more troubling, because they suggest that whatever we do, reform will not work and could even make things worse. The second argument gives in to fatalism. There are certainly good grounds for doubting whether intentional institutional change can be easily achieved. But there is no reason to rule out that idea if it can be delivered successfully. Moreover, it appears counterintuitive to think that liberal democratic systems forged through nineteenth-century political values and institutions should remain unchanged in perpetuity. There is no other area of institutional development where that would be tolerated.

Change can of course have unintended consequences but again it seems wrong to assume that they will always be negative. The original designers of mobile phones added texting as an afterthought and were taken aback when it became more common than talking. Texting in its own modest way has contributed to the advancement of human exchange. Some modest reforms in politics may not always work as intended but may still achieve some benefit for democracy. A move to a proportional voting system, for example, where seats allocated in an assembly more closely match votes cast for a political party, arguably has the virtue of being seen as fairer by voters and as a way of encouraging citizens to vote as their vote counts. Indeed, turnout is on average higher in proportional systems. But equally it changes the behaviour of political parties. It makes them reach out to broader sections of society and this gives citizens the sense that their political system is more inclusive.

Institutions, however, are not permanent and are always in a state of flux. They achieve stability through the processes of influencing the way their members think and act. But these are human processes: surprise and shocks can drive change – good and bad – as Covid-19 illustrates. Citizens are getting more vocal in their demands for change. Politicians may think they are doing a good job but eventually it dawns on them – when no one else agrees – that they are not. The constant 'drip' of such challenges can turn people from one way of understanding to another, stimulating radical change.

Reimagining democracy: a reform strategy

Is it possible to imagine a strategy for diagnosing and reforming politics? The answer provided in the rest of this book is that not only can we re-imagine democracy, but we can begin to provide an account of what it looks like. Saving democracy does not mean creating a utopian world but rather one that is better than the current one. Saving democracy does not demand the creation of a new group of super citizens but rather can rely on the capacities (modest as they sometimes are) of existing citizens. Saving democracy does not involve a new cadre of politicians. It may well require changes in where politicians are selected and drawn from, improvements in behaviour and institutional incentives to ensure that they collaborate with and are more accountable and responsive to their electors, but it does not require their wholesale replacement with a new group of randomly selected citizens. Finally, saving democracy, in the main, does not involve ideas drawn from the wild blue yonder or a journey to a place that is faraway, unfamiliar and mysterious. There are many successful examples of the practice of changing democracy to draw upon.

In terms of strategy of reform, we favour an approach that does not start with a grand new theory of democracy but a vision of democracy that makes sense to most citizens. We favour a reform agenda that matches that of most citizens. Our argument is that most citizens support and approve of the current way of doing democracy, and they argue not that its form should change but that it should be done better. We are in the 'start where people are at' school rather than 'go with a new theory' school.

So, what do people understand by democracy? This is a question that has interested social scientists for a considerable time, and three recent studies give us an up-to-date picture. The first uses data from the 2005 World Values Survey (WVS) that covers a large range of countries. It shows that there is a fairly common and consistent understanding among citizens across the world that democracy means that governing follows valued procedures, including free elections to choose leaders, the extension of civil liberties, and equal rights and the occasional involvement of citizens directly in decision-making through referenda.[36] Democracy is also seen as providing instrumental benefits (more wealth, fair taxation, welfare support) because it delivers better governance. People are also largely clear that the opposite to democracy includes political systems where the army or religious leaders take control.

Another more detailed study with rather better questions than the WVS focuses its attention on European countries in particular. It produces a parallel sense of how people see democracy. The main conclusion is expressed as follows:

Europeans mainly conceive democracy as a political system in which free and fair elections are regularly held, the courts treat everyone, including political authorities, in the same way, the government takes measures to alleviate poverty, and as a system in which it is crucial for governments to explain their decisions, for citizens to be able to obtain reliable information about these decisions, and for courts to monitor and control them.[37]

This European view of democracy combines the same procedural (fair elections, rule of law, etc.) and instrumental (dealing with poverty) elements noted in the WVS but adds the importance of open public debate about decisions and access to information through the media to hold politicians to account. There is also recognition of a need for occasional direct participation by citizens in decisions, although not so strong an emphasis on the importance of public deliberation as held by many democratic theorists. Equally much of the focus is on democracy and decision-making within the nation state and perhaps surprisingly, given the importance of the European Union to politics in that region, citizens appear to have not fully incorporated the idea of supranational decision-making into their ideas about democracy.

The third study on how people around the world see democracy was conducted by the Pew Research Center (a nonpartisan American think tank based in Washington) in 2020.[38] It confirms our previous findings that globally people are more dissatisfied than satisfied with the way democracy is working. The thirty-four-country survey reports that dissatisfaction is evident in the most established democracies (e.g. France, 58 per cent; Greece, 74 per cent; Japan, 53 per cent; the UK, 69 per cent; and the United States, 59 per cent) and that dissatisfaction is higher among those with sceptical views of elected officials. Notably a 'fair judiciary' (34 out of 34 countries), 'regular elections' (34 out of 34 countries) and 'equal rights' (32 out of 34 countries) are seen as the highest democratic priorities worldwide. Large majorities support 'free speech' (31 out of 34 countries), 'free religion' (30 out of 34 countries), 'free media' (30 out of 34 countries) and 'free internet' (29 out of 34 countries). The principles of a 'free civil society' (22 out of 34 countries) and 'free opposition parties' (22 out of 34 countries) are more polarizing and expose differences between mature democracies and new democracies. The findings show that in different contexts people develop different ideas of democracy. Broadly in established liberal democracies citizens understand and prize democracy as the protector of their freedoms, whereas in more authoritarian cultures people view democracy as a guarantee of good leadership, or even benign leadership that should be obeyed, turning democratic thinking on its head. In sum, as Christian Welzel observes, 'democracy always has been and continues to be a strongly culture-bound phenomenon'[39] and at its core is people's commitment to emancipatory values and their willingness to live by the principles of freedom for themselves and others.

In conclusion – in praise of democratic pragmatism

The first lesson we draw from starting where people are at is that there is much work to be done to deliver on even this grounded and pragmatic understanding of democracy. The study of European attitudes alone reveals 'a demanding conception of democracy, since they attribute a high importance not only to those elements pertaining to the liberal model of democracy, but also to those elements that correspond to the social and direct democratic views of democracy'.[40] This observation was further validated in a recent Australian national survey we conducted on political trust in times of coronavirus. Respondents were asked to consider whether their views about democracy had changed in consequence of Covid-19 and to identify the changes they wanted to see. As Figure 2.2 demonstrates, in general there is overwhelming support for representative democracy but with a focus on making the representative system of government more representative, accountable and responsive to the citizenry underpinned by a new politics which is 'cleaner', 'collaborative' and 'evidence-based'. Two further lessons can be drawn from these findings for our reform strategy. First, reform is as much about improving existing democratic practices as designing new ways of doing democracy. Second, citizens think that participatory reforms can be used to bolster the legitimacy of representative democracy and enhance trust between government and citizen. It appears that it is the mixture of reforms that matter most – bridging the weaknesses in the system stretching from how inputs are made to enable critical citizenship, to how throughputs work to improve the quality of decision-making to the generation of outputs that enhance the quality of life of all democratic citizens. This is the focus of our attention in the rest of this book.

Can Democracy Be Saved?

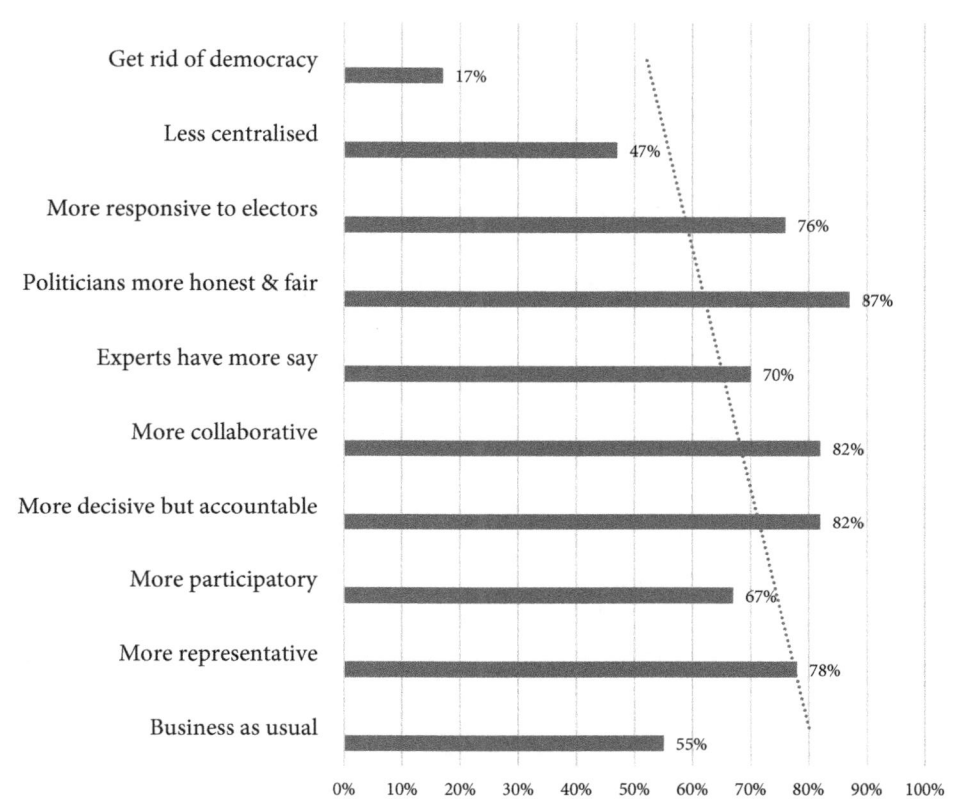

Category	Percentage
Get rid of democracy	17%
Less centralised	47%
More responsive to electors	76%
Politicians more honest & fair	87%
Experts have more say	70%
More collaborative	82%
More decisive but accountable	82%
More participatory	67%
More representative	78%
Business as usual	55%

Figure 2.1 What would you like Australian democracy post-Covid-19 to look like?
Source: Mark Evans, Viktor Valgardsson, Will Jennings and Gerry Stoker, *Political Trust in Times of Coronavirus – Is Australia Still the Lucky Country?* (Canberra: Democracy 2025/Trustgov, 2020), p. 24.

PART I
INTERVENTIONS AT THE INPUT STAGE TO ENABLE CRITICAL CITIZENSHIP

Input legitimacy refers to the responsiveness of liberal democracies to citizen concerns and the framing of political demands to enable critical citizenship.

CHAPTER 3
BUILDING PARTICIPATORY GOVERNANCE SYSTEMS

So far we have established that declining political trust is best understood by most citizens not as the product of a careful and considered calculation but rather as a constituent element of a wider sense of political disenchantment with democratic practice. Lack of political trust is tied to experiences of politics that tell you that powerful interests dominate other than your own, that governments and governors do not perform to your satisfaction and that political engagement seems a rather pointless activity.

But what is the answer to the multi-dimensional problem of declining political trust? We argue in Part I of this book that bridging the trust divide between government and citizen requires improving the framing of political demands so that new forms of citizen voice are institutionalized and embedded in the practices of democratic governance. A key mechanism for achieving this is through the establishment of participatory governance systems that reconnect citizens with their democracy through various modes of governance or forms of public participation that enable active citizenship such as direct democracy, deliberative democracy, digital democracy and community localism.[1]

Public participation is difficult to define because it means different things to different people and organizations. In a political sense, defining participation in decision-making is straightforward if it refers purely to whether the people decide. If not, then they don't participate meaningfully. A key feature of distrust in the political class is the public perception that the rhetoric of policy-makers so often emphasizes the importance of citizen participation when in practice they really mean consultation between decision-maker and citizen. Indeed, the idea of sharing the process of decision-making itself is still unpalatable to most policy-makers. This is why one of the key challenges in contemporary governance is the problem of sharing power whether with citizens, stakeholders or other jurisdictions of governments in a meaningful sense. Moreover, the purposes of participation are increasingly diverse in the contemporary age. The purpose may be to educate the citizenry or government, to market test a new intervention, facilitate feedback on the quality of public service provision or generate ideas about future governance. This enlightenment function of participation is no less valid.

But what would this look like in design terms? Suffice to say that while the path to renewal would need to be culturally defined, there are four design principles that should guide the language of reform with the principle of integrating representative and participatory modes of governance as our starting point.

Saving Democracy

Recognizing the intrinsic democratic value of public participation

Participatory democratic reforms are required to rebuild and maintain the trust of the citizenry as they speak directly to some of the negative impacts of the lack of political trust: they can provide new and different opportunities for engagement for those who have been turned off by mainstream politics; the experience of engaging in a participatory governance initiative could easily persuade citizens to think more generally about being better citizens and make them likely to do their civic duty; and participatory democratic innovations provide ways in which long-term issues neglected by mainstream politics can be addressed and public support developed for tough policy decisions. Participatory reforms also potentially provide a buttress to the representative system of government through enhancing the power of citizen oversight, and the testing of policy judgements.[2] Citizens want more of a say as they become more challenging and critical; having a say in a decision increases the prospects of trust.

Over the past two decades the number of social researchers and institutions arguing that public participation is essential for good policy-making has been on the increase.[3] This literature can crudely be organized around normative and instrumental justifications for extending public participation into policy and operational delivery. A normative lens understands participation as an essential ingredient of a liberal democratic way of life. From this perspective there is more to democracy than exercising a vote every three, four or five years. Citizens increasingly expect to be included and an ongoing role in policy-making and delivery is viewed as an important method for generating legitimacy and social ownership of government interventions. Certain authors also argue that it can be used as a tool for enhancing trust and confidence in public institutions; for as Marc Hethrington puts it, 'people need to trust the government to support more government'.[4]

The value of participation in policy-making can also be conceptualized through an instrumental lens – it is worth having as an instrument for achieving better public policy outcomes. Many practitioners, for example, do not see participation as having anything to do with politics or democracy but see it simply as a more efficient and effective way of developing and implementing projects and programmes. Public participation can assist in collating the best available evidence and providing opportunities for technocrats to be better informed about the consequences of different options, hence reducing uncertainty and risk.[5] Public participation may also assist in leveraging resources by creating opportunities for finding partners that can support the implementation of policy solutions.[6]

Technological advances and mature consumerism should also make participatory decision-making more feasible and helpful: with problems of information overload through the intelligent filtering of information and disaggregation of preferences; provide basic information about rights and responsibilities of citizenship; inform and educate about politics and about issues of public concern; help voters to make up their mind about candidates, parties and issues in election processes; promote opportunities for citizens to deliberate on public issues, on draft (in preparation) laws, social problems; provide opportunities for communication between citizens and politicians; and guide citizens through the growing jungle of publicly available government and other official information to combat truth decay. Public participation in policy-making may also be seen as a tool to resolve the complex or 'wicked' problems faced by public administrators from climate change and energy conservation to social inclusion and sustainable growth. The term 'wicked' in this context refers to resistant to resolution because of incomplete, contradictory and changing requirements.[7]

A multi-dimensional problem requires multiple solutions – integrating representative and participatory democracy

There is a tendency in both democratic theory and practice to emphasize the importance of either representative or participatory roads to renewal in a zero-sum or binary game.[8] This neglects three important factors:

1. that the involvement of politicians is integral to the long-term sustainability and legitimacy of participatory governance systems;
2. that the evidence suggests that it is easier, not to mention more efficient, to build reform on stable, respected representative institutions;[9] and
3. that the recent rise of populism is in part a product of the inability of mainstream political institutions and actors to reach out and empower disaffected citizens.[10]

Hence, the importance of building participatory governance systems that place communication at the heart of political practice, move beyond the zero-sum road to renewal and see participatory modes of democracy as a methodology for reinforcing the quality of representative democracy appears a sensible way forward.[11]

In more recent times, a growing band of academics and practitioners have developed hybrid justifications for public participation which argue that effective public participation is important in both normative and instrumental terms. For example, some deliberative theorists couch this observation in the context of the notion of deliberative systems that link deliberative mini-publics to a wider deliberative system.[12] In contrast, we prefer the looser concept of participatory governance systems as it doesn't make sense to confine citizen engagement to deliberation as a range of other engagement methods are needed to make sense of the diversity of public policy questions confronting policy-makers, citizens and communities. In sum, a multi-dimensional problem requires multiple solutions.

How you tackle the present democratic malaise depends on how you define the problem, and our data demonstrates that the problem is multi-dimensional requiring a broad range of responses. Participatory governance systems shouldn't just focus on developing deliberative spaces, such as the use of various forms of mini-public or deliberative polls but should also embrace direct forms of democracy, as well as new methods for deepening the quality of democratic engagement.[13] For example, certain methods of direct democracy (e.g. referenda or community-driven development) or processes of policy learning with citizens (e.g. gamification) are not necessarily deliberative in a formal sense but have proved effective in unlocking divided government and societies.

Solutions can be compromised by the way they are practised

Although participation has become an essential ingredient in public policy decision-making, delivery and learning, the problems of participation in practice are not widely understood. The conclusion from much of the academic and practice-based literature is not that more participation is needed but that better participation is needed. The various solutions to the trust divide offered here – whether, for example, more participation or a stronger focus on government performance – if poorly practised can become a way of reinforcing problems rather than resolving them. For example, a commitment to public participation that in reality is tokenistic and unwilling to share power can ultimately generate more cynicism and negativity among citizens.[14]

Matching engagement methods to engagement purposes

For at least half a century, public policy thinkers have developed various taxonomies of engagement to explain different degrees of citizen engagement in public policy-making.[15] Few of these taxonomies have been devised to match different engagement methods to different engagement purposes never mind the domain of decision-making most appropriate to the task.[16] While such taxonomy may be useful for determining what form of engagement may be necessary in different circumstances, policy-makers also need to identify where citizen engagement can be useful at different decision points in the policy process.

Table 3.1 illustrates the possibilities, understanding good policy-making as a process of continuous learning which involves the integration of strategy, policy and delivery and the absorption of citizen knowledge and expertise into various decision points in the policy process. There are three main justifications for adopting such an approach. The first is that all that we do in policy and delivery requires co-production with and adaptive behaviour from citizens and stakeholders. Secondly, policy is made and remade in the process of implementation and is largely a product of inheritance rather than choice, hence we will only know what people need and desire through an ongoing process of engagement. Thirdly, joining up policy and delivery through a process of strategic learning with those most affected ensures the best possible conditions for successful outcomes.

There are at least four formal decision points in the policy process that potentially benefit from citizen's involvement: (1) strategic decision-making, (2) policy design, (3) policy delivery and (4) policy learning. We have sub-divided strategic decision-making to recognize citizen involvement via direct democratic engagement such as referenda

Table 3.1 Participatory governance systems

Spectrum of participation[17]	Purpose	Method	Governance domain
Inform	*To provide the public with balanced and objective information to assist them in understanding the problem, alternatives, opportunities and/or solutions*	• Digital information platforms • Digital crowdsourcing • Gamification • Online forums • Parliamentary discussion papers	• Policy learning • Programme and service design and delivery
Consult	*To obtain public feedback on analysis, alternatives and/or decisions*	• Open space technology • Govhacks • Gamification • Planning cells • Citizen experience panels • User surveys and focus groups	• Policy design • Policy learning • Programme and service delivery
Involve	*To work directly with the public throughout the policy process to ensure that public concerns and aspirations are consistently understood and considered*	• Appreciative enquiry • Community power networks • User simulation labs • Citizen experience panels	• Policy, programme and service design
Collaborate	*To partner with the public in each aspect of the decision, including the development of alternatives and the identification of the preferred solution*	• Co-design, consensus conferences/dialogues, deliberative mapping • Citizen experience panels	• Strategic decision-making • Policy design • Policy learning • Programme and service delivery

Empower	*To directly place decision-making in the hands of the public*	• Direct democratic mechanisms such as referenda, the power of recall, community-driven development • Deliberative democratic mechanisms such as mini-publics (citizen assemblies, citizen juries, deliberative polls, participatory appraisal) depending on consequential outcomes • Action learning	• Strategic decision-making • Policy design • Policy learning • Programme and service delivery
Self-empowerment	*Citizen-led initiatives*	• Everyday makers	• Civic action

and citizen involvement via deliberative democratic engagement. The former refers to the role of direct democracy in allowing citizens to propose constitutional amendments, propose and vote on laws or advise on laws depending on its constitutional role in different nation states. As Matt Qvortrup observes, it 'addresses the legislature's "sins of omission" rather merely its "sins of commission"'.[18] Deliberative democratic engagement refers to 'decision-making by discussion among free and equal citizens ... that democracy revolves around the transformation rather simply the aggregation of preferences'.[19] This can involve citizens deliberating in various forms of mini-publics on spending priorities in big City participatory budgeting,[20] or on 'wicked' problems such as the *2019 French Citizens' Convention for the Climate* or the *2020 UK Climate Assembly*.[21]

The second and third sites of decision-making relate to the direct involvement of citizens in the design and delivery of policy. Here the use of consensus dialogues and citizen panels has gained in adherents within government in recent years.[22] And the fourth site of decision-making involves the generation of knowledge from citizens about public sector performance, public attitudes on specific issues or long-term thinking: ' ... shifting foresight from a traditionally elite occupation to a process of creating collective intelligence that is shared and used by many'.[23] There is, of course, a fifth site of decision-making that can impact on the formal policy process but is best understood as an informal political domain. This is the domain of civic action in which everyday citizens seek to solve local problems often because of the absence of government support or action.[24] It is noteworthy that decision points 1, 2, 3 and 5 involve greater decision-making competency for citizens and are by implication the most controversial as they challenge dominant conceptions of representative democracy and the traditional role of elected representatives. They also tend to involve a plurality of different forms of mini-publics or engagement methods and there is an inevitable overlap in the methodological choices available.

What does a participatory governance system look like in practice?

An ideal-type participatory governance system would be one where a variety of participatory methods are used to solve a governance problem to address deficiencies within the representative system of government and bolster the legitimacy of public policy-making.

For example, Box 3.1 refers to the case of creating a new constitution for Mexico City through the establishment of an appropriate participatory governance system. It reveals that a range of engagement methods in addition to deliberation were necessary

Box 3.1 Creating a constitution for Mexico City through a participatory governance system[25]

Context and opportunity

For decades, the population of Mexico City was politically disenfranchised because, like many federal districts, it had no status as a state and citizens were not given the opportunity to vote for local representatives.

Response

Laboratorio Para La Ciudad, the experimental arm of the city government, was tasked with developing a public engagement process for the development of the new constitution. This included a writing platform co-developed with MIT Media Lab; an online petition system, which generated 342 petitions and gathered 278,000 signatures; a process for facilitating citizen-driven encounters (over 20); and the Imagine Your City project, which gathered over 34,000 effective surveys. Public engagement spanned residents of poor neighbourhoods engaged by local survey brigades, concerned citizens using online petitioning and committees of legal experts co-drafting documents.

Outcome

The participatory nature of the process and guarantees for including issues and ideas with strong support meant that a diversity of progressive issues were enacted in the constitution, which became law in September 2018.

to achieve a legitimate outcome, including digital methods of direct democracy and processes of policy learning with citizens and technocrats.[26]

Three chapters follow, each representing a mode of governance for framing political demands, and institutionalizing and embedding new forms of citizen voice into the practices of democratic governance. This includes direct democracy in Chapter 4 and deliberative democracy and digital democracy in Chapters 5 and 6. The three chapters review the most common engagement methods used in different sites of decision-making (noting that they are applicable to more than one site) through the review of a range of case study illustrations that illustrate the methods in action. These examples have been selected on the basis of the following criteria:

- Evidence-based – *the case has been evaluated through the use of credible theory and method.*
- Place – *the case is deemed successful from the perspective of the country's democratic history.*
- Novelty – *the case demonstrates a leap of creativity from existing democratic practice.*
- Significance – *the case successfully addresses an important democratic problem of 'public' concern.*
- Utility – *the innovation strengthens democratic practice.*
- Effectiveness – *the case achieved tangible results for the citizenry.*
- Longevity – *the case looks set to achieve results over time.*
- Transferability – *the case, or aspects of it, shows promise of inspiring successful replication by other liberal democracies.*

The examples are drawn from practices in the United States, three European states representing very different political cultures: the UK (Western Europe), Denmark (Northern Europe), Switzerland (Central Europe), and Mexico and Australia.[27]

Towards quality participation

It is important to note from the outset that we do not view public participation to be a panacea for all our democratic problems. Given the flourishing of participatory methods around the world a key question arises – why are they having so little impact on decision-making in high politics? Our main conclusion is not that more participation is needed but that quality participation is needed aimed at integrating citizen input into policy-making processes, building active but critical citizenship and safeguarding public trust. This requires the establishment of participatory governance systems that are:

- clear in scope and purpose
- deploy appropriate engagement methods

- inclusive in composition with co-designed processes
- underpinned by evidence-based outputs and clearly articulated outcomes to guide decision-making and operational delivery
- sensitive to context
- responsive to participants through ongoing engagement that demonstrates the value of their participation; and
- subject to ongoing evaluation and review, to ensure continuous improvement.

This final observation is particularly important. Quality participation requires more understanding of the difficulties of working with citizens to change the ways decisions are made and implemented. Despite the enormous growth of participatory practice and theory, there is still little shared understanding of what works. Participatory practice has emerged from many disciplines and in many sectors, often quite separate from each other, and the lack of effective communication across these disciplines and communities of practice has limited the opportunities for shared learning and the effective development of theory and practice. However, there is significant evidence presented in Chapters 4 and 5 that developments in design thinking can provide public managers with a unique opportunity to establish a community of practice in citizen-centric governance devoted to the co-creation and delivery of policies, programmes and services that the public genuinely values.

CHAPTER 4
DIRECT DEMOCRACY

We argued previously that direct democracy can be a useful component of a broader participatory governance system but can be mad, bad and dangerous for democracy when either used in isolation from deliberative institutions or without the enactment of certain prudential conditions. It is also a more effective decision-making tool when the issue under consideration is succinct, knowable and insusceptible to political manipulation. We also know that there is significant public support for direct democracy. A recent thirty-eight-nation Pew Research Center survey found that 66 per cent of respondents polled considered direct democracy a 'very' or 'somewhat' good way to govern their country, second only to representative democracy (78 per cent), providing further evidence of support for the participatory governance system approach.[1] Direct democracy neither should be seen as panacea for all our political problems and an alternative to representative democracy nor should it be rejected out of hand as inherently populist. The merits of direct democracy are rooted in where sovereignty lies within a liberal democracy. Does it lie with the *demos* – the people – or the *kratos* – the constituent power or source of sovereign decision-making in a nation state?

This chapter presents a range of comparative evidence that suggests that at its worst direct democracy is a dangerous tool of what the Nobel laureate Danny Kahneman refers to as 'fast thinking' but at its best is an effective method for making highly politicized legislation more robust and legitimate.[2] Kahneman and cognitive scientists in general distinguish between two processes of decision-making. Type 1 decision processes such as joining a queue or following traffic signage are deemed 'fast' and not requiring conscious thought, and Type 2 decision processes such as buying a house or a car are seen as 'slower' and more careful tasks, requiring time and effort to be put into evidence collecting, reflection and deliberation. We argue that history-making decisions through referenda require citizens to 'think' slowly but this self-evident empiric observation is often ignored at the detriment of social progress.[3] A set of prudential conditions are then presented for judicious application to complex problems noting that this is contingent on the model of democracy in operation in a particular country.

A broad range of instruments of direct democracy have also emerged at the local level over the past century to promote local democracy and offset the power of local and national elites or ensure more effective delivery of public policy through principles of subsidiarity and participatory localism. We will consider some of these devices in the penultimate section of this chapter.

Saving Democracy

Origins and purpose

The main policy instrument of direct democracy – that the will of the people be expressed through a public vote – is the popular referendum.[4] The name and use of the popular referendum are thought to have originated in the Swiss canton of Graubünden as early as the sixteenth century and were modelled on the ancient tradition of Landsgemeinde, annual open-air meetings where all the men of the canton would engage in direct decision-making on local matters.[5] Since the end of the eighteenth century, popular referendums have become common around the world. Unsurprisingly, Switzerland has been the greatest consumer, with almost 600 national votes being held since its inauguration as a modern state in 1848.[6] The term 'plebiscite' has a similar meaning and derives from the Latin *plebiscita*, which originally meant a decree of the *Concilium Plebis* (Plebeian Council), the popular assembly of the Roman Republic. Notably Italy currently ranks second to Switzerland as the greatest consumer of direct democracy with seventy-two national referendums.

Citizen initiatives and popular referendum serve both to moderate and to check the political legislative process. A citizen's initiative works like a compass, guiding the direction that future laws take through the collection of a sufficient number of signatures triggering a ballot. In contrast, a popular referendum stops the drafting of a law by the legislative body. Direct democracy impacts the legislature in two ways. First, initiatives and referenda can override decisions made by the political class. Second, the threat of citizens taking up a ballot ensures that the political class enact laws in the interest of the people. It is a corrective mechanism for representative democracy to ensure popular control of the political class.

Referenda have often been used by both democratic and autocratic regimes, to confirm newly written constitutions by what many constitutions regard as the ultimate sovereign – the people. History-making examples include the 1958 French constitutional referendum and subsequent 1969 referenda that led to the resignation of President de Gaulle, the 1992 South African Apartheid referendum, the 1993 Malawian democracy referendum or most recently the 2019 Cuban constitutional referendum.[7]

Practice

In recent times, governments around the world have appeared increasingly willing to submit issues to voters and let them have a greater input in key decision-making processes. At the same time that Donald Trump was elected to the US presidency in November 2016, 154 state-wide ballot measures were certified in thirty-five states.[8] Of these measures, seventy-six were put on the ballot by citizens through signature petitions, rather than by state legislatures.[9]

Arizona voters, for example, rejected marijuana legalization, but voters in California, Nevada, Maine and Massachusetts approved it. Medical marijuana measures were approved in Arkansas, Florida and North Dakota, and the programme in Montana was expanded by removing the three-patient limit for providers. The minimum wage was increased in Arizona, Colorado, Maine and Washington but voters in South Dakota overturned the state legislature's attempt to decrease the minimum wage for those under eighteen. Gun control expansion was defeated in Maine but approved in California, Nevada and Washington and attempts to repeal the death penalty were rejected in California and Oklahoma. Over 205 million US residents were affected by the results of ballot measure elections in November 2016.

A popular referendum can be binding or advisory but voting in referenda tends to be compulsory because they have constitutional authority. Plebiscites are nearly always 'advisory referendums' because the government does not have to act upon its decision; although there may be a moral obligation to do so. Nor do plebiscites deal with history-making, constitutional questions but focus on issues where a government seeks approval to act. A popular referendum usually offers the electorate a choice of accepting or rejecting a proposal, but not always. Some referendums give voters the choice among multiple choices and some use transferable voting.

Controversies

The most contested aspect of popular referendums tends to be around the level of public support required to force constitutional or legislative change. It seems reasonable, as He Beogang notes that 'if the approval rate of a referendum is too low, it ought to be discredited. A nearly simple majority does not provide sufficient legitimacy'.[10] This has proved the main source of acrimony surrounding the June 2016 Brexit referendum on European Union (EU) membership, in which 51.9 per cent of Britons voted to leave. In contrast, the condition of a supermajority requirement, albeit a small one, and an eligibility requirement were used in 2006 in Montenegro. The law stipulated that independence would be approved if supported by 55 per cent of those eligible to vote. The total turnout of the referendum was 86 per cent; 55.5 per cent voted in favour and 44.5 per cent were against breaking the state union with Serbia.

Sveinung Arnesen, in his empirical work on conditional legitimacy governing referendums, observes:

> Its' perceived legitimacy in the eyes of the public heavily depends upon the level of turnout, the size of the majority, and the outcome of the specific referendum in question. Thus, whether a referendum legitimizes a political decision in the eyes of the public is conditional upon these three dimensions.[11]

The use of referenda has a checkered history, for as David Altman notes, 'the list of nondemocratic regimes that abuse plebiscites is pathetically high'.[12] Daniel Lewis further argues that the empirical evidence demonstrates that direct democracy (ballot measures and traditional legislation) 'endangers the rights of minorities and perpetuates a tyranny of majority'. Although this, of course, depends on whether the majority oppose minority rights and there are examples of majorities both extending and limiting minority rights as the cases of same-sex marriage across US states, ethnic minorities in California and naturalization in Switzerland amply demonstrate.[13]

What is certain is that referenda of history-making proportions should always be measured against the highest measures of legitimacy and certainly benefits from the establishment of a participatory governance system such as the one noted above in Ireland to inform deliberation on the termination of pregnancy. Direct democracy can be dangerous unless public sentiments are refined by filtration through deliberative institutions. The Brexit decision by the UK government provides an illustration of the complexities involved here.

A June 2016 referendum endorsed exiting the EU. However, implementing the decision became much messier than anyone, especially the public, anticipated. This was largely because a narrow popular majority was confronted by a larger percentage of MPs who wished to remain in the EU, creating a classic stand-off between parliament and the people. A year later, with a 'Brexit' plan nowhere in sight, former Prime Minister David Cameron stated that 'the lack of a referendum was poisoning British politics', and that he had 'put it right'.[14]

Taking into account that Brexit was supposed to happen by the will of the people, but had not, *The Economist* diagnosed a constitutional crisis, stating that the referendum has brought into light the question of where sovereignty lies in the UK.[15] As Donald Tusk, the former president of the European Council, put it in February 2019: 'I've been wondering what the special place in hell looks like … for those who promoted Brexit without even a sketch of a plan of how to carry it safely.'

Significantly then, Brexit can't be viewed as a citizens-led initiative. It originated in the positions taken by two prime ministers. David Cameron said that he was bound to hold a referendum because that commitment had been contained in the Conservative Party manifesto for the 2015 General Election. Theresa May said that she was bound to give effect to the outcome of the 2016 referendum because it had expressed the will of the people. The bedrock principle of representative government is that 'the people' do not decide issues, they decide who shall decide. And once a legislature abrogates its responsibility and resorts to a referendum on the doubtful premise that the simple way to find out what people want is to ask them, it is difficult to avoid political sclerosis.

Remarkably, in 2017, University College London's Constitution Unit ran a Brexit citizens' assembly. It was representative of the UK electorate, with more 'leavers' than 'remainers' and in a 'soft Brexit' versus 'no-deal' trade-off, its members favoured staying in the single market and customs union, and seven in ten thought free movement of people should continue.[16] This illustration demonstrates the power of deliberation in enhancing the knowledge base for decisions that require slower, reflective thinking. Hence deliberative democracy can provide safeguards against emotional 'fast' decision-making.

Direct democracy as a tool of localism

It is almost impossible to conceive of a strong liberal democratic system without a vibrant system of local democracy augmented through various localism strategies. Although a contested term, for the purposes of this chapter we would define localism as an umbrella concept which refers to the devolution of power and/or functions and/or resources away from central control and towards front-line managers, local democratic structures, local institutions and local communities, within an agreed framework of minimum standards (see Table 4.1).[17] Simply put, different central governments in

Table 4.1 Three strategies of localism

	Managerial localism	**Representative localism**	**Participatory localism**
Defining mechanism	Conditional devolution of decision-making based on achieving agreed objectives.	Provision of powers and responsibility to local government elected on universal suffrage	Rights and support given to citizens in communities to directly engage in decisions and action.
Delivery mechanisms	Intergovernmental networks.	Hierarchical delivery networks	Community network governance, direct and deliberative democratic initiatives.
Metrics for judging success	Targets and evidence.	Electoral triumph or failure	Cohesiveness and capacity of network arrangements. Attainment of network goals and fairness of process.
Strengths	Makes sense in the context of multi-level governance and complexity.	Delivers clear identification of responsibility and accountability and capacity to meet localized needs	Delivers ownership, local knowledge and engagement by citizens in defining problems and supporting solutions.
Weaknesses	Can be too 'top-down', lack of downward accountability, associated with a 'government knows-best' narrative for change, ignores locally derived sources of knowledge. Focus in the end is on externally imposed objectives rather than local choices.	Resource issues (both financial and technical) may undermine delivery; accountability in practice may be weak	Potential for network capture by local elite interests persists. Uneven distribution of capacity among communities to respond leads to engagement of some but not all. Accountability structures can be opaque with weak democratic control. Minority voices can be silent.

different nation states deploy different strategies of localism to deliver different tasks. We can normally identify three strategies of localism at work – managerial, representative and participatory community localism – reflecting different degrees of community involvement in decision-making. While all three forms of localism have always existed, representative localism was always first amongst equals at least in terms of its political dominance. This is no longer the case; in an era of governance it is the mix that matters and the balance between the three will differ from jurisdiction to jurisdiction.

Managerial localism involves the conditional devolution of delegated decision-making or delivery functions from the centre to the locality based on achieving agreed objectives. Policy is decided at the centre but policy settings and delivery functions are devolved to the locality under a strict regulatory framework. Success is evaluated on the basis of their ability to meet centrally derived performance targets. In representative localism, powers and responsibility for specific governance tasks are devolved directly to elected local government (e.g. rates, roads and rubbish). Success is evaluated on the basis of re-election. In the context of collaborative governance (initiatives augmented by either central, or state, provincial or regional government), the role of local government would focus on its community leadership role and its ability to harness the resources of the community (including private and civil society organizations) more than a traditional direct service provider role. In practice, however, a top-down managerial tradition has tended to dominate in most countries in which devolution of functions occurs but not devolution of power or resources.[18] In contrast, participatory localism involves the devolution of rights and support directly to citizens in communities to allow them to engage in decisions and action. This is underpinned by a participatory view of democracy which is based on the notion that legitimate governance requires ongoing engagement with the citizenry and their inclusion within certain realms of decision-making.[19]

In times of instability, such as the coronavirus pandemic, participatory localism becomes more important in delivering national as well as local goals. Crucially, however, there is increasing evidence to suggest that the top-down managerial approach to localism does not work.[20] The reason for this is not new or surprising. In an era of governance, citizens' engagement in policy and delivery has become crucial to the achievement of social progress. Not least because all that public organizations do requires co-production and adaptive behaviours from citizens and often stakeholders. Moreover, the critical challenges confronting policy-makers in a complex, fragmented world require the most adaptive form of power to enable local interests to blend their capacities to achieve common purpose. This is called soft power or *the power to persuade*. Localism is a key policy instrument for achieving soft power.[21]

In theory, localism provides central and local authorities with a range of strategies (managerial, representative and participatory) for inputting citizen preferences into formal decision processes which shape the development of local communities. The arguments in support of localism can be organized into three categories: capacity development benefits, political benefits and operational delivery benefits. The potential benefits of localism for local institutional capacity development crystallize around issues of political and policy education, and training in political leadership for local leaders. Political education teaches local populations about the role of political debate; the selection of representatives; and the nature of policy-making, planning and budgetary processes. And training in political leadership creates fertile ground for prospective political leaders to develop skills in policy-making, political party operations and budgeting, with the result that the quality of national politicians is enhanced.[22]

Several sources of political capital can be derived from localism strategies. Political stability is secured by enhancing public participation in formal politics, through voting, local party activism and deliberative and direct democratic initiatives. This strengthens trust in government and fosters community solidarity.[23] In addition, new institutional venues are created to give expression to local identities. The achievement of political equality through institutional processes that afford greater political participation reduces the likelihood of the concentration of power. Localism strategies can distribute political power more broadly, thus becoming a mechanism that can, in theory at least, meet the needs of the most disadvantaged. Public accountability can also be enhanced because local representatives are more accessible to the public and can thus be held more easily accountable for their actions than distant national leaders. Moreover, the existence of cyclical elections provides local electors with a mechanism for voicing grievances or satisfaction with the performance of local representatives.[24]

In sum, direct democratic instruments can be used as key tools for establishing participatory localism as the traditional arguments against direct democracy wither away at the local scale given the acceleration of technological change. For example, it is no longer possible to make the argument that direct democracy will inevitably lead to information overload and ungovernability when we have the technology to enable local citizens to directly input preferences online through various digital platforms.[25] Digital era governance, as we will see in Chapter 6, brings direct democracy within easy reach of government and citizen but whether this is appropriate in all areas of decision-making is a different matter. As we have noted on frequent occasions, digital democracy only makes sense in the context of a broader participatory governance system; in this case, as a tool of localism. Moreover, if democracy is about getting what you want all the time then all politics is on a hiding to nothing, but perhaps citizens merely want to have a say over decisions that directly affect them. Can we use direct democratic instruments to help aid such ambitions? Let's look at three practices that can help bolster the legitimacy of representative democracy at the local scale: the right of recall, consultative and binding referenda, and community-driven development.

The right to recall local members

The right of local citizens to directly recall their local member of parliament is linked to the application of the concept of the mandate in representative parliamentary democracies. A mandate is the authority granted by a constituency to act as its representative as a consequence of winning a fair democratic election. It is normally derived from an election manifesto that sets out the case for election. The power of recall is largely used for the removal of MPs who engage in corrupt practices or personal misconduct such as the use and abuse by members of Parliament of their expense allowances or taking bribes from special interests to ask questions in parliament or congress or allocating grants or procurement projects without reference to due process.[26] But it has also been used to remove MPs for political or policy purposes such as deviating from election commitments or failing to respond to community policy perspectives.[27, 28]

The key problem with the power of recall lies in the clash between local and national interests. This issue is extremely well illustrated in the following excerpt from a June 2012 report from the UK House of Commons Political and Constitutional Reform Committee report into the recall process:

> *A system of full recall may deter MPs from taking decisions that are unpopular locally or unpopular in the short-term, but which are in the long-term national interest ... [w]e note that expulsion would not prevent the person concerned standing in the resulting by-election. We recommend that the Government abandon its plans to introduce a power of recall ... We have not seen enough evidence to support the suggestion that it will increase public confidence in politics, and fear that the restricted form of recall proposed could even reduce confidence by creating expectations that are not fulfilled.*[29]

The British Parliament introduced a Recall of MPs Act 2015 on 26 March of that year. The empowering idea of electorates being able to recall their representatives through petition does have significant risks involved which would need to be addressed. As Anne Twomey observes:

> *The rationale for introducing the recall needs to be clear as does its intended consequences. A system that allows the rich to buy a new election or political parties to harass each other is unlikely to satisfy the wishes of voters. Consideration also needs to be given to the existing political and constitutional system and how a system of recall could be accommodated within it, rather than clashing fundamentally with it.*[30]

On balance, however, the guidance provided appears to miss the mark. Why should MPs be a law unto themselves and subject to dismissal only through electoral defeat? Everyday citizens are subject to modern working practices – ongoing performance review, annual reporting, monitoring and evaluation, capability development – why are politicians treated as a different species? The power of recall ensures that MPs both adhere to codes of conduct and are responsive and accountable to their constituents ('we the people').

Consultative and binding referenda

At the local level, consultative and binding referenda, subject to the prudential conditions outlined above, can play an important role in cementing the legitimacy of representative democracy. It should be noted that in developing democracies the demand for direct democracy in local government is related to previous experiences with inefficient and nondemocratic forms of local government which prevailed under previous regimes. Some developing democracies in Eastern Europe (e.g. Hungary, Bulgaria and Slovakia) make it obligatory to hold local referenda on specified local matters such as cadastral changes, the amalgamation of communes or the sale of land. In Russia and Albania, legislation requires referenda on unspecified but important local issues. Most states also allow local initiatives to hold referenda. Local self-governments in Slovenia are obliged to hold referenda if requested by more than 10 per cent of local voters. The results of local referenda may be binding if they satisfy certain conditions (such as a greater than 30 per cent participation rate in Poland and 50 per cent in Macedonia).

The local referendum is probably the best and most widely recognized instrument of direct democracy at the local scale, although the growing number of countries with directly elected mayors (replacing election of mayors within the local council) does reflect a shift in response to pressure for direct democracy to enhance local democracy.[31]

Participatory budgeting

In 1989, Olívio de Oliveira Dutra, the newly elected mayor of the southern Brazilian city of Porto Alegre, worked with community groups to empower citizens to directly propose and vote on local investment projects to be funded by the municipality.[32] Participatory budgeting was born. Since then, participatory budgeting has spread across the globe, and is lauded by international organizations and knowledge institutions as a 'best practice' to be replicated.[33] The rise of participatory budgeting initiatives in cities like Glasgow, New York, Paris and Madrid is testimony to the latest wave of direct citizen participation in budgetary decision-making. The recently published *Participatory Budgeting World Atlas* claims more than 11,000 cases of different types of participatory budgeting exist throughout the world.[34] Participatory budgeting has become a particularly popular tool of participatory localism in response to economic crisis and recovery (see Table 4.2).

In theory, participatory budgeting is a process of democratic deliberation and decision-making which empowers ordinary citizens to identify, deliberate and prioritize public spending. It can take place at the level of the local neighbourhood, service or at the city or state levels. For example, in the aftermath of the Global Financial Crisis when confronted with deep cuts to local government budgets, many English local authorities created participatory budgeting processes to ensure broader community ownership of priority investments. In an evaluation of thirty-four of these initiatives in 2011, commissioned by the Department for Communities and Local Government, participatory budgeting – directly involving local people in making spending priorities for a defined public budget – was deemed most effective 'as part of a package of community engagement and empowerment' and was viewed to be a successful instrument for building community trust, confidence and knowledge.[35] This involves a combination of deliberative and direct democratic processes. Residents and community groups that are representative of all parts of the community are brought together to discuss spending priorities and develop spending proposals. A set of options are then voted on by the community as a whole. A representative group of citizens will then be deployed to scrutinize and monitor the arising budgetary processes.[36]

In this context, direct democracy as applied to formal decision-making liberates representative institutions from bearing full responsibility for high-impact decisions. It shares the risk and provides for common ownership of the problem under scrutiny. Direct and participatory democratic initiatives both concern non-elected citizen involvement in decision-making, or their participation in decision-making processes outside the main elected local government institutions such as local councils or the formal committee system. With the coronavirus pandemic and other social developments undermining public trust in governments, it is likely that we will see an upsurge in the use of participatory budgeting mechanisms as a crucial tool for rebuilding trust at the local scale. For example, in February 2021, Paris Mayor Anne Hidalgo relaunched the city's participatory budgeting process, whereby residents propose projects and vote on how they want to allocate up to 25 per cent of municipal spending. The initiative will allow citizens to deliberate on the impact of Covid-19 and identify their post-pandemic priorities.[37]

Table 4.2 Examples of participatory budgeting (PB) processes around the world

Inception	Initiative
1989–2021: Porto Alegre, Brazil[38]	Established in 1989, the Porto Alegre programme was the first in the world. Its success inspired countless similar projects both in Brazil and around the globe. Porto Alegre's budget process involves an estimated 50,000 people annually who decide how to spend as much as 20 percent of the city's budget.
2009–21: Chicago, Illinois[39]	The first PB project in the United States was launched in Chicago's 49th ward in 2009 by the Participatory Budgeting Project led by Chicago Alderman Joe Moore. Today, nearly 3,000 citizen participants decide how to spend $3 million of taxpayer money to improve local schools, streets, parks and other public spaces.
2012–21: Seoul, South Korea[40]	Seoul's PB programme has been running since 2012. The most recent budget involved allocating 50 billion KRW (around $50 million) into initiatives voted on by members of the Participatory Budget Council, which comprises a wide range of people from school children up to elders. The top-voted projects have included expanding the facilities for people with disabilities at a local sports centre; creating community projects to stop bullying and school violence; and installing gas safety valves in homes of low-income retirees living alone.

Direct Democracy

2004–13: Seville, Spain[41]	Between 2004 and 2013, the city of Seville in Spain conducted a PB process in which residents decided on roughly 50 per cent of local spending for their city districts. It remains a model of successful participatory practice which spread to other cities. Spain currently has the highest rate of growth of participatory budgeting in Europe largely in response to the impact of economic crisis.
2004–21: Yaoundé, Cameroon[42]	Through an 'experimental initiative' supported by the World Bank Institute and the World Bank's Open Development Technology Alliance, citizens of two local municipalities of Yaoundé, the capital of Cameroon, use mobile phones to participate in the PB process. Using text messaging to inform citizens of issues, meetings, budget data and more, the project was able to mobilize thousands of citizens in support of local issues around sanitation and water safety.
2019–21: Glasgow, UK[43]	In the 2019 budget, £150K was allocated to Glasgow's open spaces and the City Council agreed for it to be spent using a Participatory Budgeting Framework administered through the Glasgow Friends of Parks Forum.
2014–21: Paris, France[44]	Paris Mayor Anne Hidalgo pioneered the use of PB in France. Hidalgo's latest initiative allows 25 per cent of the city's outlay from now until 2026 to be decided with the input of Parisians. This will include major consultations over any flagship projects or neighbourhood redevelopment in the city.

Despite its popularity as a tool of participatory governance, participatory budgeting has been criticized for being a forum of local elite action and failing to provide inclusive representation and a plurality of perspectives on policy problems.[45] This is not a criticism of participatory budgeting per se, rather an observation that it is often poorly practised.[46] We will outline the conditions informing authentic deliberative engagement in the next chapter.

Evaluation – prudential guidance for the use of direct democracy

The Brexit process demonstrated that the use of direct democratic institutions for political decision-making processes is controversial and suggests that at the very least nine prudential criteria should be introduced to guide their use.[47]

1. First, process design with a clear intervention logic mindful of consequences of action is critical to achieving a legitimate and credible outcome.

2. Secondly, given that referenda are both a check on representative government and an agenda-setting mechanism, they should be initiated by citizens through petition. The power of petition should be knowable and accessible to all citizens eligible to petition. Allowing parliament or executive government to decide on what matters citizens should have a say on is inconsistent with the notion of a sovereign people. It automatically heightens the potential for either the abuse of power (as in the case of the recent introduction of constitutional amendments in Turkey) or in political sclerosis (as in the case of Brexit).[48] If confidence in the executive government depends on approval of a proposition by the voters, referenda are likely to be used as a political tool.

3. Thirdly, power asymmetries between parliaments, executives and citizens need to be eliminated to reduce the likelihood of abuse. Referendums called by the executive or legislative body give ruling politicians additional power over citizens. The fact that such plebiscites are often not legally binding but consultative reinforces power asymmetries.

4. Fourthly, all popular decisions should be considered fallible and reversible to stay apace with social and political change.

5. Fifth, referenda require a politically literate public, so it makes sense to encourage the use of direct democracy at the sub-national and local government levels. This also allows for comparison and the progressive diffusion of innovations across territory.

6. Sixth, the core element of referendum or initiative law is that it should be enshrined constitutionally or through the highest source of law in a country to avoid risk of short-term manipulation through amendments that would favour a certain interest group or sectional interest.

7. Seventh, for direct democracy to be credible and legitimate, voters should be able to voice their opinion and make decisions in an authentic way free from constraints. The historic evidence suggests that this requires that the proposed legislation should deal with one subject only to allow the voter to form and express their opinion with clarity. In other words, if a proposed legislation includes several substantive questions, the voter's capacity to make a free choice may be severely constrained.

8. Eighth, referenda should not undermine minority rights. Any potential conflicts with existing rights should be explicitly declared prior to the vote. Newly proposed legislation may be in contradiction with existing public laws and human rights protected by the constitution or through international law. The easiest way to address this issue is to include a rebuttable presumption that assumes that newly formulated initiatives intend to respect existing fundamental rights.

9. And, ninth, the validity of a ballot proposition should be considered a legal matter decided by a legal rather than a political authority and confirmed as legitimate prior to the ballot.

These criteria can be used both to guide the application of direct democratic measures and to assess their impact.

In conclusion – direct democracy as an instrument of democratic symmetry

Direct democracy is an important component of a participatory governance system, but it is crucial to understand the pitfalls of direct democratic decision-making processes and how this powerful tool can be implemented in a safe and effective way to strengthen the broader democratic system. The single most important quality of direct democracy is that it provides the powerful with a constant reminder that the legitimation of political power emanates from the people. As the British parliamentarian Tony Benn put it in his farewell speech to the House of Commons, in which he talked widely on his view of the role of parliament and the wider question of democracy:

> *In the course of my life I have developed five little democratic questions. If one meets a powerful person – Adolf Hitler, Joe Stalin or Bill Gates – ask them five questions: 'What power have you got? Where did you get it from? In whose interests do you exercise it? To whom are you accountable? And how can we get rid of you?' If you cannot get rid of the people who govern you, you do not live in a democratic system.*[49]

While not the target that perhaps Tony Benn had in mind direct democracy might be seen as falling foul of the last question. If the people rule, who is to be held accountable for its decisions? Who could replace the people if they got the decision wrong? The next generation might be an answer. There are many opponents of Brexit in the UK or proponents of independence in Scotland that might question whether waiting for a new generation to be formed is an attractive political option. Direct democracy has a role in saving democracy but it cannot replace other democratic instruments.

CHAPTER 5
DELIBERATIVE DEMOCRACY

John Dryzek and Simon Niemeyer define deliberative democracy as a field of political enquiry that is concerned with 'improving collective decision-making'. It emphasizes the 'right, opportunity, and capacity of anyone who is subject to a collective decision to participate ... in consequential deliberation about that decision'. Consequential means that the deliberation must have some influence on decision-making.[1] We argue in this chapter that deliberative democracy plays an essential role in a participatory governance system. The key debate around the merits of deliberative democracy does not focus on its intrinsic value but on whether it has a specific domain of utility. As noted previously in Chapter 3, we prefer the looser concept of participatory governance systems rather than deliberative systems as it doesn't make sense to confine citizen engagement to deliberation as a range of other engagement methods are needed to make sense of the diversity of public opinion on public policy questions. For example, Box 5.1 provides an illustration from the Irish context where a participatory governance system was established to inform deliberation on the termination of pregnancy. Ireland has been a trailblazer in the use of deliberative mini-publics to discuss important topics of constitutional reform at a time when the Irish Parliament was too divided to make a change. The Constitutional Convention (ICC) of 2012–14 and the Citizens' Assembly (ICA) of 2016–18 were established by the Irish government and tasked with considering a series of constitutional reform proposals.

Membership of the mini publics in both cases comprised random selections of regular citizens; however, in the case of the ICC one-third of the members were professional politicians representing all the political parties in the national parliament. Successful referendums on marriage equality in 2015 and abortion in 2018 suggest how democracies can bring citizens into the heart of discussions over constitutional and political reform through combining representative and participatory modes of governance that enhance the quality of decision-making and provide deep legitimacy to the process of change.

These were not deliberative in a formal sense but proved effective in unlocking a highly politicized policy environment. Deliberative democracy makes room for many other forms of decision-making such as bargaining politics and, as we shall see in the next chapter, co-design. It should also be noted, once again, that without good practice, deliberative methods can be subject to politicization and manipulation.[2] We will assess what this notion of better practice might look like in the concluding section of the chapter.

Our discussion of deliberative democracy is organized into four sections. In part one we review the guiding principles of deliberative democracy. Parts two, three and four evaluate the role of deliberative democracy in strategic decision-making; policy, programme and public service design; and policy learning. In conclusion, we identify six ingredients of better practice to guide deliberative practice.

What is deliberative democracy?

At its essence, deliberative democracy establishes the argument that there is more to democracy than voting. There is a need through democratic governance to justify decisions made by citizens and their representatives.[3] It has four key features. The first and probably most important characteristic is its public reason-giving requirement. Citizens should not be treated as subjects of the political class, and passive subjects to be ruled, but as autonomous agents with the critical capacity to take part in the governance of their own society.

Box 5.1 Participatory governance system informing deliberation on the termination of pregnancy

2016–17: Citizens' Assembly

In 2016, the government set up a Citizens' Assembly to debate the need for another referendum on the 8th Amendment, among other constitutional issues. The Assembly was made up of ninety-nine randomly selected people from across the country and chaired by a Supreme Court judge. This group's job was to consider the issue and recommend to the government whether to keep, change or remove the 8th Amendment.

The results of the Citizens' Assembly, published in April 2017, were as follows:
87 per cent of the members voted that Article 40.3.3 (the 8th Amendment) of the constitution should not be retained in full.
56 per cent of the members voted that Article 40.3.3 (the 8th Amendment) should be amended or replaced.
57 per cent of the members recommended that Article 40.3.3 (the 8th Amendment) be replaced with a Constitutional provision explicitly allowing the Oireachtas to legislate on the issue of abortion.

20 December 2017: Joint Committee on the Eighth Amendment of the Constitution

Following the Citizens' Assembly, the Assembly's report was referred to a Joint Committee in the Oireachtas for consideration. The Committee brought together T.D.s and Senators from different political parties, as well as independents, to consider the report from the Citizens' Assembly and make a recommendation to the Dáil.

The recommendations made by the Committee included that:
Article 40.3.3 of the Constitution should be repealed.
Termination of pregnancy, with no restriction as to reason, should be allowed with a gestational limit of twelve weeks.
Termination of pregnancy should be allowed where there is a fatal foetal abnormality that is likely to result in death before or shortly after birth, with no gestational limit.[4]

29 January 2018: Announcement of referendum

It was announced on Monday 29 January 2018 that the government is to hold a referendum to remove Article 40.3.3. from the constitution and replace it.

A Yes vote in the referendum would allow for the removal of the 8th Amendment from the constitution, and the introduction of an 'enabling clause' which would allow the Oireachtas to legislate for abortion in Ireland – something they are restricted in doing now because of the 8th Amendment.

26 May 2018: Irish referendum on the termination of pregnancy

The Irish people responded to the referendum question: *Do you approve of the proposal to amend the constitution? The amended text would read: 'Provision may be made by law for the regulation of termination of pregnancy'.*

66.4 per cent voted for yes to 33.6 per cent for no and on a record turnout of 64.51 per cent, to repeal the eighth amendment of its constitution, which since 1983 has effectively prohibited abortion in all bar exceptional circumstances.

The Irish taoiseach, Leo Varadkar, who had campaigned for repeal, welcomed the result. "What we have seen today is the culmination of a quiet revolution [that has been taking place] for the past 10 or 20 years."

The amendment to the Constitution was signed into law by the Irish President Michael D. Higgins on 18 September 2018.

A second characteristic of deliberative democracy is that the reasons giving rise to the deliberative process should be accessible to all citizens affected by the decision. The issue should not be the preserve of political elites in an imprisoned zone of decision-making.

The third characteristic of deliberative democracy is that its process should aim at producing a decision that is binding for a period but should be considered fallible and debated on an ongoing basis. This notion of the ongoing nature of debate and the fallibility of decision-making illustrates the fourth characteristic of deliberative democracy – its process is dynamic. Mocracy is a living thing and needs to be fostered and renewed through ongoing deliberation and engagement.

Deliberation and strategic decision-making

A variety of deliberative democratic methods have been used to integrate citizen input into strategic decision-making largely focusing on the use of various forms of mini-publics. America-speaks deliberative design, founded by Carolyn Lukensmeyer in 1997 and operating until 2014, has been emulated throughout the world. Box 5.2 describes the case of the UK European Citizens Consultation which combined deliberative design and polling. This involves the recreation of '21st century Town Meetings' in one day events involving between 500 and 5,000 people deliberating on a specific issue and culminating in a poll. Selection procedures vary but there is normally an attempt to establish a degree of representativeness. They operate through moderated small group discussions at demographically mixed tables of representatives consisting of ten to twelve people. Feedback from these tables is aggregated via networked computers and filtered to form the basis for subsequent discussions. Large video screens present data, themes and information in real time over the course of the deliberations: as themes emerge and votes are taken, recommendations gel. Key stakeholders produce background materials and, together with public authorities, typically attend the events.[5]

America-speaks deliberative design methodology has been effective in engaging citizens: in shaping New Orleans' recovery plan after Hurricane Katrina,[6] developing participatory budgets in Washington through neighbourhood action (later emulated in Chicago and New York), and healthcare priority setting in California.[7] America-speaks was also instrumental in influencing the establishment of President Barack Obama's Open Government Initiative in 2009 but Obama was arguably more successful in ensuring access to open data than extending public participation.[8]

Deliberation and policy, programme and service design

This section explores innovative examples of policy, programme and service design using deliberative input from citizens. Here we focus on two types of mini-public – the role of consensus conferences and the use of citizen panels.

Box 5.2 The 2007 European Citizen's Consultation

Context and opportunity

This deliberative process was held in the aftermath of the European Union's abortive attempts to establish a European Constitution. All European Union member states were instructed by the Council of Europe to: (a) engage a non-governmental organization to facilitate a deliberative engagement with a representative sample of 300 citizens using state of the art interactive technologies; (b) the deliberation would be held over a weekend and focus on developing policy statements on four key issues confronting the European Union – defence, immigration, economic development and climate change. The case study illustrates the key challenges confronting engagement specialists when designing a large-scale national deliberation drawing on international better practice guidelines.

Response

The European Citizens' consultations provided the first-ever opportunity for members of the public from all member states to debate the future of the EU across the boundaries of geography and language. The deliberative format of the events ensured that every voice was heard through a combination of professional facilitation and instant transfer of information by interactive technology. The agenda was entirely citizen-led as the main topic areas to be discussed were defined by citizens of all EU member states at an Agenda-Setting Event held in Brussels in October 2006. The whole process was structured towards allowing the participants to refine their own views and define their highest priorities, asking them 'What Europe do we want?' The key topics chosen were: Energy and the Environment; Family and Social Welfare; the EU's Global Role and Immigration.

In design terms, the European Citizen's Consultation combined elements of thinking derived from America Speaks approaches with Deliberative Polling. A deliberative poll measures what the public would think about an issue if they had an adequate chance to reflect on the questions at hand by observing the evolution of a test group of citizens' views, as they learn more about a topic. Deliberative polls are more statistically representative than many other approaches due to their large scale. Deliberative Polls gather a random sample of between 150 and 300 citizens to deliberate on specific policy questions. They hear evidence from experts, break up into smaller groups (up to fifteen in each) to frame questions to put to experts, reassemble in plenary sessions to pose those questions to panels of experts. Before and after surveys of participants are taken to measure the existing knowledge base of citizens and attitudinal change over the period of deliberation. The results of a Deliberative Poll are partly prescriptive, pointing to what an informed and reflective citizenry might want policy-makers to do.

Outcomes

While the consultation was evaluated as successful in design terms its impact has been negligible in terms of shaping policy outcomes due to the lack of consequentialism and the sovereign decision-making role of the Council of Ministers. However, the deliberation has subsequently been repeated on a bi-annual basis which suggests its significance as a learning opportunity for policy-makers.

Consensus dialogues

The Danish Board of Technology Foundation (DBTF) is internationally renowned for its work on public participation.[9] It was formerly the Danish Board of Technology – an independent counselling institution connected to the Danish Ministry of Science, Innovation and Higher Education.[10] It employs a variety of methods for engaging citizens. These include cafe seminars, citizens' and parliamentary hearings, citizens' juries and summits, future panels and voting conferences. Perhaps the most well-known engagement method associated with the DBTF is the consensus conference or dialogue.[11] In Denmark, there is an expectation (although no formal legal requirement) for Parliament and political parties to respond explicitly to the recommendations of Consensus Dialogues organized by the DBTF. Consensus Dialogues originally began in 1987 and have received much attention for their role in engaging citizens in pre-decision-making processes.[12] They involve a small group of up to fifteen lay citizens who hold two-weekend-long preparatory meetings to set the agenda for a four-day public forum at which experts give testimony and are questioned and the lay panel retires to write a paper. The paper is then presented to a press conference. In Denmark, the public forum is followed by a series of local debates.[13, 14] Box 5.3 presents a recent example from the United States.

Citizen experience of public services

A citizens' experience panel is a large, demographically representative group of citizens used to assess public preferences and opinions. Citizens' panels are made up of a representative sample of a local population and are used by statutory agencies, especially local authorities, to identify local issues and consult service users and non-users. Potential participants are generally recruited through random sampling of the electoral roll or door-to-door recruitment. They are then selected so that membership is made up of a representative profile of the local population in terms of age and gender. Once they agree to participate, panel members participate in surveys at intervals over the course of their membership and, where appropriate, in further in-depth research such as Focus Groups.

Citizens' panels have evolved from opinion polling and market research and can be used to assess service needs, identify delivery issues and determine the appropriateness of service design. Large panels can also be used to target specific groups for their views on issues. Citizens' panels measure the views of a large body of people over a period of time, thereby assessing the impact of developments. Here deliberative mapping tools are used to discern differences in perspective between citizens and technocrats. Participants rate different policy options against a set of defined criteria. The citizen and expert participants are divided into panels (often according to gender and socio-economic background to ensure that people are comfortable voicing their views). The citizens' panels and the experts consider the issue both separately from one another and at a joint workshop. This allows both groups to learn from each other without the experts dominating. The

Box 5.3 University of Michigan consensus dialogue on autonomous vehicles[15]

Context and opportunity

In December 2016, Michigan passed the most 'permissive' autonomous vehicle (AV) laws in the United States, allowing cars on public roads without safety drivers or steering wheels. Washtenaw County roads are expected to be early hosts of AVs. Thus far, industry and academic experts have driven the conversation and policy development. Missing though are the critical perspectives and values of the community. The conference was therefore organized as an opportunity for community members to learn about and voice their opinions on a potentially society altering technology – autonomous vehicles (AVs). The event was designed to enable the public to contribute to the discussion around technologies that impact their lives. The event looked beyond industry experts to those who will be most impacted; community members themselves.

Response

Eleven citizens were selected to represent Washtenaw County in a consensus dialogue using the methodology outlined above and convened three times to learn more about AV technology, engage with experts and formulate recommendations.

Outcome

In overview, the citizens viewed AVs as an opportunity to not only reduce traffic accidents but also as a technology that could potentially address some of the social injustice issues facing Southeast Michigan, including providing access to communities that lack mass transit access. They also viewed the rise of a new industry (AV testing facilities and development) as a chance for job creation and believe that strengthening the education pipeline to ensure that residents of Southeast Michigan are competitive for new jobs should be a top priority. The citizens were concerned, however, that these opportunities may not be realized if industry leaders are the only voice in the policy-making process. The auto industry's primary objective will be to sell AVs, and thus it is up to citizens and their representatives to direct the advancement and 'roll-out' of these vehicles in a way that is safe, transparent and equitable. The findings were accepted by the local municipal government as an advisory paper to inform local policy development.

---

emphasis of the process is not on integrating expert and public voices but understanding the different insights each offer the policy process. The groups themselves determine which criteria they will use to score the options against, thereby limiting any structural bias, and arrive at a ranking. Deliberative mapping incorporates both quantitative and qualitative methods and participants work both individually and as a group.

Saving Democracy

Deliberation and policy learning

Methods for exploring new policy directions and long-term policy thinking have been a feature of many mature liberal democracies for over two decades. Policy learning involves the ongoing engagement of citizens in the monitoring and evaluation of public policies or services and in horizon or future scanning of alternatives. This is often explored using a set of similar devices for either getting feedback on performance or identifying social attitudes on specific problems or initiatives. Here we will explore the role of citizens' assemblies and juries in policy learning.

Citizens' assemblies and wicked problems

The use of citizens' assemblies is very much in vogue in policy arenas featured by political sclerosis. As noted above, Ireland became a trailblazer in the use of deliberative mini-publics to discuss important topics of constitutional reform at a time when the Irish Parliament was too divided to breakthrough and make a change. In the context of high-risk political management, the Constitutional Convention (ICC) of 2012 to 2014 and the Citizens' Assembly (ICA) of 2016 to 2018 were catalytic deliberative events that made action on historically contested constitutional reform proposals possible. As Tom Ritchy observes, citizen assemblies are a particularly useful device for making progress on wicked problems, issues that are

> ... ill-defined, ambiguous and associated with strong moral, political and professional issues. Since they are strongly stakeholder dependent, there is often little consensus about what the problem is, let alone how to resolve it.[16]

A recent Ipsos poll conducted in fourteen countries found that two-thirds of citizens consider the climate crisis as serious as Covid-19 and want their governments to prioritize climate action in the process of economic recovery.[17] Two of the highest profile citizen assemblies of recent times were established just prior to the Covid-19 outbreak in the UK and France to make progress on the issue. The UK citizen assembly – Climate Assembly UK – was sponsored by the House of Commons via six parliamentary committees with the remit of evaluating how the UK should respond to the climate emergency and what policies they would like to see implemented to meet the target of net-zero carbon emissions by 2050, already enshrined in UK law.[18] The 110-person assembly was chosen by sortition and convened by MPs (see Box 5.4).[19] In the UK since 2018 citizens assemblies have been initiated on how adult social care in England should be funded long term, the future of Scotland and Wales, congestion, and air quality and public transport, amongst others.[20]

In contrast, the French government is yet to legislate on emissions targets. France's citizens' assembly was launched following 'yellow vest' protests ignited by a 2018 hike in fuel tax. It was empowered by President Emmanuel Macron to generate measures to reduce the country's carbon emissions by 40 per cent by 2030 from 1990 levels 'in a

Deliberative Democracy

Box 5.4 How sortition or a civic lottery works: the case of Climate Assembly UK

> On 6 November 2019, 30,000 letters were sent to citizens across the UK inviting them to take part in Climate Assembly UK. To ensure the most representative sample, 80 per cent of those receiving an invitation were randomly selected from every UK household address in Royal Mail's Postcode Address File. The remaining 20 per cent were randomly selected from the most deprived areas within the Royal Mail's Postcode Address File, simply because response rates are estimated to be lower from these postcodes. People receiving an invitation could reply by phone or online. This created a pool of potential participants free on the relevant dates.
>
> *Climate Assembly UK* used random stratified sampling (also termed sortition), undertaken by a computer, to select the 110 participants who together are representative of the UK population aged sixteen years and over in terms of age, gender, educational background, ethnicity, location, urban/rural and attitudes to climate change.

spirit of social justice'. Macron initially guaranteed that their proposals would be put to parliament 'unfiltered', 'transformed into executive decrees' or even used as the basis for a referendum. However, he subsequently reneged on the agreement undermining public trust in the process. Both assemblies were then suspended and moved online to continue their work due to the need for social distancing restrictions to contain the spread of the virus.[21] Notably they have both adapted their agendas to ensure that climate action is linked to post-Covid-19 recovery.[22]

Citizens juries, reviews and policy learning

Citizens' juries and initiative reviews are engagement events similar in design to citizens' assemblies but on a smaller scale. Initially introduced in the United States by Ned Crosby and the Jefferson Center, juries have been used sporadically in different countries to provide feedback on initiatives or scope new issues. They are called citizens' juries, as they are similar to juries in criminal trials. A typical design for a citizen jury would involve twelve to twenty-four citizens, selected by stratified sampling to promote demographic representativeness deliberate for two to four days to provide advice on a specific policy issue. The jury receives information, hears evidence, cross-examines witnesses and deliberates on the issue at hand (see Box 5.5 for an illustrative case study).[23] Citizen juries have increasingly become recognized for their capacity to deliver outcomes that are trusted by the broader community.

Citizens' Initiative Reviews provide an interesting twist on the citizen jury model and an important link between the direct democracy ballot measures discussed in Chapter 4 and used in the United States and deliberative methods. Here a group of twenty-four registered voters from around a state are selected from a random sample of 10,000 registered voters to study an active ballot measure. They undergo training in dialogue and deliberation techniques to prepare for deliberation on the issues raised and campaign advocates for and against the measure make their case and are questioned by the citizen panellists. In addition, independent experts provide information and respond to request and questions from the panel. At the end of the deliberation, the forum uses a combination of voting and consensus tools, to generate a statement that includes key facts, the rationale for voting for and against the measure. The statement is then distributed as widely as possible so that all of the state's voters can read and consider the statement when they cast their ballot. For example, in Oregon, where the Citizens' Initiative Review is an official part of state elections, the CIR statement is sent to every registered voter as part of the official Voters' Pamphlet.[24]

Box 5.5 The democracy in Geelong Citizen's Jury Project[25]

Context and opportunity

Following the dismissal of the City of Greater Geelong Council in Australia in April 2016, the Victorian Government decided to engage with the community on the structure of its future local council. It was decided to create a citizen's jury.

Response

MosaicLab[26] was engaged by Local Government Victoria and DemocracyCo to design and facilitate discussions and activities for both the online and face-to-face components of the process, which asked 100 randomly selected and descriptively representative Geelong residents to deliberate on the following question: 'Our council was dismissed. How do we want to be democratically represented by a future council?'

The Geelong Citizen's Jury was drawn representatively from the City of Greater Geelong. Over an intensive period of face-to-face and online forum work the Jury developed recommendations for the Victoria Minister and Cabinet to consider for the 2017 Geelong Council Election and beyond.

Outcome

The jury recommended a bi-annually elected mayor and deputy mayor; greater emphasis on community engagement in decision-making through the use of citizens juries and committees; the use of four wards (with 11 or preferably 15 councillors); and the establishment of a Geelong online Portal, a Junior Council and a Junior Mayor.

The Democracy in Geelong project was a ground-breaking engagement process given that no other community in Australia had ever had the chance to design its own council's structure.

Evaluation – the conditions for effective deliberation

A systematic review of best practice in participatory engagement by Nicole Moore highlights six principles of engagement that may well hold the key to their success:[27]

1. **Inclusive representation of affected people and professionals**
   It is not possible to involve all people in every decision-making process. What is important is to ensure that those most affected by the issue, along with those who will ultimately be responsible for implementing solutions, are represented in the process. Affected people and professionals offer unique insights that collectively ensure solutions respond to the real-world contexts in which issues arise.

2. **Autonomy and equality of participants**
   The freedom to form and transform views on a particular issue is an indication that participants are engaging with autonomy and not constrained by fixed ideas or coerced by higher power interests. Without autonomy, participants can't genuinely consider the viewpoints of others in order to be open to new possibilities. Autonomy and equality go hand in hand since power imbalances must be addressed and participants must feel listened to and respected to contribute equally to engagement processes.

3. **Plurality of viewpoints and engagement methods**
   It is important to ensure a range of viewpoints are considered when making decisions on matters of public interest. Modern societies, however, are diverse and not everyone will engage in the same way. Offering multiple engagement methods can increase the range of perspectives that contribute to public sector decisions and enhance the quality of potential solutions.

4. **Quality process design and facilitation**
   High-quality engagements recognize that participants are experts in their own experiences with valuable insights to share. This requires a shift in thinking from being the experts on a particular topic to being facilitators with expertise shared between participants. Public engagements must carefully balance the need for respectful collaboration between diverse 'experts' with the ability to provoke different opinions to enable innovation. Often this involves mixed methods that allow people to contribute individually, in small groups and in large group discussions.

5. **Transmission of citizen engagement outcomes to formal decision-making bodies**
   Engagement processes usually occur in informal public spaces rather than through formally constituted decision-making bodies, hence requiring some form of transmission to take effect. Transmission can, however, be impacted by whether or not citizen-generated recommendations are transferred indirectly via other stakeholder groups, or directly, to those with the power to make decisions. When recommendations are transferred via stakeholder groups, it is important to ensure the original intent of the recommendations is retained.

6. **Citizen participation as an accepted democratic value**
   Political support for citizen participation has the power to increase the legitimacy and acceptance of public sector decisions. Committing to accepting, at least in principle, the solutions offered by citizens recognizes the value that citizen participation makes to identifying workable solutions. While it is likely to be unfeasible (and perhaps unwise) to agree in full to solutions before knowing what they are, the level of commitment should be made known before citizens agree to give up their time to participate. This includes making clear the boundaries and constraints that are not open to discussion and providing a clear remit or guiding question to focus their involvement.

In conclusion – enhancing the quality of participation through deliberation

There is considerable evidence to support the observation that deliberative methods can enhance the quality of participation and decision-making and provide for greater legitimacy.[28] Mini-publics of various kinds are useful in generating a representative view of what the public considered; identifying what deliberated opinion might look like; enhancing the political literacy of participants; increasing public understanding of an issue through broadcasting or streaming the event online; and they often include people who would not normally be chosen to be involved (the 'silent' majority).

As public service organizations increasingly strive to enhance public trust and improve the legitimacy of decision-making, effective engagement that represents those most affected by the decision is crucial. It is not sufficient that public sector organizations seek the views of those most vocal in their communities (the 'noisy minority') or the technocratic elite. Representation must be inclusive, equal and diverse and give voice to the more numerous 'quiet' citizens. Participants must be autonomous and supported by quality processes that allow them to be active contributors. And both governments and public sector organizations must value the input of citizens as democratic agents and commit to integrating their views and recommendations in decision-making.

CHAPTER 6
DESIGN-LED DIGITAL DEMOCRACY

The disconnection between the way in which citizens go about their daily lives and the ways in which democracy is practised is no better illustrated than in the area of digital democracy. Democratic institutions around the world, with few exceptions, continue to go about their business in remarkably traditional ways and have hardly been affected by new technologies. Most parliamentary debates continue to require the physical presence of speakers and members to discipline and conclude proceedings and limited use is made of digital information management systems to underpin parliamentary debate. Moreover, the fundamentals of an enabling IT infrastructure in a contemporary working environment are often conspicuous by their absence. Public sector organizations are better resourced in this regard, but operations still tend to be shrouded in secret and are largely contained within closed information systems. While citizens want to engage with open public services, in the main contemporary governance systems continue to operate in a world with secrets. Hence early proclamations that digital democracy would lead to 'a democratic revolution in politics and public governance' or a 'technological fix for basic problems of political activity and the trust of citizens in government' have thus far proved hollow.[1]

Nonetheless, digital media remains a fundamental tool of participatory governance that can be used by governments and citizens alike to enhance public participation in formal politics and strengthen democratic practice. This chapter uses the concepts E-democracy, E-government, *e*Participation, digital democracy and internet democracy interchangeably to describe the impact real and potential of digital media on democratic practice.[2] We can observe two digital domains where progress has been made: first, state-directed digital governance and, secondly, citizen-directed digital politics. In state-directed digital governance, digital governance is generally perceived as integral to central government operations in all advanced industrial states, albeit with a 'culture lag' compared with certain private sector and civil society adaptations. The evidence suggests that progress is occurring in the design of public service provision but is less apparent in other areas of policy formulation and learning. This is largely due to the failure of digital governance to institutionalize citizen input into various decision-making points in the policy process and establish authentic deep participation.[3]

Digital media has been deployed successfully by citizen-led initiatives and some new digital parties as a mobilization tool for enhancing *e*Participation in civic action.[4] Indeed citizen-led applications in *e*Participation appear to have been more successful than governmental-led ones. However, in the main, these too have ultimately fallen short because of their failure to impact successfully on formal political arenas of decision-making.[5] We therefore argue that the core democratic puzzle to be solved in digital democracy is how we can connect up the domain of civic action with the formal political domain through digital governance in a way that strengthens democratic practice. The Covid-19 response is providing some exciting illustrations in this regard and early evidence suggests a renewed global interest in digital democracy.

This chapter is organized into five parts. Part one examines the rise of digital governance. Part two explores the contribution of design thinking to online citizen experience of public service provision. In part three, we review specific innovative examples of where citizen voice has been digitally embedded in formal decision processes focusing on service design, artificial intelligence, Big data analytics and gamification. In part four, we evaluate the impact of digitization for the enablement of civic action and identify lessons for enhancing the quality of digital governance from the Covid-19 response. Part five maps out a framework of principles for connecting up the domain of civic action with the domain of digital governance.

The rise of state-directed digital governance

Digital change made feasible by internet and web-based technologies and applications is beginning to move to centre stage in most countries around the world although progress appears to be contingent on the country's state of development and levels of public and private investment. Most countries in the world are currently undergoing a historic shift towards the establishment of Digital Era Governance (DEG) supported through Government 2.0 technology.[6] This process of change often challenges the established ways in which policy is made and public services are delivered, monitored and evaluated. Most significantly, it questions dominant public sector cultures and (sometimes) values and provides evidence of the differences in adaptive capacity experienced by different public services in response to new governance realities. We now live in a digital era, where public organizations are playing catch-up in response to rapid and disruptive change in societal behaviour and industrial and economic patterns.

Table 6.1 presents a heuristic framework that organizes the key features of IT/digital creation over the past two decades into four models of public management reflecting different uses and trajectories of IT/digital governance deployed in advanced and certain developing societies. We can use this heuristic to map the trajectory of DEG across the world. New Public Management (NPM), the dominant mode of public sector management for at least the past three decades, with its focus on managerial control through instruments of economy, efficiency and effectiveness provides the baseline for patterns of IT organization. NPM marginalized technological changes in favour of a managerial emphasis on organizational arrangements and strong corporate leadership. This reflects a long-running tendency of public administration to downgrade technological factors; a view that some experts have argued is being fundamentally reappraised.[7]

Table 6.1 Four models of bureaucracy and the role of IT and digital technology

Model	Service architecture	Role of IT/ digital technology
New Public Management Focuses on managerial control through economy, efficiency and effectiveness and assumes *a world with secrets*	Managerial modernization focusing on disaggregation, competition and incentivization	*Peripheral* – initial tokenistic IT adoption for better service, but strong oligopolistic IT markets, weak e-Gov, no citizen/consumer role
Digital Era Governance 1 Deploys new technology to enhance government's nodality obligation at the epicentre of society's information networks	Reintegration through shared services; digitalization of paper/phone-based systems, basic nodality; some system integration and user design	*Central* – first wave transactional e-services and static websites, portals – still at periphery
Digital Era Governance 2 Assumes *a world without secrets* and embraces the internet of things to enhance nodality	Acceptance of Moore's Law[9] (digital services reduce costs of delivery) and cost containment strengthens reintegration; proactive systems integration; more nodality; user design by default	*Core* – social media, rich media, co-production, cloud/ utility IT, early 'time-stream' starts
Digital Native Governance *Services co-designed with and for digital natives*	Inherently digital-by-design services, free or low-cost scalable services displacing legacy models. Intelligent centre/devolved delivery architectures; state bureaucracy is the key nodal actor in the societal time-stream.	

Digital Era Governance 1 (DEG1) interventions use technology to 'join up' governmental activity across departments or tiers of government or involve attempts to create client-focused agencies driven by 'end-to-end' user-focused redesign of services or the development of digital platforms for the electronic delivery of services. In 2020, the top performers in e-government development with very high E-Government Development Index (EGDI) scores included Denmark, the Republic of Korea, Estonia, Finland, Australia, Sweden, the UK, New Zealand, the United States, the Netherlands, Singapore, Iceland, Norway and Japan. The EGDI assesses e-government development at a national level and is based on three components: online service index, telecommunication infrastructure index and the human capital index. These key performance indicators largely correspond with the implementation of DEG1 interventions.

The highest performing countries have five features in common: high investment in online technologies; user design by default; digital first targets for the delivery of core transactional public services; a whole of government approach with coordination across the public service; the existence of digital coordination and design agencies; and certain

Saving Democracy

countries such as Denmark and Singapore even mandate that most of their citizens use public services online and receive email, rather than postal mail, from the government.[8]

Digital Era Governance 2 (DEG2) interventions both build on Digital 2.0 technologies and embrace the 'internet of things' exploiting opportunities afforded by the social web. In many ways, DEG2 interventions are driven by the need for government to catch up with patterns of consumer behaviour. Most citizens expect to transact with government digitally and online in the same ways that they transact with their internet or telecommunications provider. Moreover, increasing volumes of digital information relevant for public policy-making are now generated in society.[10] The distinguishing feature of DEG2 is that it assumes a world without secrets and embraces the 'internet of things' to maintain the centrality of government information within domestic information networks.

Digital Native Governance (DNG) suggests the next destination of future digital governance in which government services are co-designed with and often by digital natives. DNG emphasizes the central role of citizen-centric design thinking in digital governance.

Citizen-centred design

Public sector leaders around the world are facing a common set of challenges to meet the increased expectations of their 'customers', 'consumers', 'clients' or 'citizens' in an era of declining public trust. The core challenge faced by every organization (public and private) is how to service its citizens and businesses better and at a sustainable cost. To address this, public organizations need to find ways of improving the efficiency and effectiveness of their service delivery functions. This means providing value for money by improving quality of service (accessibility for all and satisfactory citizen experiences and outcomes), and where possible and appropriate, reducing the costs involved in providing those services. We argue in this chapter that digital public services can be a critical space for trust-building between government and citizen but this requires the development of citizen-centric service models that place the language of the citizen at the centre of service culture, design and delivery and embrace the mantra – 'Citizens not customers – keep it simple, do what you say and say what you do'. 'Citizens and not customers', because the notion of citizenship engenders trust through an informal social contract based on rights and obligations. It helps establish a trust system between government and citizen that is based on parity of esteem and creates common ground for transactions to take place. In contrast, given imperfect access to resources, in the marketplace customers are inherently unequal and the concept is potentially a force for distrust.

Meeting citizen expectations inevitably requires both a better understanding of the service needs and aspirations of an increasingly segmented citizenry and a service culture that sees like a citizen and not a customer. This is why design thinking and especially co-design have moved centre stage in public sector production around the world for both online and offline citizen interactions.

What is co-design?

Co-design is a methodology of research and professional reflection that supports inclusive problem solving in policy formulation, project development and service design. It places the citizen or the expert stakeholder at the centre of a planned process of collaborative learning. The process of learning focuses on the achievement of very specific outcomes, such as a fit for purpose action plan or digital service. It draws on ways of working that are commonplace in product design and formulates interventions through understanding the lives of others and walking in their shoes. Co-design has been widely used in the development of online services, interventions to combat various forms of marginalization, new governance practices or policy innovation.[11] In sum, design thinking has become a fundamental tool of public policy design and analysis and, as we will see in the next section, is now commonplace in DEG1 public service delivery.

Co-design tends to involve three ideal-type agile stages of learning; all of which are iterative and require engagement and re-engagement between researchers, practitioners and citizens. These include (1) discovery and insight, (2) prototyping and (3) evaluating and scaling co-design interventions. Figure 6.1 provides an illustration of an ideal-type co-design process used in the design of digital interventions. As Richard Buchanan observes:

> *One of the most significant developments of system thinking is the recognition that human beings can never see or experience a system, yet we know that our lives are strongly influenced by systems and environments of our own making and by those that nature provides. By definition, a system is the totality of all that is contained, has been contained, and may yet be contained within it. We can never see or experience this totality. We can only experience our personal pathway through a system.*[12]

Stage 1: Discovery & Insight — Search for domestic and international best practice; explore how the 'system' works with the target group identifying barriers to progress; and, co-discover what needs to change and desirable outcomes.

Stage 2: Prototyping — Co-design the design principles to underpin the new intervention or product, engage in collaborative learning about what will work and experiment with plausible alternatives.

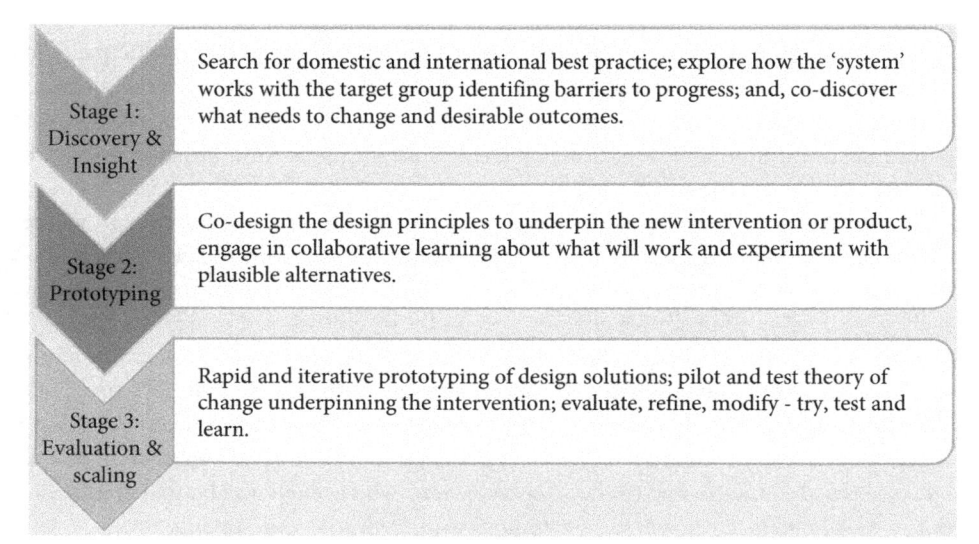

Stage 3: Evaluation & scaling — Rapid and iterative prototyping of design solutions; pilot and test theory of change underpinning the intervention; evaluate, refine, modify - try, test and learn.

Figure 6.1 Service co-design.

The first stage of learning involves establishing a shared representation of concerns and problems with the target group; it draws on evidence that is synthesized and tested for its robustness but it also generates a broad range of perspectives on an issue as seen by different citizens. This requires creating a learning environment that allows citizens to tell their own stories, rather than making assumptions about their preferences. This is based on the observation that citizens never experience the delivery system as a whole, just pathways through the system. We therefore seek to understand the problem through the eyes of the user. It doesn't require big numbers unlike a statistically significant survey but it does require spending quality time with a small number of participants, mapping their journeys, identifying obstacles and developing mitigating strategies.

The second stage is about creating a safe space where participants can imagine and progress towards a future rather than becoming trapped in past models or ways of thinking. It uses a creative design dynamic to encourage new ways of thinking. Some of the techniques that can be used here include getting practitioners to experience the world from the perspective of citizens, getting citizens to draw or capture in non-written form their perceptions of a better future and generally trying to encourage emancipation from past certainties and developing a space where creativity and learning, and taking risks, are encouraged. Beyond these process elements, this stage also involves a search for alternatives, options and innovations that address the issue in focus. Ultimately, this stage of learning focuses on developing prototype interventions based on a joint commitment with key partners and developing appropriate rapid feedback research methods to support that dynamic. Here the logic is of a design experiment. The experiment focuses on the design of an intervention as the core research problem. The techniques used at this stage will be contingent on the amount of time available to the project team. For example, the ideal-type experiment would allow sufficient time to observe and manipulate the intervention over a period usually in one location, until acceptable results emerge. The experiment would progress through a series of design–redesign cycles with ongoing engagement with core participants to ensure that the intervention adjusts to the local context. The design experiment claims to provide an evidence base about 'what works' in the early stages of the development of an intervention; in addition, it may provide a staging post for a broader and more generalizable test in the future.

The third stage of learning then reverts to a more traditional evaluation phase where collaborative options analysis takes place on the basis of assessing pilot interventions through the use of randomized controlled trials[13] or other robust forms of evaluation such as qualitative comparative analysis.[14] In addition, enlightened practitioners would seek to evaluate the quality of their practice throughout the process of learning. This would include (1) pre-engagement surveys in live cases to determine participant characteristics and the diversity of viewpoints represented in each process; (2) post-engagement surveys to assess participant experiences, perceptions and agreement on the recommended solutions; and (3) targeted interviews with a small number of participants or key stakeholders to unpack survey findings using reflective questioning.[15]

Citizen-centric digital innovation

In a recent survey of IT thought leaders in Westminster-style democracies, informants were asked their views on which countries were trailblazing in citizen-centric DEG1 and 2 innovations and which were playing catch-up (see Table 6.2).[16] Most informants were sceptical about international league tables, observing that data was provided by governments without any regard for the quality of implementation.

The majority of respondents agreed that different countries excelled in different aspects of digital innovation. Anglophone countries, for example, have particular areas of expertise such as the Australian Tax Office's *My Tax* and New Zealand's *Integrated Data Infrastructure*.[18] And those impacted most profoundly by the Global Financial

Table 6.2 Most frequently mentioned government exemplars of digital innovation

Area of innovation	Exemplar	Methods
Unified digital vision	ICT Vision (Estonia) eGov2015 and *Smart Nation Initiative* (Singapore) *Digital Strategy 2016–2020* (Denmark)	Design-led, whole of government, citizen-centred, behavioural insights
Governance enablers (institutional mechanisms to enable and exploit digitization)	*Digital Transformation Agency* (Australia, www.dta.gov.au/), *Digital Service Standards Agency* (Singapore, www.tech.gov.sg/digital-service-standards/) *Agency for Digitization* (Denmark, https://en.digst.dk/)	Big Data analytics, design labs with users, random control trials, small-scale experiments
Digital Era Governance 1 Enablers digital by default online services, reintegration through shared services	UK's *Government Digital Service*; Australian Tax Office's *My Tax*; New Zealand's *Integrated Data Infrastructure*; and the US government's data.gov.	User and stakeholder design, small-scale experiments
Digital Era Governance 2 Enablers via 'The internet of things' and high-tech defence enablers that fully exploit the opportunities afforded by the social web or build capability in Big Data analytics or Artificial Intelligence	Big Data generated via satellite and drone technology (Australian *GeoScience Data cube*)[17] in areas such as environmental protection (e.g. eBird.org), and transport planning; co-production of public health interventions (e.g. Singapore's 'TraceTogether'), and for futures thinking, gamification (e.g. 'Magnetic South', New Zealand).	Drone, satellite and robot technologies; Big Data analytics; co-production; and gamification

77

Saving Democracy

Crisis appear to have embraced digital-first service delivery such as New Zealand and the UK. Stand-out countries also tend to have a unified vision for change and invest in technical centres of excellence using design methods and behavioural science. As Box 6.1 illustrates, Singapore's *eGov2015* initiative which now forms part of the *Smart Nation Initiative* is a case in point. The unifying vision of change (*eGov2015*) became a disruptive force for affecting public sector reform stimulating cross-agency collaboration,

Box 6.1 Digital vision – the case of eGov2015 Singapore[20]

The challenge

The Government of Singapore has been a leader in providing digital services to its citizens for over two decades successfully tapping into advances in information and communications technology (ICT) but until recently this was generally a one-way process with limited government–citizen interaction predominantly focused on delivering information to the public.

The intervention

Singapore's 'eGov2015' aimed at shifting a 'government-to-you' approach to a 'government-with-you' approach in its delivery of e-government services. This DEG1 vision of collaborative government is featured by high levels of co-creation and user design and significant interactions between government, citizens and the private sector.

Critical success factors

The intervention has greatly improved the citizen service delivery experience largely due to the inculcation of a citizen-centric service culture that leverages multichannel and cross-government service systems, deploys proactive communications through the use of social media, and underpins its vision with public programmes to enhance IT literacy.

The public impact

Citizens and businesses in Singapore can access more than 1,600 online services and more than 300 mobile services provided by the government. Levels of citizen satisfaction and public trust have increased with the level of service maturity.

Limits of the example

Singapore is a City State featured by limited democracy and strong executive government. Few significant checks and balances constrain the operations of the executive regarding balancing privacy, cyber security and data use. Singapore citizenship is limited regarding the exercise of freedom of expression and association.[21]

Design-Led Digital Democracy

whole of government data integration and procurement, and outcomes-driven reform in the design and delivery of citizen-centric public services.[19]

There are four promising streams of DEG2 innovation for enabling digital citizen-centric governance – robotic process automation (RPA) and Artificial Intelligence, 'Big Data' enabled decision-making, digitally enabled co-production of services and gamification for deepening *e*Participation.

Robotic process automation (RPA) and artificial intelligence

The NADIA project developed in the former Commonwealth Department of Human Services in Australia is in many ways a benchmark for measuring the degree of digital transformation occurring in mature democracies (see Box 6.2). This bold government venture into the use of artificial intelligence for delivering critical services to people with disability was for many observers a litmus test for gauging the digital imagination of public service providers. It was deemed high risk not because NADIA was unable to support the needs of Australians with disability but because it came in the wake of a high-profile public relations disaster – the 'robo-debt' debacle.[22] This was a case in which an automated debt raising and recovery system was incorrectly used to unlawfully raise $1.76 billion in debts against 443,000 clients. In response to a class action in June 2021, the Australian government agreed to repay at least 381,000 people $751m and wipe all debts – worth $1.76bn – that were raised using the unlawful method of 'income averaging' tax office data to check welfare payments.[23]

It is also noteworthy that the successful deployment of NADIA would have led to the closure of call centres in key marginal constituencies in an election year! NADIA was thus stalled due to political pressure. But think of the potential role of machine learning informed assistive technologies such as NADIA in other areas of democratic governance. If we wanted to, we could create virtual direct democratic assemblies with our own personal avatars in attendance advancing our individual preferences compiled through machine learning. Deliberative processes such as citizens' juries, assemblies and parliaments could work in a similar way but this time we would deliberate directly through our avatars. Of course, the X, Y and millennial generations familiar with popular culture are wise to the potential pitfalls of allowing robots, AI, avatars or international corporations (e.g. the fictitious Skynet in the *Terminator* film franchise) take over the management of our democratic processes. Nonetheless, there is an urgent need for national and international conversations to take place on the ethical questions underpinning the role of technology in democratic advance to prevent democratic backsliding.

'Big Data' and better participatory decision-making

The US government has been one of the most active in leveraging Big Data to support government decision-making. In 2009, it gave open data a legal and privacy framework that led to the creation of data.gov, a repository of government tools, resources and

Box 6.2 Robotic process automation and artificial intelligence – the case of NADIA[24]

The challenge

The National Disability Insurance Scheme (NDIS) was introduced by the Gillard Labor Government in Australia on 1 July 2013. It is being progressively rolled out and is not due to be completed until 2020. It represents a major reform of disability support in Australia and emerged from years of heated debate about problems with existing disability support arrangements. Under the NDIS, people with disability and their families and carers co-design a plan of supports which is developed and tailored to their individual needs. The NDIS is thus viewed as an empowering social policy. However, as a consequence of early piloting of the scheme it became evident that participants would require significant assistance to help them navigate the complex information landscape in the disability space. The 'NADIA project' was therefore established to help people navigate the NDIS with the help of a virtual assistant ('NADIA') – a highly advanced artificially intelligent communication system.

The intervention

NADIA is an avatar – an artificially intelligent public servant who works for the National Disability Insurance Agency (NDIA). She was created by Dr Mark Sagar from the University of Auckland, creator of Baby, an Oscar winner well known for his CGI work on *Avatar*, *King Kong* and *Spider Man 2*. Nadia possesses qualities of emotional intelligence co-designed with a group of Australians experiencing various forms of disability and their carers. Oscar winner Cate Blanchett is the voice of Nadia.

Critical success factors

This was a classic example of the integration of design thinking with the latest cognitive technology developed by the then IBM Watson team.

The public impact

Despite outstanding success in pilots and the approval for roll-out from the NDIA Board, the programme has been frozen. Sources close to the project suggest that a combination of fear for a repeat of the ABS Census and Centrelink's 'robo-debt' debacles stymied government's appetite for risk in what was an election year.

information on a broad range of policy-oriented data.[25] In all, more than 200,000 data sets are available to help businesses, knowledge institutions and private citizens conduct research, develop web and mobile apps, and create design visualizations. Data.gov's tenth anniversary in May 2019 coincided with the Open Government Data Act, which, as part of the Foundations for Evidence Based Policymaking Act, became law.[26] The Open

Government Data Act requires federal agencies to publish their information online as open data, with their metadata included in the Data.gov catalogue. Competitions, such as *Apps for America* and *Apps for Democracy*, have also been established to attract talented developers to build applications that use government data. Most mature democracies are following suit.

Digitally enabled co-production of programmes and services

New technologies are proving highly effective in enabling the co-production of programmes and services with citizens in a broad range of areas from environmental protection to public health. For example, citizen science is an invaluable part of ornithology as the regular collaboration between the public and science helps scientists map the distribution and movements of birds across the world. Bird watchers around the world record their observations in the eBird database and application informing the creation of new maps showing the expected flying range of each species.[27]

In the social sciences, Volunteer Science Inc. is a C-corporation originally developed out of Northeastern University with the mission to 'make online methods of behavioral research widely available to researchers and engage people all over the world in behavioral science'. It provides an online platform enabling anyone to participate in social science research and, in particular, Massively Open Online Social Experiments ('MOOSEs').[28] A good example of a MOOSE, in this case a social survey, was launched at Imperial College London in April 2020 and posed two key questions.[29] What impact has the lockdown in response to Covid-19 had on our mental health, and what determines how people cope with isolation? These questions form part of a crowd-sourced project, *The Great British Wellbeing Survey*. The work builds on the success of the *Great British Intelligence Test*, a collaborative project with BBC Horizon that assesses the nation's intelligence and well-being. The results for the project were based on online tests and a detailed questionnaire, completed by more than 330,000 people in the UK since late December 2019.

The impact of digitally enabled technologies for co-producing services has been particularly evident in the sphere of public health, and they have experienced varying degrees of success. Prior to the invention of the Kardia, basic electrocardiogram (ECG) application for iPhones, iPads or the iWatch, ECG analysis required an attending GP, a hospital room with a large ECG machine, full-time technicians to operate and maintain the machines, and appointments were made days in advance. ECG applications for iPhones, iPads or the iWatch now allow for daily (or more frequent), convenient heart rate and pattern monitoring with auto-uploads of results to the Cloud and via email to physicians.

Possibly the highest profile and controversial current example of a digitally enabled technology for co-producing a public health intervention are contact-tracing applications used to combat the spread of the Covid-19 virus. Many countries have either developed their own applications (e.g. Australia's, 'COVIDSafe', Hong Kong's 'StayHomeSafe', India's 'Aarogya Setu', Israel's 'The Shield' or Singapore's 'TraceTogether'), which retrospectively analyse GPS location data from those who later test positive (e.g. China, South Korea and Taiwan) or utilize Bluetooth Google-Apple technology (e.g. Germany and the UK).

Saving Democracy

Gamification

Gamification can be used to strengthen citizen participation in online engagement of different kinds – policy deliberation, futures thinking, service design – through amusement or fun deploying game mechanics or game-design elements in nongame contexts.[30] Through games, participants can experiment, explore options and evaluate trade-offs in a safe, pressure-free environment. Play builds greater knowledge of the problem from both the perspective of designers and citizens and allows for a more targeted approach that fits the behavioural features of a segmented audience.[31] Gamification can include multiplayer computer games involving large, diverse audiences, or single-player computer games for a small target audience. Gamification does not have to be hi-tech. It can also include more traditional board games or role plays.[32] Box 6.3 provides examples of different forms of gamification deployed to enhance the quality of public participation.

Citizen-led digital democracy

We noted at the outset of this chapter that digital media has been deployed successfully by citizen-led initiatives and some new digital parties as a mobilization tool for enhancing eParticipation in civic action.[33] Indeed, there is significant evidence that citizen-led applications in eParticipation appear to have been more successful than governmental-led ones.[34] Two prominent examples are worthy of detailed examination here – digital parties and online national issue forums.

The rise of the digital parties

The concept of the 'digital party' has over the last decade become a new blueprint for political party organization and has been behind the success of the Pirate Parties in Northern Europe, Podemos in Spain, France Insoumise in France and the 5-Star Movement in Italy. The digital parties or 'digital populist' parties, coined because of their integration of populist rhetoric with digital campaigning techniques, began as online protest movements and transitioned into political parties due to their ability to capture the political imagination of young activists due to the promise of political transformation. As Paolo Gerbaudo, author of *The Digital Party* (2019), observes, traditional forms of party organization based on delegate democracy and the establishment of mass party memberships are slowly giving way to digital movements in which we find younger political activists who have been politicized by events such as the 2010 student protests and the Occupy movement:

> *These people tend to be suspicious of delegate democracy, of the heavy intermediation that it involves, and of the cadres who carry out these tasks. They are less keen on endless physical meetings, when compared to older and more ideological militants, and believe that all members should be empowered to participate directly in important decisions whenever possible.*[35]

Box 6.3 Examples of the use of gamification for enhancing the quality of public participation

Massive multiplayer games

Magnetic South was one of a series of Christchurch City Council-supported public engagement activities following the major earthquakes in Christchurch, New Zealand, which destroyed much of the city. The project used the Foresight Engine, a MMORPG (Massive Multiplayer Online Role-Playing Game), run by the Institute of the Future and played with almost a thousand people over a two-day period. Players generated cards, ideas and strategies for rebuilding the city, with 8,889 micro forecasts.[36]

Single-player games

Viewpoint ACASI (audio computer-assisted self-interviewing) is a web-based method that engages vulnerable children and young people in a gaming environment and helps them communicate difficult views, opinions, wishes and feelings. Viewpoint Interactive uses graphics, speech and animated assistants. Game breaks occur to maintain interest in the topic for discussion. It is particularly useful in gaining the insights of marginalized groups into the quality of the social inclusion programmes that they receive or in family futures mapping.[37]

Traditional games

Democracy 100 is a board game designed by Democracy 2025 and ThinkPlace in Australia to help a target audience (in this case 100 members of various Australian elite networks) design a Charter for Champions of Australian Democracy. Participants were organized into groups of ten and provided with a deck of thirty-five democracy playing cards in three different colour sets corresponding with three national survey questions: What do you think are Australia's most important democratic values? What should the responsibilities of champions of democracy be? What could be done to strengthen our democracy? Each card represented one of the top 10 most frequently mentioned responses to national survey questions. Five wild cards were also provided so that participants could write in their own preferred answers if they could think of something better. Each table deliberated on each of the questions and compiled a Charter for Democracy Board from their responses to the questions. Table responses were then aggregated and distilled into one Charter representing the views of the deliberative forum.[38]

Digital parties have developed online platforms or 'participation portals' to engage directly with their activists such as *LiquidFeedback* for Pirate Parties in Northern Europe, *Rousseau* in the 5-Star Movement in Italy and *Participa* in Podemos in Spain. These platforms allow party members to make decisions on party leadership, candidates and policies; create and join local groups; donate to the movement; download campaign material and attend online training sessions for activists and prospective candidates.

Saving Democracy

These mobilization tools are available via mobile applications, allowing easy access from any point and at any time:

> *Participatory platforms such as the ones listed above have become the 'digital heart' of new political organizations: the space in which the digital assembly of members is periodically summoned to discuss and decide on important issues affecting their organization. In this context, the platform comes to substitute the multi-tier bureaucratic structure of mass party of the industrial era, which in present digital times is perceived to be too heavy and convoluted to allow for effective organization and mobilization.*

It is noticeable, however, that the most successful digital parties have only been able to link-up arenas of digital politics with formal political arenas of decision-making where they have had significant electoral success.

National Issues Forums

National Issues Forums were established by the Kettering Foundation in the United States in the mid-1990s.[39] The Foundation convenes an annual US-wide network of over 3,000 locally sponsored public forums of varying sizes and selection procedures to discuss selected issues. The Foundation then collates papers on the findings which it distributes to elected officials. The UK sought to emulate this device in June 2003 with the 'GM Nation' Public Debate. This was organized at arms-length by government as part of a national consultation on genetically modified foods involving 675 open community meetings. Organizers also convened ten 'narrow but deep' deliberative groups a fortnight apart generating views on issues that arose in the meetings.

There are a number of digital methods currently in use globally to facilitate online deliberation, ranging from the simple use of websites for information-giving to more interactive processes that allow citizens or stakeholders to 'converse' online or participate in processes that emulate conventional participative processes. The two participative processes most used are Online Forums and Structured Templates or Open Space Technology. Open Space Technology (often referred to as 'Open Space') is a meeting framework that allows unlimited numbers of participants to form their own discussions around a central theme. The method is highly dynamic and effective at generating enthusiasm, as well as commitment to action. These types of initiatives can be used to monitor public opinion on key issues, as a source for participants to engage in more in-depth processes, such as focus groups, and engaging the public in the development of new policy issues.

Digital participatory governance systems

This final section draws on an exemplar case study of a government-led participatory intervention prompted by citizen pressure that led to the creation of a vibrant, multi-

Box 6.4 The City Council of Madrid's 'Decide Madrid'

The challenge

Austerity measures following the Global Financial Crisis, combined with high-profile instances of political corruption, combined to exacerbate low levels of citizen trust in traditional politics, politicians and political institutions. This created the space for the emergence of new movements such as the '15M movement' committed to challenging the established political order, cleaning up politics and introducing participatory governance. The success of this movement led to the rise of new political parties such as 'Podermos' which formed a coalition with other political parties under the banner 'Ahora Madrid', won the election and governed the city of Madrid from May 2015 to May 2019.

The intervention

'Ahora Madrid' included a commitment to 'encourage the participation of citizens in the management of the city, involving them in the generation of innovative and viable ideas and proposals, in order to improve their quality of life' ('Decide Madrid').[40] This aim manifested in the creation of an eParticipation system with five channels of participation (debates, proposals, polls, processes and participatory budgeting) allowing for citizen impact in agenda-setting, policy analysis and preparation and policy formulation and monitoring.

Critical success factors

In Spain, the right to direct citizen participation is recognized in the 1978 Constitution (articles 23 and 29) and Law 40/2015 provides for online petitions with 10 per cent public support. 'Decide Madrid' also enjoys strong political support; high rates of broadband connectivity (91.7 per cent); robust technical capability; and a culture of co-production of public services through vibrant neighbourhood associations. 'Decide Madrid' also utilized open-source software, Consul,[41] which has been successfully operated in more than 100 organizations around the world and drew rational lessons from the award-winning online consultation forum *Better Reykjavik*.[42]

The public impact

'Decide Madrid' achieved significant impacts in terms of internet reach, platform accessibility, guidelines and procedures, increased online capability and citizen influence on decision-making for proposals and participatory budgets.[43]

Limits of the example

Limitations were also identified in terms of sustaining citizen interest, transparency, facilitation of and feedback on certain initiatives and the security of the platform.[44, 45]

dimensional eParticipation initiative – 'Decide Madrid'. This will help us establish some key lessons for how we can connect up civic action with digital governance which will have particular resonance in a post-Covid-19 world. Box 6.4 presents the key features of the case in terms of the innovation challenge, the multi-faceted intervention, critical success factors, public impact and the limits of the example.

'Decide Madrid' is a particularly instructive case study given that it emerged from citizen pressure for greater participation to ensure the integrity of the representative system of government. It is also an example of a government co-creating an online deliberative system to maximize participation in different areas of decision-making (policy and service design, monitoring and evaluation).

Evaluation – the conditions for effective digital engagement

So what particular lessons can we draw from the case studies explored above for connecting-up civic action with digital governance? The key lessons encompass both design and technical principles and can be used as criteria to assess progress.

Design principles

On- and offline engagements share certain common design principles. Both need to be clear in scope and purpose to maximize the value of participation. Engagement methods should be co-designed with the target group to remove any potential barriers to participation. Forums need to be broadly representative of the target group to ensure public legitimacy and avoid challenges to forum outcomes. The engagement process should be transparent with clearly articulated procedures and decision rules. Competing evidence should be translated in a meaningful way for the target group. The process should be professionally moderated and sensitive to context and culture. Forum participants should receive regular updates on progress to demonstrate the value of their participation. Forum outcomes should be subject to ongoing evaluation and review, to ensure continuous improvement and legitimacy.[46]

Technical lessons

Functional technology

Online engagement needs to be based on principles of citizen centred design with a 'mobile first approach' given its reach – intuitive, accessible in multiple ways (via search engines or while browsing through the website), reflecting different citizen journeys at different entry and exit points with jargon-free communication of information. Machine learning should be used to assess interventions with the highest levels of 'quality' participation. Landing page design must be easily navigable with linear flow of content and clear signposting for citizens to the next piece of content to read.

Intuitive content

Citizens want access to information that is seamless and easily accessible – it should not mirror the fragmented nature of government internal structures and content should not be dispersed across multiple agencies, platforms and technologies (e.g. various applications and websites). To achieve this aim jurisdictions should have a single portal for public participation – a trusted, 'one-stop-shop' that is accessible from all devices, in one location. Citizens want the language and tone of the content to connect at the individual level – 'talk to me as a citizen not as a consumer'. Content should be communicated in plain English and not bureau speak. Designers should be encouraged to think differently about how they can use content and different mediums to encourage engagement and enhance political literacy through, for example, uploading compelling case studies that illustrate the citizen story from idea to action and developing 'packaged content' that is easily sharable.

Channels of communication

The platform and its content need to be promoted through a targeted and integrated marketing strategy which includes relevant social media channels, email marketing, referrals from trusted intermediaries and referrals in the form of direct links on other government websites. Potential collaborations include educational and research institutions, industry associations, professional registration bodies and leveraging off existing networks from relevant jurisdictions of government.

Platform designers need to continue to monitor and optimize its search ranking so that it can easily be found in search engines such as Google. Citizens 'don't know what they don't know' and often turn to Google first, when searching for answers. Attracting citizens to the site through appropriate search engines is an excellent way to identify citizens looking to participate. This needs to be continually monitored and optimized, to ensure the platform is keeping up with changes to search engine algorithms.

In conclusion – connecting-up civic action with digital governance

Digital media has been deployed successfully by citizen-led initiatives and new digital parties as a mobilization tool for enhancing *e*Participation in civic action.[47] Indeed citizen-led applications in *e*Participation appear to have been more successful than governmental-led ones. However, in the main, many of these too have fallen short because of their failure to impact successfully on formal political arenas of decision-making. There remains a systemic scepticism about the merits of online deliberation in contrast with face-to-face deliberation with most leading deliberative practitioners confining online engagement to building the knowledge of participants and general monitoring and evaluation processes.[48] It will be interesting to see whether the increasing use of digital conferencing applications throughout the pandemic will break the orthodoxy of deliberative democracy. It will be interesting to see whether the operational success of the online climate assemblies in France and the UK discussed in Chapter 4 will shift practice in post-pandemic conditions.

In sum, the uptake of digital democracy rests on political will, the quality of its practice and its ability to connect civic action with the promise of digital era governance. For many politicians and senior public servants, it remains a high-risk venture, but increasing examples of good practice and the achievement of better outcomes make digital democracy an integral component of participatory governance.

PART II
INTERVENTIONS AT THE THROUGHPUT STAGE TO IMPROVE THE QUALITY AND INTEGRITY OF POLITICS

Throughput legitimacy refers to the accountability, transparency and efficiency of decision-making processes focusing on the activities of those actors (politicians, bureaucrats, experts and stakeholders) tasked with making decisions and their openness to engage with the citizenry. We explore the myriad ways in which the policy-making process works both institutionally and constructively to reach legitimate decisions in the public interest.

CHAPTER 7
REFORMING ELECTED ASSEMBLIES

In democratic theory, parliaments and assemblies are viewed to be the central institutions of representative democracy but in practice consistently come near to the bottom of the list of institutions, in their level of public trust or esteem.[1] This chapter explores how to improve the practices of elected assemblies that are at the heart of the way democracy works. We examine two main issues: how to increase the diversity of elected representatives, and how to improve the connection between the workings of assemblies and citizens. Of course, the explanation for the lack of public confidence in elected assemblies is not confined to the absence of diversity among elected representatives or the weak connection of elected assemblies with the public. Another important underlying factor is that parliaments can appear to be powerless institutions when they struggle to hold the executive arm of government to account. The erosion of that function as a source of redress and challenge open to citizens and the taking up of that role by courts, ombudsman, official regulators and the wider array of institutions captured by John Keane's term 'monitory democracy' may have helped to lessen the standing of parliaments in the eyes of citizens.[2] As noted in Chapter 1, parliaments were to a large extent sidelined in responding to the Covid-19 pandemic. There are signs, however, of parliaments fighting back by developing their own evidence gathering and enquiry functions, often delivered alongside greater engagement with the public through e-petitions and various forms of democratic innovation.

Other issues of concern have been examined elsewhere in this book. Chapter 8, for example, explores integrity problems in public governance and public scepticism with the way that political parties and election campaigns are financed. Indeed, political parties and parliaments stand out more than any other factors in eroding public trust.[3] Yet the issue of increasing diversity of representation and finding new ways to engage the public in their work remains central to the renewal of parliaments, legislatures or elected assemblies.[4] These are the two topics that provide the focus for this chapter.

Increasing diversity – does diversity matter?

Does it matter that in 2019 in parliaments around the world less than a quarter of representatives are women? Even in the Nordic democracies, often praised for their commitment to gender equality, the share of women elected representatives stands at 44 per cent. The parliament with the highest percentage of women (at 61.25 per cent) is the lower house of Rwanda.[5] Does it matter that in the UK parliament the number of former manual workers has dropped from around 16 per cent in 1979 to 3 per cent in 2015? In contrast, the same parliament has seen a rise of the career politician, with 3 per cent having had a previous job in politics in 1979 rising to 16 per cent by 2015. In 2015, 6 per cent of the members of the UK parliament were from Black and ethnic minority backgrounds, while the proportion from those backgrounds in the general population was at least double that percentage.[6]

Some could argue that diversity is not the key issue in a representative democracy, rather it is to have high-quality representatives who are good at their job. Being a politician in today's complex world of the '24-7' news cycle, international agreements, and complex layers of economic, social and cultural arrangements demands individuals with a breadth of policy knowledge, emotional intelligence, adaptive capacity and the ability to muddle through. What is certain is that we need to attract political leaders who are up to the challenge. When asked, citizens favour politicians with integrity, who are authentic or in touch with everyday concerns.[7] But competence is always in the mix; people want politicians who know what they are doing who are clever, wise and good on the international stage. It is therefore not unreasonable to suggest that getting the right people as elected representatives to take decisions on our behalf might involve selecting from the best and the brightest.[8]

There are some obvious counterarguments to the claim that meritocracy beats diversity as a virtue in a democratic system. The decision as to who is the best and the brightest depends on judgements and values that are unlikely to get universal support. A second challenge is to ask: if the system is so good at attracting the best and the brightest, why are citizens not more appreciative of the talent on display? Why too is there an exhaustive literature on the blunders of governments?[9] Many of the explanations offer group think and overconfidence as key elements in the emergence of blunders, suggesting that greater diversity might have helped.

The strongest argument against the simplistic application of the concept of meritocracy is to accept that there is always a trade-off between ability and diversity. The argument here is that solving complex problems will often require putting together a group of problem solvers with diverse backgrounds, experiences, knowledge and skills rather than assembling a collection of your version of the best and the brightest. Why? Because there is significant evidence to suggest that this makes for greater creativity and the generation of more imaginative solutions. Diversity supports collective knowledge production. A diverse and intelligent group of problem solvers will outperform a group of the best problem solvers.[10] This caveat is important, diverse groups need to contain people with skills but once a threshold of capacity has been past then a diverse group will do best. More generally, though not a panacea, human systems like natural systems thrive on diversity.

Another argument advanced by those who want to make the case that it does not matter who the representative is in terms of gender, race or other demographic factors is the importance of representatives being publicly accountable. If political equality is expressed through one-person one-vote, then if a political actor can be removed from office by disgruntled voters then their performance will reflect the need to be responsive to all voters or accept the consequences. Accountability in this case trumps the argument for diversity.

Here again we can find powerful counterarguments.[11] Leaving aside the sweeping assumption that political systems deliver public accountability to a sufficient degree to satisfy the average voter there are strong grounds that targeting a diverse range of representatives through descriptive representation will improve the interaction between politicians and voters in two ways.[12] First, those voters who are women or from ethnic minorities are more likely to feel empowered and incentivized to engage as critical citizens and enforce accountability because they will think that they can make a difference. Second, if they see people like them exercising power, the achievement of legitimacy for political decisions will be easier to forge and political trust should increase. In short, for accountability to work, diversity needs to work. It does not trump it, but rather complements it.

Diversity in those who are elected politicians will make for better decisions and greater accountability in the political system. These two pragmatic arguments can be bolstered by a third that is more normative in character: that social equality and justice demands parity of representation.[13] There is no evidence that men are more talented politicians than women, so how can it be justified to have more male than female representatives? One ethnic minority is not intellectually, morally or socially superior to another, so why should one ethnic group dominate decision-making in political institutions? If the essence of democracy is that all people are of equal value, then the case for diversity rests on the claim that social justice requires equal representation.

Is it the case that you must be a woman to represent the interests of women? Or to put the question in an even more direct manner, can a white woman speak about the lived experience of a women from an ethnic minority? Or could a young gay woman speak for and defend the interests of an ageing heterosexual married man? Our answer is that an effective democracy needs both 'descriptive representation', and a variety of decision-makers present from a range of backgrounds. But it also needs to deliver 'substantive representation', a determination to act and change the world to meet the needs and interests of a range of groups.[14] That requires mutual understanding, inclusion and a willingness to see the world from the perspective of others and of course a recognition of how power is unevenly spread and why it needs to be more evenly distributed. Or to put it another way, any elected representative needs to be tasked to both speak about their own experiences and seek out knowledge of the experiences of others. The crucial skill is not just about speaking for others but also listening to others. This argument too adds to the case for diversity of representation.

Why is diversity difficult to deliver?

Before talking about how to improve diversity in representation, it is important to consider what explanations there might be for existing limited diversity among elected representatives. Once again, a valuable way to think about the issue is in terms of supply and demand.[15] There may be factors such as those already discussed early in the chapter that could limit supply and people coming forward to stand for election. People may feel they lack the skills, social and political networks and role models. Equally there might be demand-side factors, such as gatekeepers, who purposively lock certain groups of people outside the system and by implication reduce the possibility of diversity.

The supply-side factors that limit the range of people willing to stand for office encompass both structural and agency factors. We have already touched on how nascent ambition, the willingness to think about standing, is a relatively rare attribute to be found in individuals. A national survey conducted in the UK reveals that only 10 per cent of the population had even thought of running for political office at the national or local levels. 'People who run for political office are strange that is, they are unusual, abnormal, unlike most other people', conclude Peter Allen and David Cutts.[16] They have individual qualities that mark them out. As previously noted in Chapter 2, Richard Fox and Jennifer Lawless conducted a study in the United States which found that those disposed to running for office are confident in their abilities, and more convinced than others that politics works and that the political process can be trusted and they have the support of familial or other social networks that suggest that politics is a career route for them. These factors, again matching the US research, are more commonly found in men rather than women, in the better educated, and privileged social groups, which in turn explains lack of diversity.[17]

There may also be structural features about cultural and institutional practices of politics that stop people even thinking about putting themselves forward. These might be considered inadvertent demand limitations because of the way that politics has been conducted by its current incumbents for decades. The equivalent of 'if you can't stand the heat, stay out of the kitchen' style of argument. The threat and reality of abuse particularly from social media are likely to be a powerful deterrent to many, as our unsocial demands for engagements and meetings that eat into time that could be spent with family and friends and add to the potential damaging consequences for mental health and well-being for those who become full-time politicians.[18] The reactions of friends to people who announce that they are thinking of standing for election are often one of concern and alarm for them, with a polite or not so polite version of the question – are you mad? – often in the mix.

A more obvious source of demand-side constraints is the way that the institutions of politics operate a gatekeeping role in relation to the selection of candidates. In most instances, political parties are in a key position to let some people in and keep others out since a large proportion of those elected in democracies stand for a political party. As Allen comments: 'parties are the main vehicle that can transform private citizens into public politicians due to the infrastructure and existing dominance of political life'.[19] Political parties have members to help support campaigns. They have access to the media and the institutional experience and public recognition to drive a candidacy. Most will have a baseline group of voters, already primed to support the party's selected candidate. A very hard-working and effective candidate is an attribute that can add to that mix and in the case of campaigns in some countries like the United States that might be an important factor as well. The costs involved are considerable, and successful candidates raise millions of dollars to fight their campaigns. Even getting chosen to be a candidate for an established party without a system of primaries. That is turning up to meet perhaps hundreds of party members at various selections meetings can be financially demanding.

A survey conducted by the website *ConservativeHome* found that party candidates spent on average £33, 000 (about one and half times the average annual salary in the UK) to audition for a selection that they might not get and to fight an election they might not win. These figures would deter many and make it less likely that a diverse range of individuals might stand. In addition, the ideology, preferences and potentially narrow sense of who should stand and who can win, held by a small and unrepresentative section of the wider population group of party members, may play a determining role in who is selected.

Further structural factors persist to reduce the chances of diversity in representation. We live in societies of unequal income and wealth, where in many countries the evidence indicates that the disparities are increasing rather than lessening. Peter Allen makes a plausible, if tentative, connection between the concentration of wealth and lack of diversity in who is attracted to engage in politics:

What we are seeing overall is a concentration of economic capital, and all the security and opportunity that this carries with it, in the hands of a decreasing number of people. Concurrently, we are seeing a broad withdrawal from the political process by a growing number of people.[20]

Democratic political mechanisms have always operated on the premise that there is a mismatch between political equality (all votes are equal) and the realities of economic and social inequality to ensure that the capacity to do politics is not exclusively in the hands of one group. The mismatch may not be too overwhelming in most democracies, in that resources to engage in politics are more broadly spread, but it would seem sensible to recognize that one factor driving the lack of diversity in our elected representatives is that the scale of inequalities makes engagement much more of a mountain to climb for some rather others.

Searching for solutions

The solutions to this lack of diversity in our elected assemblies must in some way address the various causes of the problem. If we start with the issue of the limited willingness of people from marginalized groups to even put themselves forward, then key gatekeepers, such as political parties and party leaders, have tried to address those concerns in a variety of ways. Sarah Childs refers to strategies of rhetoric and promotion where in speeches and through organizational processes political elites can make it clear that greater diversity is something they support.[21] Making sure that diversity is reflected in party platforms and public statements is another very modest step. More actively, mentoring programmes with role models could be established to encourage a wider range of citizens to think that 'people like them' could be politicians and seeking to foster confidence in their skills and abilities. The establishment of networks of support to help people down the tough track of seeking a nomination could also be helpful. Finally, and more directly, people from a wider range of backgrounds could be headhunted and asked to stand or think about putting themselves forward as politicians by parties or their representatives. Asking a person to participate directly can make a huge difference in that it suggests that their knowledge and skills are valued and their potential contribution to the party is welcomed.

A further set of reforms can be introduced that are aimed at making the working life of politicians commensurable with modern working practices or as Peter Allen puts it, making 'politics compatible with being a normal person'. As he observes, the long and unsocial hours and lack of opportunities to meet demands on your time outside doing politics mean for many that taking up a role in politics would be too great a sacrifice. But there are myriad small reforms that could be made to make the option of engaging in politics less daunting. These include the availability of creches and gyms, flexible working patterns, parental paid leave, sociable procedural time (e.g. putting debates on at more social hours rather than late at night), enabling voting and engagement from home by use of digital technology, and matching breaks in political activities to school holidays.

There are other reforms that are more about changing the culture of politics and the norms of political institutions as workplaces. Where you work should be a safe space for all – a fact we often take for granted.[22] In 2017, the UK Parliament was stunned by allegations of assault and harassment by male MPs. One prominent cabinet minister had to resign over his predatory behaviour; other cases await further investigation. But what also emerged was that Parliament lacked the procedures and processes to deal with these issues effectively. Allegations were dealt with in a highly charged and toxic manner and there appeared to be no mechanisms in place to deal with them. Men have dominated politics and created a club atmosphere suited to themselves, but not others. But the agenda of reform is clear and much of it is laid out in Sarah Childs report on *The Good Parliament*.[23] The details of the report relate to the particular circumstances of the UK and focus on the role of women, but its broad areas of reform concern should be of interest for democracies around the world.

Four areas of reform can be highlighted. First, the building and fabric of Parliaments need to be made suitable to meet the needs of a more diverse group of elected representatives and those concerns stretch from appropriate toilet facilities, accessibility needs, private rooms to allow for confidential exchanges with visitors, and open spaces and public meeting rooms that have a welcoming and non-intimidating atmosphere.

Secondly, the working conditions of Parliaments should meet the needs of the twenty-first century and not be bound to historic traditions and practices. These include the types of changes in working conditions identified above but could stretch further to include not only meeting the travel and accommodation costs of representatives but the additional burdens of social care or childcare that they might have to incur, and even the possibility of job sharing.

Thirdly, direct and clear procedures should be established to ensure equal representation of women on committees and working parties within Parliament. Finally, under the broad heading of workplace culture, we need to deal with issues of bullying, verbal abuse and of course the emerging evidence of sexual harassment and assault. A workplace should be a safe place for all. The current atmosphere and culture of politics appear alien to many citizens and need to be addressed. Dealing with these issues would give us an opportunity to close the current trust gap between politicians and public. We will address these behavioural issues in significant detail in the next chapter. Suffice to say that we support the deployment of incentives, training and nudges co-designed and monitored by parliamentarians and communities to combat poor behaviour and recognize the importance of shifting integrity policies from a narrow focus on deterrence and enforcement towards promoting values-based decision-making. Furthermore, if our elected representatives were required to work and behave in settings a bit more like the rest of us, we might not come to love them, but we might see them as less weird and more approachable.

The final type of reform intervention goes under the heading of strategies that guarantee more diversity of representation and rest on mechanisms to increase the proportion of particular types of candidate or make a particular social characteristic a qualification for public office. In elections where voters are asked to select from lists offered by parties and the seats are then allocated according to the share of votes given to different lists, this could mean that a mix of candidates are at the top of the list. In other cases, it might mean insisting that a quota of women or ethnic minorities is elected in winnable or target seats.

One practice to express this commitment is the idea of all women shortlists which means that only a woman can be chosen to stand for a party in that seat. This begs the question as to whether this results in less qualified candidates being selected. The evidence so far suggests not.[24] Comparing candidates selected by shortlists to those selected by more trading and 'open' mechanisms reveals no difference in talent, experience and capacities. There is a normative choice to be made between taking action to push the diversity agenda along and waiting for social and cultural norms to change sufficiently in society to make it a non-issue but given the scale of inequalities faced by many countries and the evidence of lack of diversity in representation then the case for quotas remains strong.

Quotas work where there is a relevant characteristic in social groups that can be identified such as gender but are perhaps less appropriate with lack of representation of other types of group. For example, those in manual class occupations, not least because you cease being manual class when you take up a job as an elected representative. Quotas do make a difference and although, by definition exclusionary, the degree of exclusion of other groups is normally justified on the basis that opportunities for inclusion are in general available to those who are excluded. Here there is an argument for using the Committee system to bolster the representation of certain groups when they are potentially disproportionately impacted by a policy issue (e.g. young and homeless people and affordable housing). This can be done through sortition of lay members. Belgium's

Saving Democracy

Parliament first used a sortition-based citizens' dialogue to debate the issue of childcare in September of 2017. The parliament randomly selected twenty-six East Belgians to develop a 'citizens' agenda' of the most important issues within childcare and with the support of experts formulate policy recommendations. Similar devices have also been used at the regional government level.[25]

Whether an argument driven by social justice or a desire to see more diversity giving mixed knowledge and insight to decision-making the case for a more inclusive democracy is overwhelming. The case for greater diversity in representative democracies is strong, and there are several promising levers available to reformers that appear to have some impact. There is no reason to put this reform into the 'too difficult' bracket as it is largely a matter of political will. The outstanding issue perhaps is whether diverse descriptive representation leads to better substantive representation of the interests of others. For example, there would be many who might dispute that the policy agenda for women was boosted by the arrival of Britain's first female prime minister, Margaret Thatcher. Being a woman does not automatically make someone a better defender of the interests of women. But we would argue it increases the chances. We need to achieve much greater descriptive representation to see the strength of that claim but the greater involvement of women or other under-represented groups in politics has brought some evidence of shifts in the policy agenda from equal pay to social issues, although there remains the need for more progress in terms of delivering outcomes.[26] If we are to save democracy, we need mechanisms to change the makeup of the political class and there are mechanisms in place that will enable that shift.

Improving the connection between citizen and parliament

Parliaments, it might be argued, are designed to be slightly off-putting to many citizens. The UK Parliament until 2004 used the term 'stranger' to refer to someone physically present in its buildings who is neither a member of parliament nor a parliamentary official. After 2004 the less antagonistic term of 'member of the public' has been used. But still 'men in suits' appear omnipresent in parliaments and elected assemblies featured by procedures and rules that seem part of an *ancien régime*. If elected assemblies are to be home to a wider diversity of representatives, they need to provide a more welcoming and modern work environment. This insight also applies to the challenge of how we get a wider group of citizens to engage with this central political institution. Parliaments and assemblies need to change the ways they currently engage to support better public engagement.

The pinnacle of that engagement might automatically be seen as getting citizens directly involved in the processes of collective decision-making. However, we think that it is important to appreciate the broader canvass of engagement that can be offered if there is a focus on the non-legislative roles of elected assembles within the political system. A valuable framework for thinking through these issues is provided by Cristina Leston-Bandeira in which she identifies four broad roles in which elected assemblies can mediate the relationship between governed and governors.[27]

Reforming Elected Assemblies

The first is a linkage role in which elected officials show they understand issues, share information that is important to understanding the topic and connect the public into the decisions that are being undertaken. The second is about campaigning, elected assemblies can provide a focus for the concerns of the public and in particular issues that are in danger of being overlooked or not dealt with effectively. Campaigning for a change in law should not be a process external to parliaments but rather a dynamic in which they engage. Scrutiny is a classic role for any assembly whereby it holds the government of the day to account for its policies and performance, and there would appear to be ample opportunity in performing this role to bring citizens (whose experiences are important) into direct engagement with the process. Policy development is a fourth role where assembles can engage with citizens, where the focus is not on the detailed production of legislation but rather on facilitating deliberation and discussion about how to tackle an issue. We need to re-orientate our thinking about what elected assemblies are for and to recognize that their functions are not restricted to the narrow role of law-making but have a broader set of societal roles of linkage, policy, scrutiny and campaigning. These broader roles open up considerable opportunities for citizen engagement. Some of these are illustrated in Table 7.1.

Linkage roles

The linkage role is a potentially neglected element of political systems where the focus is more on the distinct roles of institutions and actors rather than on the relationships between them. Carolyn Hendriks offers the notion of 'designed coupling' to express the need to develop innovations and interventions to support linkage processes:

Table 7.1 Non-legislative roles for elected assemblies and citizen engagement

Role	Description	Citizen involvement	Purpose
Linkage	*Getting diverse citizens views expressed to elected officials*	*Inviting engagement through outreach or 'Go-to' democracy*	*Aiming to get those groups less likely to participate to do so through outreach activities*
Campaigning	*Facilitating public campaigns to get issues on the agenda*	*Petitions, public designed and driven petitions*	*Supporting processes whereby neglected issues get on to the agenda of politics*
Scrutiny	*Review of policy and performance of government*	*Experience-based*	*Engaging citizens in the review of policy and performance*
Policy Development	*Developing better policy ideas and options*	*Citizen Assembly as a complement to Assembly-based deliberation*	*Funding a randomly selected group of citizens to reflect policy issues alongside elected representatives*

Saving Democracy

> *At minimum it would provide procedural guarantees to link the more informal (public) parts of the system with the more formal empowered sites. Institutional interventions may be important when interdependencies between sites do not exist, as is often the case between citizens' deliberations and more elite-based sites.*[28]

Linkage then is about bringing the operations and procedures of parliaments more directly into contact with ordinary citizens and thereby removing the sense of strangeness and remoteness about the work that takes place there. What do examples of linkage look like? A catch-all phrase 'go-to-democracy' refers to a range of initiatives that involve getting members from an elected assembly to conduct their work outside the assembly, in town halls, community centres or by visiting particular workplaces or areas of interest. Some of the most innovative are about trying to get groups and individuals who may be less likely to participate to engage through various forms of outreach. For citizens who cannot make it to Parliament one option is to send out a recording team to film or capture their responses (see Box 7.1). Established in 2015, the outreach team for the National Assembly for Wales conducted several initiatives.

Campaigning

The next role which could provide a focus of connection between elected assemblies and citizens is the role of campaigning. A central element in democratic politics is the opportunity for citizens to raise issues of concern themselves and to build coalition of interest to get those issues addressed. Parliaments can be part of the campaigning dynamic in a range of ways from organizing meetings between elected representatives and citizens to those elected representatives using their platform in parliament to campaign on issues.

The right to petition parliament stretches back for centuries but in recent decades has been given a new lease of life by programmes that ensure that once a certain level of support is demonstrated in terms of numbers of signatures supporting a petition then a

Box 7.1 Outreach and the National Assembly for Wales

> In 2015, the National Assembly for Wales' Environment and Sustainability Committee undertook an enquiry into the general principles of the Environment (Wales) Bill. The committee wanted to hear from the fishing industry but as the inquiry took place over the summer (a prime season for shellfisheries) this proved to be difficult to arrange. To resolve the problem an outreach team went out with the fishermen on their boats, carrying out interviews with them and filming their responses. After a process of editing, the team was able to deliver a shorter film but still a fair reflection of views expressed to show to the Committee. These inputs had a significant impact on their findings and recommendations.

response is required. Petitions are most often collected online and provide a keyway of enabling campaigning. As Leston-Bandeira observes, they perform

> ... a mobilization role, providing a focus for citizens to unite around a specific cause, and in doing so, playing a role in strengthening a group's identity, supplying groups' members the means to sustain a sense of shared identity.[29]

Petitions allow for dissemination and discussion of an issue of concern and help build coalitions of support. Where petitions do make an impact, this outcome is usually when members of the elected assembly decide to take things further by collecting more evidence or pushing government ministers to provide a more adequate response if the first response appears inadequate. It is difficult to show how a petition determines a policy outcome since they are often other factors at play, a matching media campaign, expert evidence or political support. A successful petition 'may not lead to actual changes in policy, but petitioners should feel listened to.'[30]

Scrutiny

The third role that elected assemblies can play in connecting citizens to assemblies is undertaken as part of their scrutiny role. A common feature of elected assemblies is their function in calling government ministers and officials to account for their spending and actions or inactions. This is a role that can be done with extensive citizen involvement. Citizens can offer a different form of expertise based on their experience and this evidence can have a powerful impact in the scrutiny of the performance of government. To achieve this kind of impact requires that committees make an extended effort to get

Box 7.2 e-Petitions

> A lot of petitions make no impact, but some do. And there is evidence from the UK that as the use of e-petitions has developed so has the tendency for a government response to emerge. Since 2015, once a petition has achieved enough support then a response is required and given. Of course, at times the responses from government are general or technical or not willing to take on board the policy request. One of the authors of this book had a sister-in-law, Charlotte, whose son, Tom, was killed in a tragic hit-and-run road traffic accident. Without any previous political experience Charlotte was able to organize a petition to ask for a change in the law about how such cases were treated and managed to get to the level of signatures that required a response from government. The response pointed to some of the complexities of changing the law but did try to address the concerns raised and left Charlotte at least feeling she had been listened to, indicating the strength of this mechanism to connect parliaments and citizens.

witnesses beyond the standard public call to provide evidence which tends to attract the better organized or professional interests. Failure to act without innovation can mean that 'committees suffer from a participatory bias in that they engage less with everyday citizens, or more dispersed publics who have yet to form, crystallize or articulate their interests'.[31] But the example below shows it is possible to reach out to even the most vulnerable of groups to gain insights from their experience.

Policy development

A fourth role is the direct involvement of citizens in policy development. Citizens can help elected representatives reflect on policy choices and options. There are increasing examples of elected assemblies commissioning citizens assemblies to support them in that work. The key features of citizen assemblies are described in Chapter 5, but basically they offer a random selected group of citizens the opportunity to reflect on a policy or constitutional issue, facilitated by access to expertise and with enough time to allow for extended deliberation and the generation of recommendations. The UK Parliament's first commissioned citizens' assembly dealt with the vexed issue of the future of social care. These examples of institutional devices that have been used to develop a more creative partnership between elected assemblies and citizens illustrate what can be achieved if there is a political will for change. The institutional practices are there to develop but it is important to note Carolyn Hendriks and Adrian Kay's conclusion that

> ... *successful integration of the public into parliamentary committees will involve deep cultural change, particularly on the part of elected representatives. Not only do parliamentarians have to be willing to listen to a broader range of public voices, but they have to accept that public input can come in multiple forms ... the role of individual MPs in the democratic renewal of legislative institutions has arguably never been more important.*[33]

Box 7.3 Outreach and the Scottish parliament

During an investigation by the Scottish parliament's Education and Culture Committee it wanted to hear directly from looked after children.[32] To do this, it worked closely with local charities who facilitated two private meetings for the elected representatives with young people in Glasgow and Edinburgh. These meetings made a strong impression on the elected representatives and they followed up by organizing an informal event which some of the young people attended along with support staff and they performed a play telling their experiences of being in care. The experience was described as 'uncomfortable but vital for learning'. The young people joined a discussion that followed to develop ideas for better practice.

Reforming Elected Assemblies

Box 7.4 The UK Parliament's citizens' assembly on the future of social care

> Two select committees combined to fund an inquiry to identify a broad consensus for funding reforms in the area of social care reform. The Assembly's recommendations contributed to the Committee's final report which was published on 27 June 2018. This Assembly was the first of its kind to be commissioned by the UK Parliament. The Assembly was made up of forty-seven randomly selected citizens. Participants were selected to be a broadly representative sample of the English population (as social care is a devolved issue). The joint chairs of the Committee wrote a blog about the experience and concluded that 'listening to the views of a representative group gave us a reliable insight into the solutions that could command broad consensus'.[34] The Committee might have been convinced that they had found a way forward with the help of citizens but, as yet, the Government has not taken any proposal forward. The engagement has not been consequential in the sense developed in Chapter 5.

We endorse this judgement and would add that not only do parliamentarians need to commit to doing things differently but so too do members of the executive branch of government. This requires our political leaders to be champions of democracy who put the health of democracy over short-term political expedience.

Evaluating the performance of parliamentary citizen engagement mechanisms

There is a mature literature on the broader evaluation of the democratic performance of assemblies but how should we evaluate parliamentary citizen engagement mechanisms in particular?[35] Here we have over fifty years of research to draw upon that tells us when public participation schemes are likely to succeed. As Vivien Lowndes and her colleagues observe, impact is more probable when the public:

- Can engage *(has the resources, skills and knowledge to participate)*
- Likes to engage *(has a sense of attachment to the issue or institution)*
- Enabled to engage *(is incentivized to participate)*
- Asked to engage *(feels valued)*
- Responded to when they do *(and where there is ongoing engagement with participants)*

The CLEAR model provides a useful heuristic for guiding the evaluation of public participation schemes initiated by assemblies.[36]

Saving Democracy

Conclusion – putting the health of democracy first

Parliaments face a considerable struggle to improve their standing in the minds of citizens. The reforms that we review in this chapter could provide a launching pad for change (see Table 7.2). The essential role of an elected body to represent the views and interests of voters is unlikely to be diminished during the twenty-first century. But as this century has already demonstrated whether it's dealing with a global financial crisis, climate change or a pandemic the only way to effective action is to combine the resources of formal institutions (government, businesses and professions) with the informal resources of citizens, social media and civic action. If that is going to be achieved, then Parliaments need to play their part in gaining support and affecting combined collective action. To that end making assemblies more diverse in their membership and more proactive in engaging with citizens in their political practice are crucial elements in saving democracy.

Table 7.2 Putting the health of democracy first – the reform of elected assemblies

Barrier	Proposed reforms
Remove barriers to the participation of marginalized groups	Role models, mentoring programmes, party and parliamentary champions of change, social support networks
Make politics compatible with being a normal person	Supporting the well-being of elected representative through the creation of creches, and gyms, access to flexible working patterns, job sharing, parental paid leave, sociable use of procedural time, enabling voting and engaging from home by use of digital technology, and matching breaks in political activities with school holidays. Meeting the costs of social care and child care.
Make assemblies more representative of society	Use affirmative action in party recruitment of women candidates (via headhunting or quotas), and ensure the equal representation of women on parliamentary committees. The use of functional lay representation in the parliamentary committee system for groups disproportionality impacted by certain policies.
Create a safe workplace culture	Recognize the importance of shifting integrity policies from a narrow focus on deterrence and enforcement towards promoting values-based decision-making. Introduce incentives (parliamentary pledge, performance review, constituency reports, power of recall), integrity training and nudges to combat poor behaviour codesigned and monitored by parliamentarians and communities.
Actively connect people and parliament	Ensure active citizen engagement in the linkage, campaigning, scrutiny and policy development roles of assemblies through e-Petitions, outreach or 'Go-to' democracy, citizen reviews and assemblies.

CHAPTER 8
CLEANING UP POLITICS

When an angry mob coaxed by a desperate departing president attacked the US Capitol on 6 January 2021, an objective lesson was provided in what happens when a political leader refuses to abide by the rules of democratic governance. It was also a culmination of a period of illegitimate leadership in which Donald Trump continually violated public trust systems through brazenly promoting his own business interests, interfering in the Justice Department, rejecting congressional oversight, insulting judges, harassing the media and failing to concede his election loss.[1] It would be easy to demonize Trump at this point and use him as a barometer for all the integrity challenges that liberal democracies are presently confronting but public perceptions that standards of conduct in public life are in decline and distrust of societal institutions and leaders is widely shared across liberal democracies.[2] Moreover, the sense among citizens that the political system and wider society is corrupt and driven by sectional interests has been seen as a key driver of public distrust for some time and contributed to the rise of Trump himself.[3]

Transparency International's *2019 Corruption Perceptions Index* reveals that the majority of countries are showing 'little to no improvement' in tackling corruption and corruption is generally more widespread in countries where large political donations can flow freely in electoral campaigns and where governments are influenced by powerful sectional interests. As Transparency International observes:

> The index ranks 180 countries and territories by their perceived levels of public sector corruption, according to experts and business people. It uses a scale of zero to 100, where zero is highly corrupt and 100 is very clean. More than two-thirds of countries score below 50, with an average score of just 43.[4]

In the last eight years, only twenty-two countries significantly improved their CPI scores, while twenty-one countries significantly decreased their scores, including Canada and Australia. In the remaining 137 countries, the levels of corruption show little to no change.[5]

We have already argued in his book that it is the quality of democratic governance which counts. This chapter argues that improving the quality of democratic governance requires the establishment of integrity in public governance as a democratic value, proactive integrity agencies and a set of measures for ensuring that elected and non-elected public officials exercise their powers with integrity and remain accountable for their actions. It further argues that the design of effective national integrity systems entails a broad understanding of the obstacles to the achievement of integrity in democratic governance, the options for integrity reform and the appropriate strategic framework for implementing them.

It observes, however, that the achievement of integrity in democratic governance is as much a behavioural challenge as a problem of institutional design or regulation. Over the past three decades at least there has been a fascination with responding to integrity problems either through structural reform and the proliferation of integrity policies and processes to reinforce workplace integrity or by creating new integrity institutions. These are often layered over existing institutions without due reflection on roles, responsibilities and agency creating a crowded and inefficient policy and operational environment. Public organizations consequently spend a great deal of time, energy and resources on meeting compliance obligations rather than embedding integrity values in the hearts, minds and practices of elected and non-elected public officials. The removal of this integrity paradox remains the central challenge for integrity reform.[6]

This chapter maps the integrity reform agenda in three parts. It begins by identifying an ideal-type national integrity system and the values that should underpin it. Part two explores the key ethical dilemmas confronting politicians in liberal democracies. In response, part three introduces a set of measures for ensuring that politicians remain accountable for their actions through the use of a behavioural change model for embedding norms and values in democratic practice.

The role of national integrity systems in democratic governance

As the OECD notes,

Integrity is a cornerstone of good governance. It is a pre-condition for legitimacy of government activities and – more generally – for trust in government. That is why integrity management has been a growing concern for countries around the globe for over a decade.[7]

Integrity refers to principles, standards and behaviours of right conduct not only in terms of distinguishing right from wrong and good from bad but also in terms of demonstrated commitment to do what is right or what is good.[8] The achievement of integrity in democratic governance is as much a behavioural challenge as a problem of institutional design or regulation.

The OECD identifies eight important integrity measures to inform democratic governance or what it terms the 'ethics infrastructure': (1) political commitment to integrity; (2) an effective legal framework; (3) efficient accountability mechanisms; (4) workable codes of conduct; (5) professional socialization of staff; (6) supportive public service conditions (e.g. good working conditions, professionalization and independence); (7) an ethics co-ordinating body; and (8) an active civil society performing a watchdog role.

There have been four main drivers underpinning practice-based thinking on integrity and democratic governance: the search for aid accountability in the developing world; the need to adapt the changing norms and values of public services due to the application of new public management (NPM) and its emphasis on value for-money and commercial business practices; the need to respond to various integrity crises, which have beset advanced liberal democracies; and declining public trust in government.[9]

All four drivers have precipitated a pathology for the introduction of structural reform aimed at creating new integrity systems rather than focusing on reforms with direct behavioural impacts. It is notable that since the end of the Cold War international developments in integrity thinking have set the nation state agenda in this regard. We can identify at least three generations of international discursive thinking about the concept of good governance: good governance as a methodology of market and political reform in the era of structural adjustment (early 1980s to the mid-1990s), the rise of 'good enough governance' in the era of poverty reduction (mid-1990s to the mid-2000s; and the present era of 'integrity in democratic governance' as a normative project for realizing 'good enough governance'.[10]

Integrity systems are designed to give effect to the values of democratic governance delivered through a diverse range of agencies. The most well-known is the National Integrity System, coined by Jeremy Pope and adopted by Transparency International. The metaphor used by Pope is that of a Greek temple, where all the institutional 'pillars' involved in the control of accountability and corruption in a country hold the National Integrity. These pillars include the specialized integrity agencies, such as the auditors-general, ombudsman and watchdog agencies, which are complemented by independent oversight functions within the branches of government, as well as civil society, media and businesses. We could also add conservation commissioners, data protection agencies, public prosecution, electoral commissioners, ethic commissioners and human rights commissioners.[11] Integrity Action adds the importance of collaborative methods to empower citizens to fix and resolve problems that affect their local communities and to monitor integrity.[12]

A.J. Brown and John Uhr remind us out that 'the main lesson is that no single law or institution is likely to provide a magic bullet against corruption. Rather, multiple institutions and reforms are needed to achieve and support a desired integrity "balance", the value of the whole being greater than the mere sum of the parts.'[13] In most instances integrity agencies are statutory bodies set up to perform a monitoring role on governmental activity. By implication they should not be agencies of government but should be financially and legally independent from government to perform their function: 'structured and equipped to relate well to the legislature ... at some distance from the government'.[14] Integrity agencies are increasingly required to play three roles in democratic governance.

First, they play a moral role as guardians of the good society safeguarding the principles of public life and the sanctity of the liberal democratic system of government. Secondly, they play a prudential role in monitoring, evaluating and reporting on risks to the system government brought about by maladministration. The third and probably most contested and underdeveloped role for Integrity agencies lies in their educative function. In keeping with John Dewey's argument that the key measure of the quality of a democracy lies in its capacity to develop a 'fully formed public opinion', integrity agencies should play a fundamental role in enhancing the political literacy of the citizenry through active public engagement with the citizenry.[15] These roles require political independence, the support of elected politicians, and appropriate legal, financial and human resources.

Ethical dilemmas

Politicians inhabit a unique ethical position in terms of deploying public power both within liberal democratic institutions and more broadly in the social and economic system. The core idea of representative democracy is that citizens delegate power to politicians whom they believe will best use that power to serve their interests. Political parties play a key role in aggregating interests and formulating policy agendas which they believe can be exercised for the good of the community they serve, and they present these agendas to the electorate for legitimation in elections, and then seek to deliver on the promises they make if they achieve power. However, politicians are constantly confronted with ethical choices about the way in which they exercise public power. Harold Lasswell's seminal definition of politics as the study of 'who gets what, when, how' highlights the role of politicians (depending on their political capital) as the key agents of resource distribution and redistribution within a political system.[16] This role inexorably involves ongoing ethical dilemmas, sometimes in areas of uncertainty, where there are no hard and fast rules but simply a moral imperative to do the right thing. However, most of these choices are now governed by formal codes of conduct and regulations which are openly flouted by elected and non-elected officials if it is politically expedient for them to do so.

These ethical dilemmas – where integrity principles point one way but personal or pecuniary interests potentially point in the other – include issues surrounding the acceptance of political donations, responding to the interests of lobbyists, the provision of public information about how policy is made, the use of procedural fairness in privatization or outsourcing decisions, the establishment of ethical relationships with media and business interests, among others. Three main sources of ethical disquiet require discussion here – the tensions between democratic governance and the market economy, the rise of the career politician and integrity as a behavioural challenge.

The interactions between democratic governance and market institutions

> *High levels of economic inequality lead to imbalances in political power as those at the top use their economic weight to shape our politics in ways that give them more economic power.*
>
> (Joseph Stiglitz, 2012, p. 3)[17]

As Joseph Stiglitz notes, policing the boundaries between the market and democracy is a fundamental problem in liberal democracies committed to democratic and market principles. This first source of ethical disquiet is often viewed as inevitable given that we live in a capitalist system but arguably this tension has become more acute in contemporary governance systems dominated by NPM. The marketization of public service production is integral to the practice of NPM because it involves the distribution and redistribution of public resources to non-accountable third parties to manage and deliver public programmes and services. An integrity paradox often emerges in which the quest for 'economy', 'efficiency' and 'effectiveness' through NPM, and risk management instruments, increases rather than reduces the scope for maladministration or corruption.[18] Indeed many academics such as Mark Bevir identify the interactions between democratic governance and market institutions as the key source of the liberal democratic deficit.[19]

There is another important facet to this interplay between politics and markets that requires understanding. The general dynamic of the professionalization of parties and their reliance on state and other non-membership sources of funding is known in political science as the 'cartel party thesis'.[20] Broadly speaking, instead of being rooted in civil society and taking citizens' views to government, parties have increasingly become part of the machinery of governance, an indispensable mechanism for organizing elections and choosing political leaders, and in many instances are funded and supported by government. However, political parties have also become a conduit for protecting and advancing special interests which has called into question the legitimacy of their role.

The professionalization of politics and the rise of the career politician

All the current generation of politicians, myself included, typically came up through the back offices. We're the professional politician generation, aren't we?
(Andy Burnham, UK MP, 2013)[21]

This quotation reflects broader academic and popular concern with the professionalization of politics – the idea that politicians are increasingly drawn from a small group of individuals, many of whom have worked in politics in other capacities prior to running for elected office.[22]

There are three ethical dimensions to this issue that require elaboration. The first is that career politicians are, of necessity, seeking power and by implication the profession will attract those who desire power, although they may seek to exercise it in different ways. Power is intrinsically neither good nor evil, but its user can make it so. Some may exercise it in the public interest and according to the values and interests articulated by the electorate. Others may exercise it on behalf of the electorate but in contradiction with the values and interests articulated by the electorate but for the broader public good as a trustee or steward of the public interest. And then there are others that exercise power purely through self-regard and interest.

The second ethical dimension to the problem of the career politician is the increasing evidence that the political class has become isolated from the people it represents and this is reflected in terms of what citizens perceive to be the key characteristics of the good politician. Over the past three years we have conducted forty-six focus groups with different groups of Australians with the aim of exploring how they would characterize the good politician. Within these focus groups, we asked participants to describe the characteristics of their ideal politician. They were fairly uniform in emphasizing the importance of:

Integrity – described as 'honesty', 'transparency', 'someone who does what they say' and 'consistently fair'.

Empathy – described as a person who is 'approachable and accessible', 'listens', 'cares' and 'understands'.

Delivery – described as a person who 'keeps promises', 'explains if they change their mind', 'follows up' and 'delivers'.

Loyalty – described as a person who 'has their back' and 'looks after them'.

These features of a good politician parallel those discussed in Chapter 2, and reflect the centrality of the community linkage and integrity roles to building and maintaining public trust but are not deemed to be very common in the age of the career politician. As the following testimony from Australian citizens shows:

At the moment a lot of politicians go into politics for advancement rather than service. Turning out clones of media-savvy people with sound bites and platitudes, not genuine responses. It feels like they're manufactured.
(Baby Boomer, regional and rural Australian)

Keeping your word. That's a big thing with me. Don't tell me you're going to do something and then don't do it because I'll never trust you again.
(Builder, urban Australian)

To trust a politician would mean they were approachable, reliable and consistent and that their words lined up with their actions: You're going to laugh at this from a male's point of view. When I shake hands with another male, I will know by his handshake whether or not I'm going to trust him. They look you in the eye.
(Generation X, rural Australian)

The third ethical dimension to the problem of the career politician is reflected in the failure of political parties to champion liberal democratic values and strengthen democratic practice as an ongoing mission. In theory political parties and by implication politicians perform three sets of overlapping and reinforcing functions in a democratic political system – governance, community linkage and integrity roles. The third role is of crucial relevance to this chapter. The 'integrity' role emphasizes that political parties should be considered guardians of liberal democratic norms and values with a public expectation to uphold the highest standards of conduct in public life. This crucial role is not only important in linking national and local politics and maintaining trust between government and citizen but has heightened significance in a period where democracy is on the retreat globally and there are now more authoritarian regimes than full democracies.[23]

These observations in part explain why independents that play the community-linkage role effectively can be successful. The rising minor party vote features in many liberal democracies as some voters' search for alternatives to the mainstream. If existing political parties are replaced by others that better reflect the popular will and public interest, then democracy is working. The rising minor party vote, properly understood, may also encourage existing major parties to enact reforms in their own long-term self-interest that would also be in the public interest.[24]

Integrity as a behavioural challenge

Although the establishment of efficient and effective integrity agencies is an important component of integrity reform, the achievement of integrity in democratic governance is primarily a behavioural challenge in which integrity values are embedded in the hearts, minds and practices of elected and non-elected public officials. So why do integrity reforms so often fail? Behavioural research provides us with strong clues to the answer to this question. Integrity policies are based on a rational decision-making model driven by the assumption that people will exploit an opportunity for misconduct if the benefits outweigh the costs:

> *Individuals are assumed to weigh the probability of getting caught (i.e. the strictness of internal and external control and detection mechanisms) and the ensuing sanctions against the undue gain they could obtain through action or inaction.*[25]

Evidence from three decades of behavioural science experiments highlights the range of social and psychological factors that influence decision-making. This has led to the award of two Nobel Prizes. In 2002, Princeton University psychologist Daniel Kahneman, PhD, was awarded the Nobel Memorial Prize in Economic Sciences for his ground-breaking work in applying psychological insights to economic theory, focusing on how individuals make decisions under uncertainty. Then in 2017, Chicago University economist Richard Thaler was awarded the Nobel Memorial Prize in Economic Sciences for 'contributions that have built a bridge between the economic and psychological analyses of individual decision-making'.[26]

Alongside traditional policy instruments such as tax, spend, regulate and penalize, there is growing interest in how behavioural insights can be used to improve policy outcomes.[27] Behavioural insights, drawn from experiments in behavioural economics and psychology, have increasingly been used in public policy design to tackle issues that require change in human behaviour such as climate change, obesity, saving for the future through private pension schemes, tax avoidance, dangerous driving, engaging in corrupt practices, among others.[28] Behavioural insights have also been used to improve public compliance with Covid-19 suppression measures.[29] The core insight here is to work with, rather than against, the grain of human behaviour. To make no assumptions about how people behave (as in the case of formal economic modelling) but to use experiments to find out how they behave in the real world of decision-making and how they might behave with a different choice architecture.

Behavioural insights are not about asking citizens what they think. Nor are they about public participation. It involves shifting the way government does things to give it more of a chance to see like a citizen. Seeing the world through the eyes of the citizen and responding to that vision. Most importantly, it provides a different way of thinking about implementation. A timely corrective to the dominance of 'top-down', 'government knows best' approaches to policy design which have struggled to achieve strong outcomes for the citizenry.[30]

In the context of safeguarding public integrity, behavioural insights can be used to ensure that the good or ethical choice is the easiest choice. In this context, it is important to see like a politician rather than a citizen. Recent field research has sought to explain how corrupt networks function and how they might react to incentives provided by integrity measures.[31] There are seven important lessons that we can draw from the main findings for integrity reform:

1. Ethical choices are not made in isolation, but in the context of social interaction. What others think and do matter.
2. Expect ethical failures from everyone.
3. Raise and emphasize moral reference points and encourage ethical reflection at key moments in the policy process.
4. Guilt is less when shared hence spreading the burden of responsibility over too many people can create an integrity risk.
5. Over-strict control can have adverse effects. Excessive monitoring of a trust-based rule might drive people to disregard the rule and create an entry-point for severe misconduct.
6. Provide actionable training and commitment.
7. Anticipate where politicians will fail and build integrity systems around the pressure points.[32]

The OECD therefore recommends the deployment of incentives, training and nudges to combat poor behaviour:

All three should be included in an integrity system: decision-makers need to be clearly incentivised to be objective and shielded from subtle conflicts of interests. They should be trained to know and identify biased behaviour. And the way in which they are presented with choices should be designed to favour objectivity, for example, through smart default setting or reframing questions.[33]

Cleaning Up Politics

We can therefore derive from this research and the work of the Behavioural Insights Unit a set of behavioural insights that can be used to design and pilot integrity interventions.[34] These are set out in Box 8.1.

Taking an integrated approach to building an integrity culture

There is no single 'magic formula' that has been discovered for resolving the complex ethical dilemmas politicians face. However, the evidence clearly suggests that building an integrity culture requires behavioural change and influencing behaviour is most effective when measures are combined from across four broad categories of policy tools that regulate, enable, encourage and co-govern change (see Figure 8.1). This observation reflects the importance of shifting integrity policies from a narrow focus on compliance and enforcement towards promoting values-based decision-making.

Enabling behavioural change is about building the capacity of politicians to perform their duties with integrity. In keeping with contemporary workplaces, this should involve mandated integrity training, coaching and mentoring. However, personal development plans should be co-designed with the target group to develop actionable training outcomes and ensure commitment. Parliamentarians should submit annual constituency reports for public scrutiny and review.

Regulating behavioural change requires establishing the right incentives/disincentives to prompt good behaviour. In keeping with the modernization of contemporary

Incentives
- Local election manifestos
- Parliamentary pledge
- Constituency performance reporting and review
- Integrity award schemes

Disincentives
- Co-regulation – codes of conduct, integrity reviews and enforcement through Parliamentary /integrity/ Committee
- Power of recall

Capacity building
- Codesign integrity training, coaching and mentoring schemes with target group and create spaces in the workplan for effective delivery and absorption of integrity values

'Nudge' and 'Think'
- Use behavioural insights to co-design 'nudge' and 'think' interventions with target group to trigger behavioural change

Co-governance through integrity champions
- Design and co-grovern the integrity system with national and community party elites, senior parliamentarians and integrity agencies

Integrity culture

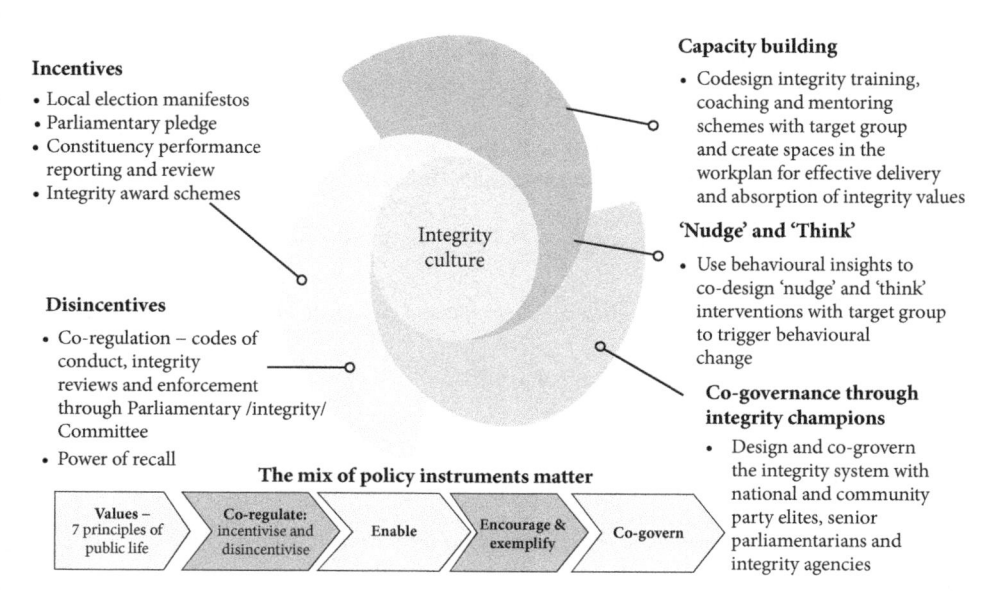

The mix of policy instruments matter

Values – 7 principles of public life → Co-regulate: incentivise and disincentivise → Enable → Encourage & exemplify → Co-govern

Figure 8.1 Building an integrity culture.

workplaces, incentives should include performance review processes governed by codes of conduct and underpinned by personal development planning processes monitored by an integrity panel including party and community representation. The power of recall or parliamentary petition should be available to electorates in the event of poor performance or misconduct. Parliamentary integrity award schemes should be introduced to celebrate exemplary behaviour.

Behavioural change should be encouraged through 'nudge' (e.g. direct messaging to parliamentarians to emphasize moral reference points) and 'think' interventions (e.g. cyclical public deliberations to assess the outcomes of integrity reviews and suggest remedial action) with parliamentarians aimed at embedding behavioural change.

Co-governing behavioural change reflects the importance of establishing broad ownership of the change process. A Parliamentary Integrity Committee should be created comprising senior parliamentary integrity champions, directors of appropriate integrity agencies and a random sample of lay citizens. The purpose of the committee is to ensure effective implementation and monitoring of integrity reform. This will require the co-development of a theory of change, intervention logic and desired outcomes and mechanisms that ensure the diffusion of innovation across the system of democratic governance.

Table 8.1 Behavioural insights for integrity reform

Behavioural insight
Who is the right messenger of integrity reform? *Politicians are heavily influenced by their national party leadership, local elites and constituents.*
What incentives need to be created to prompt good behaviour? *The response of politicians to incentives is likely to be shaped by predictable mental shortcuts such as strongly avoiding losses.*
What integrity norms will lead to appropriate behaviours? *Politicians are strongly influenced by what other politicians do and the norms they share.*
How should integrity reform be presented? *Politicians require some choice to feel valued.*
What integrity issues matter? *The attention of politicians is drawn to what is relevant and pressing to them and their electoral chances.*
What integrity values drive the behaviour of politicians? *The values of their peers nationally and locally.*
How can we ensure that politicians remain accountable for their actions? *Politicians seek to be consistent with their public promises and reciprocate acts.*
Ego *Politicians act in ways that make them feel better about themselves.*
Convenience *Make the ethical choice, the easiest choice for politicians?*

Source: Inspired by MINDSPACE.[36]

The reforms outlined above would be given moral force through the creation of a parliamentary pledge that all parliamentarians should take on entering parliament to uphold the values of representative democracy.[35] Sound ethical decision-making is maximized when politicians' decisions are made in an appropriately designed, transparent and accountable integrity system. Integrity reform along the lines suggested above should be welcomed by those wishing to strengthen ethical practice in democratic politics.

Box 8.1 The Nolan principles

Selflessness

Holders of public office should act solely in terms of the public interest. They should not do so to gain financial or other benefits for themselves, their family or their friends.

Integrity

Holders of public office should not place themselves under any financial or other obligation to outside individuals or organizations that might seek to influence them in the performance of their official duties.

Objectivity

In carrying out public business, including making public appointments, awarding contracts, or recommending individuals for rewards and benefits, holders of public office should make choices on merit.

Accountability

Holders of public office are accountable for their decisions and actions to the public and must submit themselves to whatever scrutiny is appropriate to their office.

Openness

Holders of public office should be as open as possible about all the decisions and actions they take. They should give reasons for their decisions and restrict information only when the wider public interest clearly demands.

Honesty

Holders of public office have a duty to declare any private interests relating to their public duties and to take steps to resolve any conflicts arising in a way that protects the public interest.

Leadership

Holders of public office should promote and support these principles by leadership and example.

Saving Democracy

Evaluating integrity in politics

How are we best evaluating integrity in public life? We believe that the seven principles of public life enunciated by the Nolan Committee are still the gold standard for public conduct and in some parts of corporate life.[37] In 1994, in response to several high-profile abuses of public office, the UK government established a Committee on Standards in Public Life which is still with us today.[38] The committee was chaired by Lord Nolan and was tasked with making recommendations to improve standards of behaviour in public life. What became known as the 'Nolan principles' are outlined in Box 8.1. You would be hard pushed to find anyone to argue against such noble values, but as we have seen they are not enough in and of themselves to ensure good behaviour in public life. Nonetheless, they still provide clear standards for evaluating integrity in politics.

In conclusion: it is the mix of policy instruments that matters

The evidence presented in this chapter suggests that the capacity of liberal democracies for saving democracy is potentially undermined by a fundamental democratic paradox – a cognitive dissonance between integrity reform and individual and organizational absorption of integrity norms and values. Public organizations consequently spend a great deal of time, energy and resources on building integrity systems and meeting compliance obligations rather than transforming individual behaviour. Hence the removal of this integrity paradox remains the central challenge for integrity reform. We have discovered that building an integrity culture requires behavioural change and that influencing behaviour is most effective when measures are combined from across four broad categories of policy tools that regulate, enable, encourage and co-govern change. It is the mix that matters and it is important to find space for both 'nudge' and 'think' interventions with target groups to reinforce regulatory change. At the same time, it is essential to use integrity values to guide policy choices and to deploy evidence to inform those choices.

CHAPTER 9
EMBEDDING EXPERTS AND EVIDENCE IN DEMOCRATIC GOVERNANCE

The relationship between democracy and expertise continues to be a troubled one.[1] If democracy is defined as the opportunity for citizens to decide together what they want to do collectively, then the role of experts can appear to be a threat to democracy rather than an opportunity. In this light, experts might not automatically be seen as part of the mechanisms necessary to help save democracy. Yet in this chapter, we argue that one of the key reforms necessary to improve democracy is to find a way of making expertise and evidence central to collective democratic decision-making. Indeed, we have already demonstrated how this can work in the context of mini-publics and deliberative democracy in Chapter 5.

There are strong forces that would appear to question that commitment. On the one hand, there is the growth of a form of right-wing populist movement that encourages distrust of expertise and more generally of scientific institutions.[2] And on the other hand, there are progressive democratic reformers who express considerable distrust of experts.[3] There are at least four lines of attack. Experts present their evidence as if it were indisputable when that is rarely the case. Experts claim to be value free in the advice they offer, and that position often hides their conscious or unconscious political motives. The language and style of argument used by experts are exclusionary at best and may even be designed to bamboozle and confuse others. Finally, how experts reach their advice or policy recommendations often lacks transparency and accountability and they can overstep their domain of expertise.

There is some validity in each of these lines of attack. But we want to offer an alternative position. We are not advocating for a technocratic future where experts take over the practice of governing, but rather we hold that experts are a 'hidden' but vital ingredient to successful democracy. Why 'hidden'? Because the narrow focus in democratic theory on achieving better democracy which tends to define the challenge as being about finding ways to give voice to citizens overlooks the evidence that citizens themselves often have a more pragmatic approach to the topic. Democracy is valued for the opportunity to have your say (input legitimacy) but also because it delivers effective collective action to tackle social and economic problems (output legitimacy). Experts are trusted to help in delivering that second part of operational democracy for a range of reasons.[4]

Experts bring something essential to achieving output legitimacy in three ways. First and most important, they have specialist knowledge to aid the understanding of the issues we are confronted by. This kind of specialist knowledge is becoming more rather than less important in our technologically complex and developed world.

Saving Democracy

Second, they can often be valued because they do not have an axe to grind or a tie to specialist interests, in that sense they have a perceived integrity that other actors in the policy process can lack. While not neglecting that experts can be funded by businesses, campaigners or governments there are relatively strong protocols and matching cultures in place to declare any conflicts of interest. Finally, they can help design solutions that work, a preferred outcome for many citizens. Viewed as better than all the talk or collective reflection in the world. Of course, we are not suggesting that all outcomes are equally successful from the point of view of different interests but the sense that expertise could help deliver effective action is a very attractive prospect that we should support rather than discourage. As we will see in Chapters 10, 12 and 13, these features of experts and the evidence they generate are particularly prized in times of crisis and provide strong foundational arguments for why making expertise an integral part of the policy process is supportive of rather than antagonistic to saving democracy.[5]

The issue addressed in this chapter is how best to achieve this aim because the beneficial qualities of engaging expertise are not automatically realized in practice. They have to be designed into the process of decision-making and done so in a way that minimizes the reasonable concerns about experts over-claiming, hiding their political preferences and crowding out all other voices. We start our investigation with noting that there are different types of expertise before going on to explore how both demand and supply issues will need to be addressed to make the best use of experts and evidence.

Types of expert

The case for embedding evidence through collaborative democratic governance has been made but what do we mean by expertise? Edward Page observes that expertise is best understood as 'a high level of familiarity with a body of knowledge and/or experience that is neither widely shared nor simply acquired'.[6] This is a useful definition for our purposes because in keeping with the diverse range of governance problems that social systems confront it allows for different types of knowledge as 'expertise'. In general, we can distinguish between four types of expertise that are important for problem-solving. First, scientific (e.g. natural, social) expertise attempts to understand the why, and how of the problem. For example, in the context of Covid-19, the how and why of the virus to control the spread. Here expertise comes to the fore across the full spectrum of natural and social sciences; from medicine and pharmacy, through to economics and social psychology; from genetics and data science, through to sociology and communication.

Second, policy expertise refers to knowledge of the range of policies and instruments, past and present, informing the public policy response. For this example, types of lockdown, social distancing, masks, quarantine regimes, contact tracing, economic stimulus, etc.

Third, professional expertise refers to broad interdisciplinary, experiential and practical knowledge of the nature of the treatment of the problem or similar problems and the complex processes to be followed to ensure a sensible response can be found and put into effect. For this example, professional expertise in the governance of public health.

Fourth, legal expertise refers to regulatory knowledge in how to put a law into effect, what is permissible and what is not, what could be challenged and what is likely to stand – for example, in the Covid-19 context, many countries introduced emergency powers legislation, which empowers certain elected and non-elected officials with provenance over crisis management decision-making. Tom Nichols adds additional criteria of value here:

> *Specialised knowledge is inherent in every occupation, and so here I will use the words 'professionals', 'intellectuals', and 'experts' interchangeably to refer to people who have mastered particular skills or bodies of knowledge and who practice those skills or use that knowledge as their main occupation in life.*[7]

This includes a combination of formal educational and professional credentials, peer affirmation and reputation. The technical capacity and reputation of an expert are reinforced by their institutional affiliation and brand.

Different types of expert and evidence are also required depending on the urgency with which the advice is required. In general, we live in an era of fast policy-making and knowledge institutions with the capacity to translate evidence quickly into practical recommendations for decision-makers are highly sought after. Public sector organizations will pay a premium for timely and reliable advice from one of the Big 4 public sector consultancies – Deloitte, Ernst & Young, KPMG and PwC.[8] Indeed, the temporal dimension driving advisory systems has become a key determinant in the commissioning of expertise. Academic expertise, for example, has become the preserve of post ante evaluation or long-term policy thinking where decision-makers tend to be more patient in waiting for advice. Few academics are able to meet the temporal demand for fast policy advice.

There is long-standing evidence of the tendency of governments to create durable epistemic (knowledge) communities composed of elite natural and social scientists and/or experts from any discipline or profession with authoritative claims to scientific, policy, process or legal expertise.[9] Peter Haas's seminal work in this area identifies privileged experts that dominate policy advice by virtue of their knowledge capital, strong interpersonal relationships with key political and/or bureaucratic actors and shared policy norms and values.[10] Expert advice, particularly in areas where government lacks knowledge, can be formally granted a privileged position in the policy process in the form of expert bodies that exercise a veto over policy proposals and specialist committees that can require bureaucracies to develop policies.

By way of illustration, in the Australian context, a range of expertise has been necessary to combat the virus but given the few absolute scientific truths about the pandemic, policy and process expertise has been preeminent and scientific expertise has been harvested from tried and trusted experts within the government's epistemic community, the Australian Health Protection Principal Committee (AHPPC) – the primary national health advisory body which draws on knowledge from wider sources through the creation of specialist sub-groups such as the Infection Control Expert Group. Figure 9.1 shows where the AHPPC sits within the context of Covid-19 governance at the Commonwealth government level.

Covid-19 saw the establishment of new institutional structures such as the National Cabinet and the National Covid-19 Commission. Coordination mechanisms were also established in specific Commonwealth Departments such as the Emergency Relief National Coordination Group in the Department of Social Services. In the case of Covid-19, it is the status of the expert, the content of their expertise and their institutional affiliation that appear to account for their influence.

Over fifty years of policy research also demonstrates that evidence is not a sufficient criterion for policy action as it is nearly always contested and the nature of the contestation often reflects competing social values.[11] Studies of the role of natural scientists in policy-making tend to suggest that when there is a clash of policy values between experts with competing views on the evidence base the role of science in settling the conflict is limited. This is because, as Peter Self puts it, 'scientific training often makes an expert scrupulously objective about the policy implications of his knowledge' and it is not unusual for pure scientists to adopt rigid positions when the political settings are compelling political elites towards a compromise. Natural scientists find it difficult to accept that evidence is not a sufficient criterion for policy action in a liberal democracy.[12] But what social status does expertise have in the public realm?

Decision Making

National Cabinet	National Security Committee of Cabinet	Expenditure Review Committee of Cabinet
Comprises Prime Minister, premiers and chief ministers. Coordinates Australia's national response to COVID-19	Makes decisions on Australian Government crisis response arrangements	Makes decisions on Australian Government economic response measures

Policy advice and Coordination

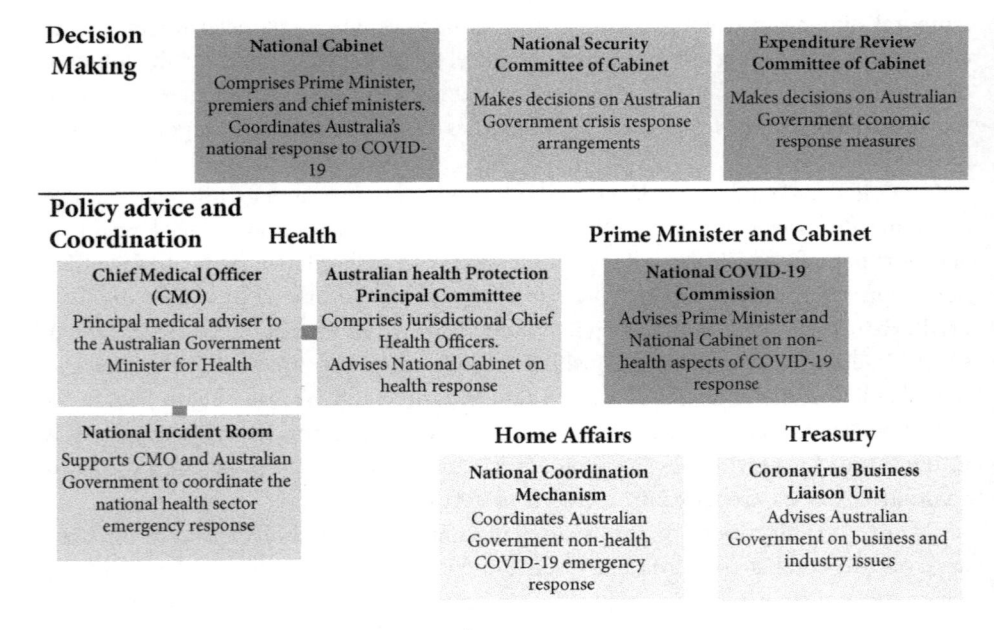

Health

Prime Minister and Cabinet

Chief Medical Officer (CMO)	Australian health Protection Principal Committee	National COVID-19 Commission
Principal medical adviser to the Australian Government Minister for Health	Comprises jurisdictional Chief Health Officers. Advises National Cabinet on health response	Advises Prime Minister and National Cabinet on non-health aspects of COVID-19 response

National Incident Room	Home Affairs	Treasury
Supports CMO and Australian Government to coordinate the national health sector emergency response	National Coordination Mechanism — Coordinates Australian Government non-health COVID-19 emergency response	Coronavirus Business Liaison Unit — Advises Australian Government on business and industry issues

Figure 9.1 Covid-19 governance in Australia.

Experts and the public

Recent evidence suggests that scientists have experienced fluctuating public attitudes both prior and during the pandemic. Before the pandemic there was strong evidence, particularly in Brazil, the United States and the UK, of anti-intellectualism – the generalized distrust of intellectuals and experts.[13] Tom Nichols wrote at the time that

> this is more than a natural scepticism towards experts. I fear we are witnessing the death of the ideal of expertise itself, a google fuelled, Wikipedia-based, blog-sodden collapse of any division between professionals and laypeople, students and teachers, knowers and wonderers – in other words, between those of any achievement in an area and those with none at all.[14]

Anti-intellectualism came to the fore in the UK during the Brexit debate in 2016 when Conservative Minister and leader of the 'Vote Leave' campaign Michael Gove famously argued 'I think people in this country have had enough of experts'.[15] In this case the word 'expert' was being used as a pejorative term for those generating evidence in support of the status quo to remain in the European Union.[16]

To add an additional level of complexity, the Wellcome Global Monitor ran a survey in 2018 on trust in science and scientists in over 140 countries and overall 72 per cent of people globally confirmed that they trusted scientists.[17] Moreover, during the pandemic 3M surveyed more than 1,000 people in fourteen different countries and found that trust in science had increased to a three-year high.[18] In short, anti-intellectualism appears to be a feature of certain cohorts in democracies that are embracing the rise of populisms – a worldview that sees political conflict as primarily between ordinary citizens and a privileged societal elite.[19]

In a recent study, Eric Merkel and Peter Loewen asked whether anti-intellectualism has shaped the mass public's response to Covid-19.[20] The research provides evidence that preferences for Covid-19 news and information from experts dissipate among respondents with higher levels of anti-intellectual sentiment. They conclude that 'anti-intellectualism therefore poses a fundamental challenge in maintaining and increasing public compliance with expert-guided Covid-19 health directives'.

We now have a good understanding of the types of expertise that are important in contemporary governance and how experts are perceived by the public. But what are the barriers to embedding the use of evidence in practice?

Supply- and demand-side barriers to the use of evidence

Crucially, we see the problem as lying with both government and knowledge institutions. For many decades now there has been much discussion about how to obtain a better match between the kinds of research that researchers undertake (the supply side) and the kinds of research governments want (the demand side). Indeed, there appears to be a significant disconnect between the two.

Supply-side barriers

What are the supply-side factors that are likely to influence the use of research in policy? We can find a strong evidence base in the health policy arena to help us with this question, although it should be noted that health policy-makers have always been the most receptive to evidence-based practice. The critical factors include the nature and relevance of the evidence to its intended audience(s); demonstration by the researcher of its relevance to the policy context; the existence of strong trust systems between researchers, research users and other stakeholders; the organization's readiness and receptivity to receive and use evidence; and the availability of, and access to, supportive resources and tools for translating evidence into practice.[21]

Academic research often deals with issues that are not central to policy and management debates and can fail to take the reality of peoples' lives into account in setting research questions. Academics are often accused of retreating into jargon and irrelevance, preferring to only interact with other scholars. Conversely, when research tries to be relevant, it can be seen as being driven by ideology dressed up as intellectual enquiry. And a frequent complaint is the lack of timeliness in academic research. Many experts, and particularly those in the academy, have abandoned their duty to engage with the public. Such are the frustrations of many policy-makers.

Experts are of course fallible and can make mistakes. The blunders are there for everyone to see from Chernobyl to the *Challenger*, to Thalidomide and Y2K. Poor advice is always a possibility, especially in response to adaptive rather than technical problems. But to ignore expert advice is not a realistic option, not least because the development of new policy proposals in most advanced democracies demands the presentation of supporting evidence to validate decision-making. Evidence-based policy-making is, in theory at least, a key feature of public accountability insofar as the 'evidence' is presented through various devices in the policy process for public scrutiny (Green and White papers, in Westminster systems, for example).

Demand-side barriers

Although integral to the quality of democratic culture, whether citizens embrace evidence-based policy-making or not is less significant than the attitudes of politicians or public servants if it is to be embedded in practice. In a series of workshops held between 2016 and 2020, we asked groups of senior policy officers in Australia, New Zealand and the UK what they perceived to be the main barriers to evidence-based policy-making. The findings suggest that they are champions of evidence-based policy-making but their political masters (with some exceptions) are not (see Table 9.1).

Embedding Experts in Democratic Governance

Table 9.1 Key features of the Westminster advisory system in Australia, New Zealand and the UK

Country	Male	Female
'Evidence is a condition of better policy-making' (per cent agree)		
Australia	94	97
New Zealand	97	97
UK	93	95
'Work time spent on developing evidence-based policy, programmes or interventions' (per cent agree)		
Australia	24	20
New Zealand	27	22
UK	18	17
'Work time spent on retrofitting evidence to decisions that have already been taken' (per cent agree)		
Australia	76	80
New Zealand	73	78
UK	82	83
'There is an ongoing tension between short-term imperative and evidence-based policy-making' (per cent agree)		
Australia	84	85
New Zealand	85	87
UK	82	84
'There is ministerial indifference over the facts' (per cent agree)		
Australia	64	62
New Zealand	59	63
UK	61	64

Moreover, because of a combination of a pathology of the short-term and the 24/7 media cycle, they spend the bulk of their time engaged in 'policy-based evidence making', retrofitting evidence to support decisions already made. When we asked our respondents to deconstruct the barriers in more detail (see Box 9.1), they identified three key barriers to bridging the world of academia and the world of practice: disconnection, mistrust and poor understanding between the worlds of ideas/research and action/practice; a static view of academic research as a product and system decision-making as an event versus a dynamic view of both as social processes that need to be linked in ongoing exchange; and the perception that there are limited capability or incentives in the system to use research.[22]

Table 9.2 What are the major barriers to getting evidence into policy-making?

Policy culture	Environmental constraints
Pathology of the short-term	24/7 media cycle
Anti-evidence culture	Public expectations for quick fixes
Ministerial indifference towards evidence	Prevailing socio-economic conditions
Culture of risk aversion	Poor strategic alignment cross government
Poor commissioning of research	

Institutional resources/constraints
Absence of clear roles and responsibilities for policy officers
Dominant agenda-setting role of special advisors
Poor engagement capacity of policy officers
Lack of support from politicians
Short-term budgets and planning horizons
Delivery pressures and administrative burdens
Poor rewards and incentives
Capability deficit in political awareness

The perspective of academic researchers on this issue has been articulated well by Peter Saunders and James Walter, in the introduction to their book, *Ideas and Influence*, the lack of attention by policy practitioners to the subtleties and qualifications of their research findings and a fear that 'those driving policy are seeking to justify actions already decided by "cherry-picking" from among the available evidence with little regard for the robustness or validity of the material selected'.[23] They go on to observe that 'those involved in policy development often have little idea of how or where existing research can contribute, or what is needed to help resolve outstanding issues'. To this observation could be added an anti-intellectual approach sometimes formed within governments, a risk-averse attitude by public servants to findings that could embarrass the Minister, the short timeframes under which governments operate, and a lack of both respect for the independence of researchers and of incentives needed for researchers to produce policy-relevant material. Not all research is undertaken to influence policy, and when it does, this tends to be through what Carol Weiss has called 'the enlightenment effect'.[24] Research may be used simply to raise awareness although it may start to shape policy thinking through ideas, theories and concepts.[25]

It is also common for policy scientists to report that the best practice principles of policy-making are often overlooked in practice. The Institute of Public Affairs in Australia recently undertook an analysis of twenty public policies using the ten criteria of the 'Wiltshire test for good policy-making' named after Professor Ken Wiltshire's rather traditional understanding of better policy-making (see Box 9.1).[26] The project was commissioned 'to coax more evidence-based policy decisions by all tiers of Government by reviewing and rating 20 high profile government decisions against the Wiltshire business case criteria' shown in Box 9.1.[27]

Embedding Experts in Democratic Governance

Box 9.1 The Wiltshire criteria

1. Establish need: Identify a demonstrable need for the policy, based on hard evidence and consultation with all the stakeholders involved, particularly interest groups who will be affected. ('Hard evidence' in this context means both quantifying tangible and intangible knowledge, for instance the actual condition of a road as well as people's view of that condition so as to identify any perception gaps).
2. Set objectives: Outline the public interest parameters of the proposed policy and clearly establish its objectives. For example, interpreting public interest as 'the greatest good for the greatest number' or 'helping those who can't help themselves'.
3. Identify options: Identify alternative approaches to the design of the policy, preferably with international comparisons where feasible. Engage in realistic costings of key alternative approaches.
4. Consider mechanisms: Consider implementation choices along a full spectrum from incentives to coercion.
5. Brainstorm alternatives: Consider the pros and cons of each option and mechanism. Subject all key alternatives to a rigorous cost-benefit analysis. For major policy initiatives (over $100 million), require a Productivity Commission analysis.
6. Design pathway: Develop a complete policy design framework including principles, goals, delivery mechanisms, programme or project management structure, the implementation process and phases, performance measures, ongoing evaluation mechanisms and reporting requirements, oversight and audit arrangements, and a review process ideally with a sunset clause.
7. Consult further: Undertake further consultation with key affected stakeholders of the policy initiative.
8. Publish proposals: Produce a Green and then a White paper for public feedback and final consultation purposes and to explain complex issues and processes.
9. Introduce legislation: Develop legislation and allow for comprehensive parliamentary debate especially in committee, and also intergovernmental discussion where necessary.
10. Communicate decision: Design and implement and clear, simple and inexpensive communication strategy based on information not propaganda, regarding the new policy initiative.

Even allowing for case selection bias and the absence of an evidence test, or effective engagement criteria, the finding that 'just 7 of the 20 policies assessed were assessed to have met the Wiltshire Criteria' underscores our workshop findings that evidence-based policy-making is the exception rather than the rule.[28] The finding is concerning

Saving Democracy

because it suggests that more and more policy is made on the basis of ideology and the politicization of expertise rather than what works.

Pathways to progress

So how do we get a better relationship between experts and practice in a way that bolsters rather than undermines democratic practice? In our view this requires acceptance of two principles of action and a shift in mindset. First, that evidence and politics are reinforcing features of contemporary policy-making. There is a tendency for many researchers to view politics as the enemy of evidence rather than as an integral tool for building efficient, effective and legitimate public policy. Politics demands that researchers demonstrate the public value of their findings. By the same token, politics demands the public accountability mechanism that evidence-based practice provides.

Second, politics also demands that experts are not first among equals but a partner in collaborative problem-solving. Researchers need to realize that they constitute one of many sources of policy advice available to policy-makers in a contested arena. This observation emphasizes the importance of knowledge institutions and researchers, developing the advocacy and brokering skills necessary for evidence to have impact.

There are four main pathways through which experts can practise these two principles of action and help to embed evidence in policy-making through establishing a culture of evidence-based practice, the creation of collaborative policy advisory and governance systems, building participatory governance systems and in combatting truth decay. Let us consider each of these pathways in turn.

Establishing a culture of evidence-based practice

As we observed in Chapter 6, in 2018, *The Foundations for Evidence-Based Policymaking Act* was introduced in the United States requiring federal government agencies to modernize data management practices.[29] It requires agencies to submit annual plans for identifying and addressing policy questions to the Office of Management and Budget (OMB) and Congress. The plan needs to include questions for developing evidence to support policy-making; details of the data the agency intends to collect or acquire to facilitate the use of evidence in policy-making; methods and analytical approaches to develop evidence to support policy-making; and challenges to developing evidence to support policy-making, including any statutory or other restrictions to accessing relevant data. Each agency is also required to designate a senior employee as Evaluation Officer to coordinate evidence-building activities and an official with statistical expertise to advise on statistical policy, techniques and procedures. As Robert Hahn notes:

> *The act is just a foundation, not the full building. Getting from this act to more effective policy outcomes means getting departments and agencies to buy into a new culture where rigorous evaluation matters more in designing and funding programmes.*[30]

Minimally, this will require appropriate enablers and tools including access to appropriate research infrastructure (capacity and resources); brokerage services that can help policy-makers formulate researchable questions; research summaries that help policy-makers answer key questions; and the development of partnerships between policy-makers, service providers and researchers to promote new research that is relevant to policy and programme priorities.[31]

Most significantly, all publicly funded new programme proposals or the recommissioning of programmes should include an evidence health check that demonstrates how the existing programme or new programme builds on or departs from conventional wisdom and provides an assessment of the level of risk involved.[32] This approach is currently practised in Canadian health policy.[33] The Sax Institute in Sydney, Australia, also currently assists Australian policy-makers to commission quality reviews of research to inform health policy decision-making. There is evidence to suggest that the discipline of the evidence health check not only helps to embed evidence-based practice in policy-making but enhances the quality of public policy debate.

Collaborative policy advisory and governance systems

The collaborative role of experts in the policy advisory system working alongside politicians, public servants, and (depending on the change opportunity, task or problem) stakeholders and citizens at different decision points in the policy process (policy development, new policy validation, evaluation and learning) is a fundamental dynamic of contemporary problem solving. But what would this form of collaborative governance look like in practice and what role would experts play within it? Chris Ansell and Alison Gash define collaborative governance as

> ... a governing arrangement where one or more public agencies directly engage non-state stakeholders in a collective decision-making process that is formal, consensus-oriented, and deliberative and that aims to make or implement public policy or manage public programmes or assets.[34, 35]

There have been cyclical attempts to identify the ingredients of best practice in collaborative problem-solving in the public sector, and drawing on the key propositions underpinning better practice in this literature it is possible to construct a model of what might work.[36] Figure 9.2 presents the critical variables that the existing evidence tells us will influence whether or not a collaboration has the best chance of success. Consider the following factors:

Starting conditions – constraints and enablers to collaboration

1. Is there a pre-history of collaboration?
2. Resource incentives – *does the collaboration have access to requisite resources – political, knowledge, financial, and human? Is collaboration incentivized through funding and performance management and measurement?*

Saving Democracy

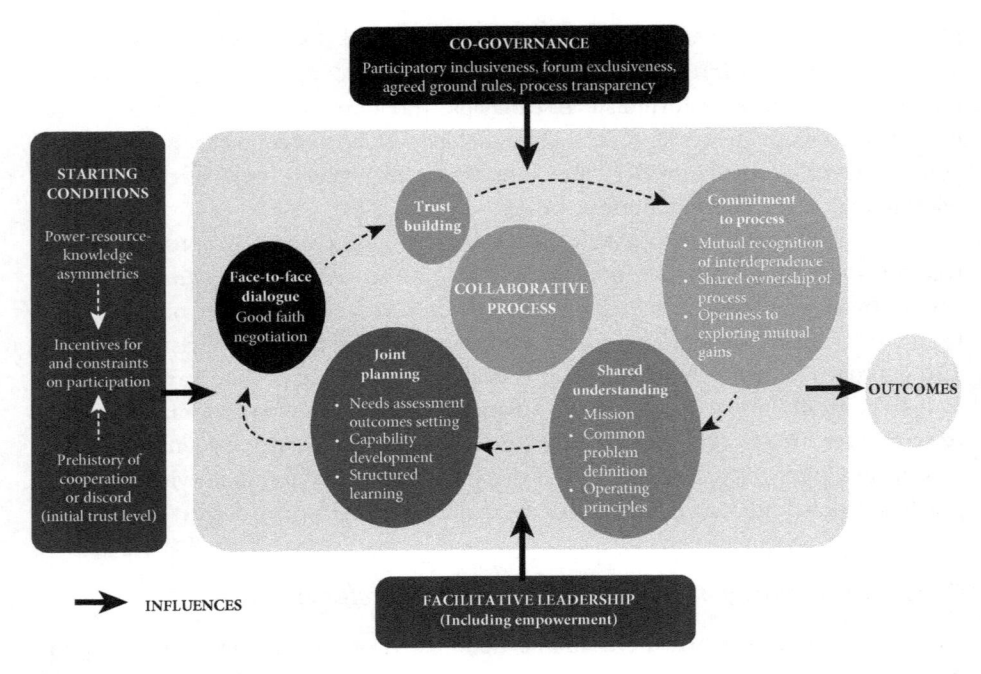

Figure 9.2 Best practice collaborative governance.

3. Trust – *do the partners recognize their interdependence? Is there parity of esteem amongst members?*

Vision and values

4. Common Purpose – *is there a clear mission, negotiated problem definition and values?*

5. Catalysts – *was the collaboration started because of an existing problem that required a comprehensive approach? What is it about the nature of the problem that requires a collaborative approach? Has that changed over time?*

Facilitative leadership

6. Facilitative leadership – *has the leadership facilitated and supported team building, and capitalized upon diversity, capability development and individual, group and organizational strengths?*

7. Clear accountabilities – *does the collaboration involve clear leadership accountabilities for action? Is there a special responsible officer with specific reporting requirements for key areas of activity?*

The collaborative process

8. Shared ownership of process – *does the collaboration involve inclusive decision-making, process transparency and accepted ground rules?*

9. Clear channels of communication and connectedness – *does the collaboration possess open and clear channels of communication? Is there an established process for communication between formal meetings? Are members of this collaboration connected and have they established informal and formal communication networks?*

10. Sustainability – this depends on the nature of the task (project, programme, etc.) but *does the collaboration have a formal plan for sustaining membership, activities and resources?*

11. Research and Evaluation – *has the collaboration access to appropriate expertise in the area of endeavour? Has it conducted a needs assessment or obtained information to establish its goals and does the collaboration collect data to measure goal achievement? Does the collaboration engage in shared learning and diffuse better practice?*

12. Policies/conventions – *has the collaboration changed existing policies, protocols and/or conventions to allow the collaboration to function effectively?*

13. Positive spill-over – *has the collaboration led to other forms of collaboration and resource sharing?*

14. Understanding the policy community – *does the collaboration understand the policy community, including its people, cultures, values and habits?*

15. Contestability – *does the collaboration have the capacity to outperform feasible alternative arrangements?*

The presence or otherwise of these four sets of factors – favourable starting conditions (identifying barriers and enablers to incentivize collaboration), common vision and values (to provide collaborative purpose), facilitative leadership (to drive collaborative problem-solving) and collaborative processes (to deliver valued shared outcomes) – can provide a measure of the quality of collaboration and a useful set of benchmarks for guiding collaboration. The role of expertise is crucial in collaborative processes for establishing a strong evidence base to underpin the intervention, needs assessment, the design of effective monitoring systems, evaluation and the diffusion of learning and better practice.[37]

The role of experts in participatory governance systems

One way to resolve the contestation between different policy values is to remove the debate about policy choices from the realm of research and place it in the arena of politics and democratic choice. We assessed the promise of deliberative democracy and co-design as arenas for enhancing the quality of democratic choice in Chapters 4 and 5 and it is evident that experts can play an important role in collaborative settings working with politicians, public servants, citizens and stakeholders in these fora to solve complex problems. The role of the expert, however, is qualitatively different in each setting. Deliberative engagements require the presentation of a diverse range of expertise by subject experts to participants. This is deemed an important hygiene factor in conducting high-quality deliberation.[38] Here the expert acts as a witness and is normally cross-questioned by participants. Deliberative designers put a great deal of thought into the role of the witness in the deliberation, witness identification and selection, the format and content of evidence provision (e.g. supporting documentation or evidence visualization), the nature of the evidence itself, and the nature of the understanding that witnesses and participants experience.

In co-design engagements, participants are experts in their own experiences with valuable insights to share with formal experts in collaborative design processes.[39] Here the role of the expert is to act as a co-designer in a planned process of learning. As we observed in Chapter 6, various methods and tools are deployed to facilitate deep engagement and learning in the process of discovering new ways of designing policies and services. These learning methods are used to improve the quality of information about the citizen or stakeholder experience of the problem under examination. This enables designers to build an evidence base on what does or does not work from the perspective of citizens and expert stakeholders to inform the prototyping of solutions. In co-design engagements, experts need to be reflexive professionals with strong interpersonal skills and the capacity to build trusting relationships with citizens from a diverse range of backgrounds.[40]

The role of experts in combatting 'truth decay'

As we will discover in greater detail in Chapter 10, the fourth pathway through which experts can embed evidence through collaborative democratic practice lies in combating 'truth decay' – defined by the RAND Corporation as the increasing disagreement about facts and analytical interpretations of facts and data; the blurring of the line between opinion and fact; the burgeoning volume, and resulting influence, of opinion and personal experience over fact; and declining trust in formerly respected sources of factual information.[41]

Given the high level of trust citizens have for public universities outside the United States, we argue that universities should be funded to provide independent, evidence-based fact-checking services in their areas of expertise. Public universities can be an effective counterweight to the epidemic of ignorance that fouls public policy debate through the internet. In this cacophony of noise, experts are often reduced to sound bites and public universities have the institutional capacity and public legitimacy to act as a sense-maker. Public universities should also deliver public programmes that build the capacity of citizens to discern and refute misinformation, disinformation and malinformation.[42]

Evaluation – assessing pathways to progress

To assess whether we are making progress in effectively integrating experts into policy-making we need to know that the ideal-type policy advisory system looks like. We posed this question to senior policy officers in Australia, New Zealand and the UK and the findings are compelling (see Box 9.2). It is evident from the findings that if we are to increase the policy capability of government, we need to embed a culture of demand for evidence-informed policy-making at all levels. The role of leaders, both political and permanent, in this process is crucial. They can emphasize the importance of evidence

Box 9.2 What does a strategic, innovative, evidence-based policy system look like?

1. Where policy professionals have the capacity to act and the competences to understand the choices available to them.
2. A policy system that works beyond the electoral cycle and focuses on long-term issues of national significance.
3. That utilizes existing capacity both within and beyond government.
4. That is pro-active to changes in the field of action.
5. Where there is room for experimentation.
6. Where innovation is incentivized.
7. Where the capacity to speak truth to power exists.
8. Where there are clear accountabilities.
9. Where policy is effectively integrated.
10. Where information systems allow for the effective flow of information from the front-line.
11. Where evidence is freely debated and shared.
12. Where better practice is shared.
13. Where there is access to evidence and by implication strong productive working relationships with knowledge institutions.
14. Where there is effective use of innovation intermediaries.
15. Where there are demand- and supply-side incentives to engage in evidence based policy-making.

by shaping their demands for policy advice in more strategic terms through placing an emphasis on the medium to long term. If leaders do not show an appetite for long-term strategic thinking and the use of evidence then policy advisors will simply not attempt to offer such thinking, preferring to offer a 'quick' win to cope with immediate budgetary concerns rather than achieving policy goals. At the same time, researchers need to recognize the importance of translating their research findings in a meaningful way for policy-makers and exploit the opportunities that politics provides for building more efficient, effective and legitimate public policy.

In conclusion – a new enlightenment?

This chapter has explored the vexed relationship between democracy and expertise. We have argued in support of the integration of the world of thought and the world of democratic action through 'enlightened' evidence-informed practice founded on strong principles of credible evidence, verifiable theory, the use of methods that matter, practical translation and strategic communication. Not just because it will improve our understanding of policy problems but because social progress demands it. The coronavirus pandemic has demonstrated the utility of this approach. However, it remains equally important for experts to stick to what they know and are good at, providing independent evidence-based advice rather than attempting to be political arbiters of the truth.

CHAPTER 10
OLD AND NEW MEDIA: POWER WITH RESPONSIBILITY

We develop a simple proposition in this chapter – a free media is fundamental to a functioning democracy as it enables freedom of speech and association, strengthens public policy debate and provides an essential check on the promiscuous exercise of political power. However, media power (particularly new media) is presently limited in its accountability to the public and needs to be subject to a new media social contract that provides for responsible content generation (including journalism), tackles truth decay and ensures diversity of media ownership. This cannot be achieved through regulation only; in keeping with the behavioural change model mapped out in Chapter 8, it requires a change in media behaviour at the individual and business levels. It also requires an educated public with the capacity to decipher and refute fake news.

In this chapter we evaluate the role of the media in a liberal democracy, the current state of new and old media in liberal democracies, the tension between the concept of the free media and its vulnerability to political manipulation and the problem of public accountability. The chapter concludes by presenting a set of public interest principles and reforms to maintain the delicate balance between the democratic value of a free media and the need for public accountability.

The role of the media in a liberal democracy

It is easy to overlook the importance of the media as a guardian of liberal democratic values particularly if you live in a mature democracy. For a reminder, on 3 May 2021, UNESCO and the United Nations' Department of Global Communications (DGC) celebrated the twenty-seventh edition of World Press Freedom Day at UNHQ in New York with a high-level event gathering UN officials, civil society organizations and experts.[1] The theme for recognition was 'Information as a Public Good' which emphasized the importance of verified and reliable information. Audrey Azouley, Director-General of UNESCO, called attention to 'the essential role of free and professional journalists in producing and disseminating this information, by tackling misinformation and other harmful content'.[2]

Since the emergence of the concept of popular sovereignty in the seventeenth and eighteenth centuries, the role of the press as 'Fourth Estate' or civil watchdog for ensuring the public's right to know, creating forums for public discussion and debate and providing a conduit between governors and the governed has been widely recognized. Given that democracy requires the active participation of citizens, the media should play a fundamental role in keeping citizens engaged in the business of governance by informing, educating and mobilizing the public. However, Margaret Scammell and Holli Semetko remind students of the mass media of two things: 'first, the central importance of media for democracy is ... virtually axiomatic [and] second, the model of democracy which media are supposed to serve is also largely taken for granted'.[3] In short, we assume both the significance of the media for safeguarding democracy and the public's regard for the institution which partly explains why recent attacks on media freedoms have become increasingly vocal.

For both media and democratization scholars, the mass media are regarded as one of the key democratic institutions for improving the quality of the electoral system, political parties, parliament, judiciary and other branches of the state, and safeguarding their democratic performance.[4] But if we turn our attention to what we know about the role of the media in transitions to democracy, despite the investment made in free media in new democracies and fragile states there is only limited evidence of the media prompting and guiding democratic transitions. There is very little research that demonstrates exactly how media deliver on their ascribed normative role. As Nael Jebril and colleagues observe:

> Mass media have often simply been assumed to play a (generically) positive role in democratic transition, particularly for citizens of transitional countries, there is in fact little evidence that fits with this assumption.[5]

Even new media's possible role in bringing about democratic transition in the aftermath of the Arab Spring is the subject of contestation. There is only limited empirical evidence of new media impact on regime changes in the Arab world. As Matthew Loveless writes: 'the real change is the cultural patterns of interaction with information, with others in the community, and with civil space, although these are much harder to see and much more difficult to estimate but arguably closer to a genuine media effect'.[6]

Unsurprisingly attempts to transform the media into a fully democratic Fourth Estate have failed historically and contemporaneously because the relationship between government and the media is at best highly ambivalent and journalists jealously preserve their independence from democratic institutionalization afraid of reducing their watchdog role in the name of the national interest. We are therefore left with two media sectors: a market-led media sector and a non-market public sector. However, most media institutions in both sectors are increasingly driven by a commercial rather than democratic logic.

We would counsel against the Fourth Estate argument on the basis that the media must remain independent and deinstitutionalized to play its watchdog role. It is doubtful, for example, that institutionalized media such as the BBC would have been able to engage in the distribution of content from the Edward Snowden Leaks (see Box 10.1).

Box 10.1 The Edward Snowden Leaks[7]

In June 2013, Edward Snowden, a National Security Agency (NSA) contractor in the United States, leaked numerous top-secret documents to certain media (*Der Spiegel, The Guardian, New York Times* and the *Washington Post*) which revealed that the National Security Administration had conducted mass surveillance of US residents. He decided not to opt for the protection of anonymity. 'I have no intention of hiding who I am because I know I have done nothing wrong', he said. 'I understand that I will be made to suffer for my actions', but 'I will be satisfied if the federation of secret law, unequal pardon and irresistible executive powers that rule the world that I love are revealed even for an instant'.

The US government disagreed with his motives and the Department of Justice brought criminal charges against Snowden under the Espionage Act. Snowden, fled to Russia in the aftermath of the 2013 disclosures and was granted permanent residency in October 2020. In the same year, an Appeals Court found that the programme was unlawful, violated the Foreign Intelligence Surveillance Act, may well have been unconstitutional and that the US intelligence leaders who publicly defended the programme were not telling the truth.

The Snowden Leaks demonstrate the importance of whistle-blowers in exposing unethical behaviour, here on the part of the NSA, and how national security issues can be used by the state to mask unconstitutional behaviour.

Declining trust in media

The main sources for evaluating issues relating to public trust in media at a global level are the World Press Freedom Index[8] and the Edelman Trust Barometer.[9] Both surveys reported in 2021 allowing us to assess supply and demand issues on media freedom and generate a series of high-level observations around declining public trust in media.

Trust in media (traditional and new) is in general decline around the world

Trust in media – traditional, social and search and owned media – is at record lows around the world but is particularly acute with social media (35 per cent). Traditional media (53 per cent) experienced the largest decline in public trust globally. As the 2021 Edeleman Trust Barometer observes:

> *Social media continues to bump along at the bottom of the trust pile, having fallen there back in 2016. Strikingly, traditional media has had the steepest annual decline we have witnessed of any media source in almost a decade of tracking.*[10]

Saving Democracy

Box 10.2 Cambridge Analytica and the Facebook data breach[11]

> In March 2018, Facebook was caught up in a large-scale data breach scandal, in which the British political consulting firm Cambridge Analytica acquired the personal data of around 87 million users without their consent and used it for political purposes, namely in the 2016 US Presidential elections but also in the Brexit Vote Leave campaign. The scandal caused Facebook to face the wrath of all those affected by the privacy breach but also of those who were indirectly, in some way, concerned by what happened. Several challenges confronted the company afterwards, such as legal actions for the lack of users' privacy protection. Nevertheless, even if Facebook put in place several measures to prevent such an event from happening again, the biggest challenge is to regain stakeholder trust and to rebuild the organization's reputation.

This can be attributed to continuing controversies over issues of ownership and control, 'fake news' and data and privacy scandals involving social media companies such as Cambridge Analytica and the Facebook data breach (see Box 10.2).

Governments distrust media in times of coronavirus

The 2021 World Press Freedom Index shows that during the pandemic, journalism has been blocked or seriously impeded in seventy-three countries and constrained in fifty-nine others, which represents 73 per cent of the countries evaluated. These countries are classified as having 'very bad', 'bad' or 'problematic' environments for press freedom. This observation demonstrates a significant example of democratic backsliding during the pandemic at a time when journalism should be playing a key role in combating disinformation.

Public trust in journalists is low

The 2021 Edelman Trust barometer reveals a disturbing level of public mistrust of journalists, with 59 per cent of respondents in twenty-eight countries saying that 'journalists deliberately try to mislead the public by reporting information they know to be false'.

The free media is in decline as a democratic value

There is growing evidence that in contrast to elites, the citizenry does not currently perceive the value of a free press as a fundamental democratic value. Indeed, the global citizenry tend to believe that the media is too powerful with both elites and citizens believing that media focuses too much on personalities and not enough on policy.

Elites also perceive a general decline in media standards. As *Reporters without Borders* secretary-general Christophe Deloire observes:

> *Journalism is the best vaccine against disinformation. Unfortunately, its production and distribution are too often blocked by political, economic, technological and, sometimes, even cultural factors.*[12]

Explaining declining public trust in media

How can we explain this worrying decline in public trust in new and old media? A combination of factors appears to be at play.

Changing business models and media fragmentation

Graeme Turner in a dystopian analysis of democracy and the media in the digital era observes that the progressive and empowering disruption created by the internet has turned out quite differently than predicted: 'It is overwhelmingly in the areas of news and information where the dream of online democratization has most categorically turned into a nightmare.'[13] The proliferation of free content, citizen journalism and the collapse of traditional revenue streams have undermined traditional journalism. The freelance labour conditions under which journalists now work are not conducive to the kind of investigative, resource-intensive journalism that is widely regarded as necessary for the media to play its watchdog role. Moreover, predictions of the emergence of a free market of voices online have proved inaccurate:

> Monetization has been the enemy of democratization [online]. The battle for attention – and the strategies used to compete in that battle – certainly attracted audiences, and it also skewed the character of what content was made available: towards entertainment, towards provocative, shareable content and so on.

Media industries such as film, music and publishing have traditionally relied on three models of revenue generation: payment by users for ownership of or access to content, advertising fees and a hybrid of the two (see Table 10.1). For a long time, the models have largely been sustainable, but in recent decades advances in information and communication technologies and changes in consumer behaviour have been so revolutionary that they pose unprecedentedly serious challenges to these models; the issue is no longer copyright infringement on its own, but how the industries respond to the changes in the market and find new, sustainable business models.

The proliferation of media sources, first through cable and more recently through the internet, has increased the problem of finding trustworthy sources of news and being well-informed. The role of the internet as a source of news has altered the way in which news moves from creators to consumers. It is also hardly a coincidence that growing

Table 10.1 Media business models

	Conventional business model	New business models
Value-adding steps covered by media companies	Content creation, distribution	Management of content, operation of digital space (apps, websites, social media), alliance with various sectors
Value chain	Fixed, controlled, supplier-led, one-way	Flexible, organic, user-centric, interactive
Value creation	Copyright exploitation	Multi-platform business
Revenue source	User payment, advertising	User payment, advertising, user subscription fees, sale of user data
Main partners	Promoter, retailer	Content/service providers, neighbouring industries in the media and elsewhere
Markey entry barriers	High: initial investment of capital required	Low
Competition	Intra-market	Inter-market
Role of creators	Strong, but moderated by the intermediary	Direct connection with users, need to be entrepreneurial
Content creation	Reserved for the professionals	Open to all
Role of consumers	Passive	Active
Traits valued by consumers	Quality of content	Social communication about content, convenient access
Primary competences of media companies	Artistic/journalistic editing, curation and distribution	Aggregating content, algorithms for matching content and users
Control of the market	Strong	Weak
Control of use	Strong	Weak
Advertisers' interest	Mass marketing	Targeted marketing

Source: Adapted and expanded from Hess, 2014 and Kawashima, 2020.[18]

distrust in media has occurred at a time when there has been less 'local' news due to the breakdown of the traditional local media business model.[14]

Reader distrust, truth decay and polarization

The key implication of fragmentation is to dilute readers' loyalty and diminish their trust in the news they receive. According to the Edelman Trust Barometer, 63 per cent of respondents agree that 'the average person does not know how to tell good journalism from rumour or falsehoods', while 59 per cent say 'it is becoming harder to tell if a piece of news was produced by a respected media organization'. These developments are characterized by the RAND Corporation as the problem of 'truth decay'.[15] This includes increasing disagreement about facts and analytical interpretations of facts and data; the blurring of the line between opinion and fact; the burgeoning volume, and resulting influence, of opinion and personal experience over fact; and declining trust in formerly respected sources of factual information.

Fabricated news is nothing new. The problem of 'truth decay' has been studied and debated in various forms for many centuries but has largely been viewed as a key instrument of the coercive apparatus of the state or state propaganda. During the 2016 US Presidential Election and UK Brexit Referendum, however, a different form of fake news rose to prominence: false or highly misleading political 'news' stories, primarily originating on new media. The role of 'moderation' by social media platforms – the process of making decisions about the content that users do and do not see, plays a key role here. This is often perceived as creating potential for the mobilization of bias. Hence the source of disinformation has refocused to new media. A 2017 survey conducted for the BBC World Service found that 79 per cent of respondents in eighteen countries were worried about what was fake and what was real on the internet.[16] Concern about fake news increased in 2020 in the wake of widespread misinformation and disinformation on social media about the Covid-19 pandemic and the 2020 US Presidential Election. Recent Chinese, Iranian and Russian interference in democratic elections is intended not just to favour one candidate over another but as an act of cyber warfare to disseminate mistrust and confusion.[17] The widespread emergence of information that is false or misleading, that is intended to persuade or confuse rather than inform, is therefore a likely contributor to the decline of trust in media.

Polarization of media criticism

There also seems to be an ideological component to this general distrust, particularly among more conservative-leaning voters, as a result of continuing attacks on 'mainstream media' by right-wing pundits and politicians. Conservative media critics have argued that the traditional press and national broadcasters are not truly objective, but rather reflect a generally liberal political perspective that purports to be unbiased.

In their book *Network Propaganda* (2018), Yochai Benkler, Robert Faris and Hal Roberts catalogue how internet-based news sites have sought to subvert the practices that enable truth-telling. They note that trust in the news media has declined in the United States but that distrust is decidedly more concentrated among voters identifying as right wing than among those identifying as left-wing. The authors attribute this to former US President Donald Trump's relentless denigration of critical or embarrassing news as 'fake news'.

There is a connection, the authors argue, between this distrust and the nature of the right-wing news media system. Benkler, Faris and Roberts make three observations: first, that the prominence of far-left news sites pales in comparison to those on the right; second, that the most visible left-wing news sources correlate at most to moderate right news sources, not far-right news sources; and third, that the traditional news media is tightly integrated with those left-wing news sources, exerting constraints of fact-checking, objectivity and evidence-based reporting. They conclude: 'Conspiracy theories, falsehoods, and rumours that fit the tribal narrative diffuse more broadly ... are sustained for longer on the right than in the rest of the media ecosystem.'[19] The skewed nature of the right-wing news media has created echo chambers that reinforce people's biases, diminish trust systems and undermine people's capacity to make sense of the world.

Ideological polarization and media fragmentation have channelled political discourse into separate 'echo chambers' reflecting group-think defined by common norms and values. Four in ten people exhibit poor information hygiene: not regularly engaging with the news, staying within echo chambers, not vetting information or checking its veracity before spreading it. The big question for liberal democracies, as Benkler, Faris and Roberts warn us, is whether 'echo chambers ringing with false news make democracies ungovernable'.[20] In sum, the disturbing combination of toxic social media, news by algorithm, declining civic discourse and information being used as a weapon in a hyper partisan war of ideas has serious implications for the quality of democratic practice.

Bridging the trust divide – media power in the public interest

> *Open societies do not support only one conception of "truth", they rather seek to establish laws and institutions, enabling people with divergent views to live together in peace. (Karl Popper, The Open Society and Its Enemies, 1945)*[21]

Once again, there is no single 'magic formula' for resolving the complexities of media power, new or traditional. However, there is evidence to suggest that building a responsible media culture requires behavioural change and by implication a behavioural change strategy. In keeping with the proposition developed in Chapter 8, influencing behaviour is most effective when it is value-driven – in this case through the democratic imperative for a free and responsible media – achieved through policy tools that regulate, enable, encourage and co-govern change. This observation reflects the importance of shifting media policies from a narrow focus on deterrence and enforcement towards promoting media freedom and responsibility as a democratic value. Clive Hollick, writing in 1994 in the context of the threat of media liberalization, warned that

> *contrary to the general view, regulation can be the defender of free speech and the forces of the marketplace the chief threat to a plurality of view. But new technologies demand new forms of regulation and government intervention may be the best way of ensuring the plurality of voice on which democracy depends.*[22]

Both supply- (media industry-centred interventions) and demand-side (citizen-centred interventions) reforms are necessary to achieve democratic progress.

Supply-side interventions

Our starting point is that the democratic value of a free and responsible media can be achieved through public interest journalism and a commitment to the professional ethical requirements of accuracy, fairness, truth-telling, impartiality and respect for persons. We would suggest that this was articulated in a public interest pledge and embedded in formal training and mentoring for new entrants to the profession.

It also requires focusing resources on public interest journalism: the reporting of parliament, the executive government, courts and powerful institutions in which the public places its trust, such as universities, cultural institutions, major corporations and political parties. This work would need to include a substantial investigative component to ensure that the media plays its crucial watchdog role.

Regulation is also needed to ensure that contested issues are treated in a fair and balanced manner on new and traditional media. We can look to history for guidance on legislation in this area. In 1949, the Federal Communications Commission (FCC) charged with issuing broadcast licenses to radio and television stations that operate in the 'public interest, convenience and necessity', issued a report that established the duty of broadcast licensees to cover controversial issues in a fair and balanced manner.[23] It was termed the Fairness Doctrine and required broadcasters to 'devote a reasonable portion of broadcast time to the discussion and consideration of controversial issues of public importance' and (crucially) 'affirmatively endeavour to make ... facilities available for the expression of contrasting viewpoints held by responsible elements with respect to the controversial issues'.[24]

It also required broadcasters to allow individuals who were the subject of editorials or personal attacks to be granted an opportunity to respond and established that candidates for public office are entitled to equal airtime.[25] Over the subsequent three decades, a period featured by the incremental liberalization of the media system, most broadcasters complained that the Fairness Doctrine inhibited their coverage and free speech and that growth in the media industry rendered it outdated. The debate reached its peak in the mid-1980s and in June 1987, the Democrat-controlled House of Representatives and Senate passed legislation to codify the doctrine into federal law but the sitting president, Ronald Reagan, vetoed it. It wasn't until August 1987 that the FCC voted to abolish the doctrine on the grounds that it violated the First Amendment and stifled democratic debate.[26] As Dylan Matthews observes, this led not to the development of a free market of ideas but to the explosion of conservative talk radio in the late 1980s and early 1990s and the growth of 'echo chambers' in both traditional and new media.[27] Though it has not been enforced since 1987, the Fairness Doctrine was not technically repealed until 2011.[28] At the time Kathleen Ann Ruane noted that it 'does not appear that the Fairness Doctrine may be applied constitutionally to cable or satellite service providers' as broadcast news is viewed as 'distinct from cable, satellite, and the Internet, which are all services for which consumers must pay'. In short, it was deemed impossible for governments to regulate broadcasting or the internet because the technologies that enable them are beyond national governments.

However, the case for state intervention can now be made on the basis that liberalization has led to polarization and the only way we can protect the further erosion of freedom of expression and the plurality of perspectives that lie at the core of the liberal democratic ideal is to ensure a diversity of voices. This requires ending geographical (global, national, regional and local) and sectoral monopolies (newspapers, radio, terrestrial television, internet, cable and satellite) through setting maximum levels of market share and ensuring balanced content through the Fairness Doctrine. As Clive Hollick observes, 'Complex technical change should not divert governments from addressing the more predictable consequence of the enduring human instincts which drive media organizations.'[29] Moreover, although media outlets remain entitled to be partisan in their opinions, when it corrupts the news coverage, the public trust is betrayed.

An additional supply-side reform of increasing salience would be to end anonymity in particular spaces on the internet and recalibrate the relationship between professional mass media and social media. The original defence of anonymity was to provide a technical instrument for subverting any attempts by the state to engage in censorship and restrict personal liberty. In keeping with John Stuart Mill's 'harm principle' – no one 'should be forcibly prevented from acting in any way he chooses provided his acts are not invasive of the free acts of others'.[30] However, given that social media companies have been reluctant to operate the harm principle in practice and trolls have engaged in hate crimes free from constraint, there are only very limited philosophical grounds for a right to anonymity. There would of course be a need for certain areas of exemption. For example, anonymity is extremely effective for promoting freedom of expression for whistle-blowers, and victims of various forms of abuse or for sharing and debating sensitive issues.[31] It is also unlikely that any reform of this kind would be foolproof given that censorship on the internet is impossible because there is always a technological solution which can circumvent the problem. The reform would therefore be of moral imperative.[32]

Demand-side interventions

On the demand side, enabling behavioural change requires building the critical capacity of citizens to discern and refute 'fake news'. The Media Literacy Index for 2021 conducted by the European Policies Initiative (EuPI) of the Open Society Institute based in Sofia assesses the 'resilience potential' to fake news in thirty-five European countries, using indicators for media freedom drawn from a range of surveys (Freedom House and Reporters without Borders), education (PISA), e-participation (UN) and trust in people (Eurostat).[33] Finland (1st), Denmark (2nd), Estonia (3rd), Sweden (4th) and Ireland (5th) are at the top of the ranking of the Media Literacy Index 2021. These countries have the highest potential to withstand the negative impact of fake news and misinformation due to the quality of education, free media and high trust among people.[34]

Finland has an effective weapon to combat fake news: education: 'high-quality education and having more and more educated people is a prerequisite for tackling the negative effects of fake news and post-truth', the Media Literacy Index's authors wrote. 'While some regulation is necessary, education seems to be the best all-round solution.'

Studies show a positive relationship between the level of education and resilience to fake news, with more knowledge and better critical-thinking skills guarding against fabricated information.

As Jean-Pierre Bourguignon, president of the European Research Council, told the World Economic Forum's Annual Meeting of the New Champions in September 2020:

> We need to train a new generation of critical minds ... We must tackle this issue through improved news literacy, and it is the task of our educators and society at large to teach children how to use doubt intelligently and to understand that uncertainty can be quantified and measured.[35]

It is noteworthy that Finland, Sweden and the Netherlands include digital literacy and critical thinking about misinformation in their national curriculum. Moreover, Finnish fact-checking organization Faktabaari (FactBar) utilizes professional fact-checking methods for use in Finnish schools, focusing on three areas of vulnerability: misinformation (defective information or mistakes), disinformation, such as hoaxes, and malinformation, stories that intend to damage. This is where public universities can play a critical role by being mandated to provide independent, evidence-based fact-checking services in their areas of expertise. In short, public education which builds the capacity of citizens to discern and refute misinformation, disinformation and malinformation is essential to combating truth decay.[36]

Assessing the democratic performance of the media

What does liberal democracy require of a media system? Here we will turn to the criteria deployed in the Democratic Audit of the UK and currently being applied in Australia, many of which have already been investigated in this chapter. Box 10.3 presents the key criteria for evaluation, noting the centrality of the concepts of media pluralism and competition, public interest journalism and regulation.

In conclusion: a free but accountable media – power with responsibility

There is a delicate balance to be struck between affording the media the freedoms it requires to perform its civil watchdog role and guaranteeing the public's right to know and ensuring that it performs its democratic role responsibly. Unfettered, the drift to the former enables political fragmentation, polarization and populism and the slide to the latter, the spectre of George Orwell's dystopian *Nineteen Eight-Four*.

The supply and demand reforms outlined above are designed to maintain the fragile equilibrium between media power and responsibility. Driven by a commitment to the democratic value of a free and responsible media, legislating against the concentration of media ownership and the right to online anonymity, funding public interest media and building citizen capacity to address truth decay.

Saving Democracy

Box 10.3 Criteria for evaluating the democratic performance of the media[37]

1. The media system should be diverse and pluralistic, including different media types, operating under varied systems of regulation, designed to foster free competition, and strong accountability of media producers to citizens and public opinion.
2. The media regulatory system should guard against the distortions of competition introduced by media monopolies or oligopolies (dominance of information/content 'markets' by two or three owners or firms), and against any state direction of the media.
3. A free press is a key part of media pluralism – that is, privately owned newspapers, with free entry by competitors and only normal forms of business regulation (those common to any industry) by government and the law.
4. Because of network effects, state control of bandwidth and the salience of TV/radio for citizens' political information, a degree of 'special' regulation of broadcasters to ensure bipartisan or neutral coverage and balance is desirable, especially in election campaign periods.
5. Where government funds a state broadcaster, this should be set up at arm's length, and with a quango governance structure. Government ministers and top civil servants should avoid forms of intervention that might seem to compromise the state broadcaster's independence in generating political, public policy or other news and commentary.
6. Journalistic professionalism is an important component of a healthy media system, and the internalization of respect for the public interest and operation of a 'reputational economy' within the profession provide important safeguards against excesses, and an incentive for innovation. Systems that strengthen occupational self-regulation within the press are valuable.
7. The overall media system should provide citizens with political information, evidence and commentary about public policy choices that are easy to access, at no or low cost. The system should operate as transparently as possible, so that truthful/factual content predominates, and incorrect content and 'fake news' are rapidly counteracted.
8. People are entitled to published corrections and effective redress against any reporting that is unfair, incorrect or invades personal and family privacy. Citizens are entitled to expect that media organizations will respect all laws applying to them and will not be able to exploit their power to deter investigations or prosecutions by the police or prosecutors.
9. Public interest defences should be available to journalists commenting on possible political, state and corporate wrongdoing, and media organizations should enjoy some legal and judicial protection against attempts to harass, intimidate or penalize them by large and powerful corporations, or by the state.
10. At election times especially, the media system should inform the electorate accurately about the competing party manifestos and campaigns and encourage citizens' democratic participation.

PART III
INTERVENTIONS AT THE OUTPUT STAGE TO IMPROVE THE CAPACITY OF POLITICS TO DELIVER QUALITY SERVICES AND POLICY OUTCOMES

Output legitimacy refers to mechanisms that are introduced to enhance the capacity of politics to deliver quality services and policy outcomes that are driven by agreed values and responsive to community needs.

CHAPTER 11
IMPROVING THE PUBLIC SERVICE EXPERIENCE: THE SEARCH FOR PUBLIC VALUE

Our purpose is not simply to tinker with the liberal democratic settlement but to set a course for its renewal. Central to advancing this goal is the transformation of our public services – a key component of democratic governance which is often either ignored or downplayed in contemporary democratic thought. This chapter seeks to debunk two myths that became dominant ideas in the zeitgeist of the Global Financial Crisis and are currently permeating the discourse around Covid-19 recovery: that governments are powerless in responding to 'wicked' policy problems and that distrust in government is inevitable. We have argued throughout this book that there is a positive correlation between public distrust and dissatisfaction with liberal democratic arrangements, and by implication, the higher the level of public trust, the more robust democratic institutions and practice. Supply-side theories of trust tell us that public trust must in some way correspond with the trustworthiness of government.[1] From this perspective it is the performance (supply) of government that matters most in orienting the outlooks of citizens, together with commitment to procedural fairness and equality. We term this condition of trusted government, performance legitimacy and it emanates from the public's assessment of the government's record in delivering public policies and services.[2] If important, as commonly assumed, then public confidence should relate to perceptual and/or aggregate indicators of policy outputs and outcomes, such as satisfaction with the performance of public services, the economy or the government's record in specific arenas of intervention such as defence, education and healthcare. Performance legitimacy also focuses on whether citizens feel that the public services they receive are appropriate and fair, irrespective of their impacts.[3]

In this chapter, we argue that public services are not only a critical space for building trust between government and citizen but that they are potentially creative instruments for addressing the challenges of social inequality and personalization and thus ensuring that government is responsive to the rising expectations and aspirations of the public. However, we also argue that the problem of performance legitimacy requires an authentic commitment to public value management and the search for public value. Hitherto, the evidence suggests that attempts to drive public service production using public value management instruments have been insufficiently citizen or politician-centric to achieve publicly valued outcomes and performance legitimacy. Indeed, they are often either captured by technocratic elites and cynically manipulated for their own ends, used

Saving Democracy

to undermine politically mandated outcomes or restricted to stakeholders that share common norms and values with the bureaucracy. In short, the current practice of public value management often undermines rather than strengthens democratic governance. This chapter therefore examines the rise of public value management as a challenge to the dominant new public management (NPM) paradigm, explores the promise of public value management and reviews the evidence on the barriers and enablers to its achievement as a governing methodology for improving the quality of democratic governance. In keeping with previous chapters, we also provide criteria for evaluating the contribution of public services to the quality of democratic governance.

Table 11.1 The new public management toolkit

Market-inspired reform	Governance reforms
• *Privatization* of state assets, and certain services	• *Decentralization* – moving responsibility for programme delivery and delegating budgetary authority from central government to provincial or local governments or neighbourhoods
• *Internal markets* – separating purchasers from providers within the Public Sector to create new markets, e.g. care for the elderly	
• *Performance budgeting* – results-oriented, target-driven budgeting	
• *Performance Contracts* and *Pay-for-performance* – establishing performance targets (PSAs) for departments and individualized pay scales for public employees	• *Open Government* – freedom of information, E-Governance and public engagement mechanisms – e.g. Citizens Juries and other deliberative forums
• *Programme Review* – systematic analysis of costs and benefits of individual programmes	• *Standards in Public Life* – constituting effective public administration frameworks (e.g. executive machinery, departments, planning and coordinating mechanisms)
• *Compulsory Competitive Tendering* – services delivered by the private or voluntary sectors	
• *One-stop-shops* – coordination of programmes through one delivery system to eliminate duplication	
• *Invest to save Budgets* – venture capital for oiling the wheels of government	• Development of *codes of ethical practice* (e.g. codes of conduct, transparency, accountability, effective audit, monitoring and evaluation)
• *Quality Standards* – applying principles of quality management, e.g. Citizens' Charters, 'Best value' or 'Comprehensive Performance Assessments', Public Service Agreements	• *Collaborative governance with stakeholders*
	• *Co-production with citizens*

Deregulatory/regulatory reform

- *Personnel deregulation* – open competition in recruitment, performance-related pay and elimination of civil service controls over hiring, firing, promotion, etc.
- *Purchasing Deregulation* – permits individual organizations to make decisions about procurement, rather than using centralized purchasing organizations
- Creation of *new regulatory bodies* to supervise privatization and collaborative governance

Competence reforms – increasing the capacity of public servants to act

- *Staff audits* to determine what personnel is on hand
- *Getting the right people into the administration*, partly by stronger incentives to attract and retain them, partly by changing objectives and procedures in an effort to make the work situation more challenging and rewarding, and
- *Establishing integrated training programmes* through the establishment of a civil service college/schools of government and professional skills for government/occupational skills/professional accreditation
- Coaching and mentoring
- Capability reviews

The rise and fall of public value management

NPM is a short-hand term for describing a toolkit of techniques used initially in the English-speaking world to implement administrative reforms geared around the achievement of 'economy', 'efficiency' and 'effectiveness' in service delivery (see Table 11.1). Most of these reforms – largely market-inspired and deregulatory and/or regulatory reforms – were introduced in the 1980s in response to cyclical economic crisis and restructuring and incrementally around the world thereafter. In the 1990s the toolkit was supplemented with a range of governance and competency reforms as described in Table 11.1. Although NPM has always been practised very differently in Australia, the United States, the UK, New Zealand and elsewhere, it remains the dominant paradigm for managing public services, and mature liberal democracies have been regular plunderers of the NPM toolkit.[4]

By the 2000s, however, it became increasingly evident that the success of NPM was largely confined to improving the efficiency of the public sector in delivering outputs and enhancing transparency and accountability in governance systems. Its problem-solving capacity and ability to deliver progressive outcomes for citizens were less evident. Indeed there emerged significant evidence that NPM tools could be used to embed dominant administrative norms and values and insulate bureaucratic elites from meaningful citizen engagement and reform.[5]

Most significantly, the NPM toolkit is not attuned to the challenge of public service reform. This is because NPM tends to privilege the role of public servants at a time when there is a need for broader citizen ownership of social problems. Collective problem-solving requires co-production and adaptive behaviours from citizens and often stakeholders. Moreover, as we have already argued, the critical challenges confronting liberal democracies in a more complex, fragmented world require the most adaptive form of power to enable community interests to blend their capacities to achieve common goals. *New power* or *the power to persuade*. Indeed, in a post-Covid-19 world, the most difficult problems confronting public administration tend to require soft power solutions rather than managerial ones.

Although the adoption of NPM was an important phase in the modernization of public services, it is simply unequal to the challenge of public service provision in an era of soft power. This is because it privileges the role of technocrats, takes the politics out of public policy deliberation and its market orientation is at odds with the concept of public service and sits more easily with the language of the consumer rather the language of the citizen. The politicization of policy advisory systems and the corresponding erosion of public service ethics and institutional memory are evident manifestations of the hollowing-out of 'government by the rules'. There are also problems with the NPM approach that are brought about through attempts to affect cultural change in large-scale bureaucracies. Historically, NPM signalled a shift in administrative structures, systems, staffing and superordinate culture from traditional forms of public administration and sought to change dominant public service norms and values. The marketization of public service production gave rise to further governance problems because it involves the increasing use of non-accountable third parties to manage and deliver government services. As we saw in Chapter 8 an integrity paradox often emerges in which the quest for 'economy', 'efficiency' and 'effectiveness' through NPM actually increases rather than reducing the scope for maladministration or even corruption.[6]

In contrast, public value management offers a broad framework in which to comprehend the public management challenge in an era of citizen-centric governance and aims at improving the performance legitimacy of government. Mark Moore, who developed the concept, basically argues that public services can add value to society in the same way that private for-profit organizations create value for their shareholders and other stakeholders.[7] By implication, public intervention should be circumscribed by the need to achieve positive social and economic outcomes for the citizenry.

Crucially what is and what is not public value should be determined collectively through inclusive deliberation involving elected and appointed government officials, key stakeholders and the public. Public value governance thus represents a significant challenge to both traditional forms of public administration and the dominant form of public management used in Western democracies – new public management (see Table 11.1).

The public value approach demands a commitment to goals that are more stretching for public managers than those envisaged under previous management methods.

Public managers are tasked with steering networks of deliberation and delivery as well as maintaining the overall health of the system. The questions they must ask of themselves in searching for public value are more challenging and demanding than those of new public management. They are asking more than whether procedures have been followed or targets met but whether their actions are bringing a net benefit to society. Public value governance emphasizes the role of reflection, lesson-drawing and continuous adaptation to meet the challenges of efficiency, accountability and effectiveness.

Its strengths lie in its redefinition of how to meet the challenges of collective problem-solving in democratic governance and in its ability to point to a motivational force that does not rely on rules or incentives to drive change. People are, it suggests, motivated by their involvement in networks and partnerships, by their relationships with others formed in the context of equal status and mutual learning. The core insight here is that the public realm is different from that of the commercial sector. Governing is not the same as buying and selling goods in a market economy. The distinctiveness of public value management comes from advancing valued social, cultural or economic outcomes. The concept of public value is an attempt to create a framework in which judgements about how to achieve valued outcomes can be made as soundly as possible and co-produced with the wider public that is paying for services.

Why has public value management failed to take hold?

The obstacles to the effective application of public value management in representative democracies have been well documented elsewhere and include professional and political resistance, the lack of political will, resource constraints to engage differently and issues of complexity.[8] The notion of public value, so the argument goes, doesn't sit easily with representative democracy as it introduces a concept of public interest that is not determined by the government of the day, but by public servants in consultation with communities and providers. These factors, amongst others, have led Francesca Gains and Gerry Stoker to conclude that 'this new "public service contract" is likely to be easier to adopt in a local setting than in the core executive although in neither case is the adoption of new modes of working between politicians, officials and citizens unproblematic'.[9]

It is noteworthy, however, that the majority of the criticisms advanced in critique flow from a minimalist conception of public value which views public value management as a method for privileging the role of bureaucrats in policy processes which was not Moore's intention.[10] On closer inspection it is evident that public value experiments tend to be characterized by different models of decision-making underpinned by different conceptions of democracy and reflecting different modes of public engagement. Figure 11.1 situates these models of decision-making along a continuum in which 'bottom-up' deliberative decision-making and 'top-down' 'government-knows best' consultative forms of decision-making can be found at each end of the spectrum. The

Saving Democracy

Deliberative decision-making	*Scope of public involvement in decision-making*	Consultative decision-making
Maximum opportunity structures for public value	⟵⟶	Minimum opportunity structures for public value
	deciding satisficing incrementalism	
Co-design	deliberative citizen juries polling assemblies	Top-down 'government knows best' decision-making

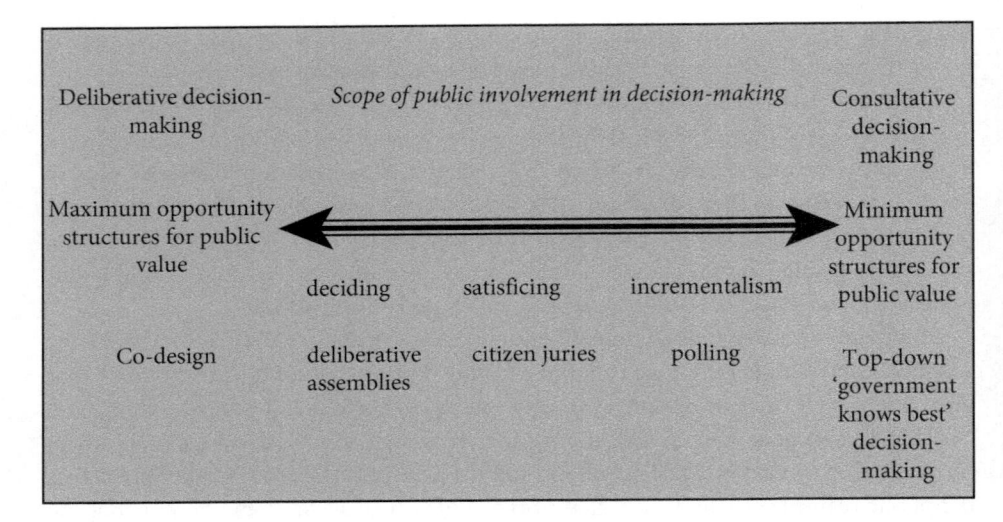

Figure 11.1 The scope of public involvement in public value decision-making.

further you move towards the participatory end of the continuum, the greater the ability for the citizen to affect policy outcomes.

There are also barriers that emerge from the persistence of administrative practices that subvert the transition to public value management and undermine the strategic approach necessary to re-culture dominant public service norms and values. There are at least seven main areas where difficulties arise in the implementation of strategy in government aimed at public value creation.

1. Analysis. Strategic analysis can either be too short-term and trend-based to help steer the organization or too far-fetched and improbable to hold the attention of policy-makers.

2. Poor 'Line of sight'. Strategy work can seem to be exclusively about high-level goals, or it can seem to be purely about a particular set of policies, or it can appear to be a preoccupation with functional strategies or with delivery planning. Line of sight is achieved when there is a clear line between delivery in the community and the high-level goals the organization has set itself. This requires the strong integration of policy, programmes and delivery.

3. Product but not enough process. Strategies that create change within organizations and in the world beyond are the result of a process driven by those who work in the organization and its stakeholders. Yet too often they are simply documents produced by a small group or by consultants who do not create new understanding, still less change. These strategies act like tightropes, from which the organization must eventually fall, rather than as a compass enabling it to set and reset its direction. This suggests the need for inclusively generated change management process with clear performance accountabilities enshrined in performance agreements and appraisal.

4. Insufficient innovation and challenge. A common complaint in government and the wider public sector is that public servants are poor innovators. Strategy requires new understanding and a preparedness to do things in new ways, challenging received wisdom. Yet government tends to incentivize compliance and conformity in its employees and restrict challenge. Commitment to continuous improvement should be embedded in performance agreements and appraisal.
5. Uncertainty about public value. Outcomes can be identified using sound analysis, but they also need both the mandate of political leaders and their sustained interest. This means that the organization as a whole must be capable of focusing on a set of publicly valued goals and returning to them again and again.
6. Lack of strategic policy capability. Political leaders regularly bemoan the absence of strategic policy capability within their organizations often resulting in the increasing use of special advisors.
7. Delivery burdens. Daily operational pressures (the 24/7 media cycle and the budget cycle) on both the political and permanent leadership can tend to 'squeeze' strategic working out of the system.

In sum, if public value management is to be successful it needs to be practised as an instrument for enhancing democratic governance rather than bureaucratic elite action. So how does public value management need to be practised to support this aim?

Authentic public value practice

What would authentic public value management look like? There are six design principles which we would advocate to support its achievement.

Public value is that which the public values

Improved stakeholder engagement, purposeful government communication, heightened levels of citizen engagement including in the novel forms proposed in Chapters 4–6 will all contribute to achieving public value. Important within this strand of thinking is, on the one hand, an understanding of members of the public as individuals, which is where an understanding of policy interventions as corrections to market failure, of NPM and of methods of service transformation all sit best and, on the other hand, of the public as citizens who seek goods for society as a whole, which is where the addition of public value thinking is particularly helpful.

Public value is a system of mandates

The delivery of public goods through the unique authority of government (e.g. to levy taxes, to imprison, to police, to provide welfare payments, etc.) depends on two forms of mandate: the endorsement of elected politicians, who are able to legitimate the actions

Table 11.2 Approaches to public management

	Traditional public administration	New public management	Public value management
Core purpose	Politically provided inputs, services monitored through bureaucratic oversight.	Managing inputs and outputs in a way that ensures economy and responsiveness to consumers	The overarching goal is achieving publicly valued outcomes and this in turn involves greater effectiveness in tackling the problems that the public care most about; stretches from policy development to service delivery to system maintenance.
Role of managers	To ensure that rules and appropriate procedures are followed.	To help define and meet agreed performance targets	To play an active role in steering networks of deliberation and delivery and maintain the overall capacity of the system.
Definition of the public interest	By politicians/experts. Little in the way of public input.	Aggregation of individual preferences, in practice captured by senior politicians or managers supported by evidence about customer choice	Individual and public preferences produced through a complex process of interaction which involves deliberative reflection over inputs and opportunity costs.
Approach to public service ethos	Public sector has monopoly on service ethos, and all public bodies have it.	Sceptical of public sector ethos (leads to inefficiency and empire building) – favours customer service	No one sector has a monopoly on public service ethos. Maintaining relationships through shared values is seen as essential.
Preferred system for service delivery	Hierarchical department or self-regulating profession.	Private sector or tightly defined arms-length public agency	Menu of alternatives selected pragmatically and a reflexive approach to intervention mechanisms to achieve outcomes.
Contribution to the democratic process	Delivers accountability: competition between elected leaders provides an overarching accountability.	Delivers objectives: limited to setting objectives and checking performance, leaving managers to determine the means	Delivers dialogue: integral to all that is undertaken, a rolling and continuous process of democratic engagement and exchange between politicians, stakeholders and citizens.

of government through the authority of election and popular appointment, and the endorsement of the public through their ongoing expression of support via elections and through their participation in participatory governance systems.

Public value provides social purpose

In the private sector companies must make a profit, and the level of dividend shareholders receive, and the value of the shares they own, will be closely related to the level of profit and to the prospects of future profit. However, shareholders are additionally interested in how a company is run, and in how it is seen by its customers, its competitors, by the media and society at large. Some shareholders will be concerned that the company behaves as a good corporate citizen, though others will not care. To some extent these concerns are a function of profitability, but they go wider than that – perhaps because shareholders are also citizens and have democratic concerns as well as shareholder concerns. In a similar way, public value reflects the concern citizens have in seeing that their taxes are spent properly and efficiently, that they receive good services, and that government is value for money. This 'delivery of goods' might be seen as the equivalent of the balance sheet in the private sector, but citizens aren't only concerned with government's *delivery* of goods; they also want to see that their government is *achieving* good; that it has a sense of how to develop public goods in the future – the greatest of these goods being society itself. However, all three of these public value practices require a strategic focus to drive the search for public value and energize the democratic governance system.

Public value creation requires strategic focus and politically mandated outcomes

The identification and pursuit of publicly valued outcomes is the purpose of public value. But this cannot be achieved indiscriminately. It requires strategic focus. The term strategy is very much part of the vocabulary of public service production, but it is used quite arbitrarily. It is attached to a wide variety of statements without much apparent thought and often used only to confer importance and seriousness. Moreover, there is little analysis of the impact of strategic working on policy outcomes.[11]

Strategic organizations develop an understanding of their likely future operating environments. This brings obvious advantages for companies in the private sector, helping them to develop new markets, goods and services in advance of competitors and to increase profitability. For government, whether at national, departmental, regional, agency, local or sectoral level, a stronger understanding of potential futures gives it the capability to track which future is emerging, enabling organizations and policies to be more robust and resilient. Many parts of government do use strategic analysis to improve their planning and performance. But it is not a sufficient ambition for government simply to understand how to survive in a particular future. The job of government is to *change the future*, that is, to set out a vision of a desired future and, through policies and achievement of those policies, facilitate outcomes for citizens that bring that vision to fruition.[12] This is called establishing 'line of sight'.[13]

For example, the aim of HM Treasury in the UK is to maintain 'control over public spending, setting the direction of the UK's economic policy and working to achieve strong and sustainable economic growth'.[14] The Ministry of Social Development in New Zealand helps New Zealanders to be 'safe, strong and independent'.[15] And, of course Bhutan's prime minister famously introduced the concept of 'gross national happiness' to a United Nations forum as a paradigm for alternative development in 1998. The concept was first coined by the fourth King of Bhutan, King Jigme Singye Wangchuck, in 1972 when he declared that 'Gross National Happiness is more important than Gross Domestic Product'.[16]

To ensure 'line of sight' from problem definition and analysis, to high-level goals, to policies to delivery and to achievement of outcomes; all public organizations should have a politically mandated strategic vision which is clear in its provenance, coherent and consistent (because trade-offs have been identified and dealt with as a part of developing the strategy) and rich in outcomes.[17] The vision should be capable of providing an organizational core purpose that everyone in the organization and beyond understands and can support (and helped to create), and it should be written in compelling, motivating language that describes the desired future the organization seeks to help create (see Figure 11.2).

Each of the outcomes it describes should, in turn, act as the end goal for a policy process that the organization will develop and foster. These policy processes will, in their turn, frame a series of programmes, projects, campaigns and other activities to be delivered in some part by the organization but also by a range of stakeholders and, in our view, by citizens as co-producers. Although good leadership, sensible structures and a strong delivery system can all help to provide line of sight, in the absence of a clear strategic vision and politically mandated outcomes there is nothing to have line of sight to.

In terms of international practice, the UK and New Zealand governments have a strong track record in using high-level outcomes-driven performance management. The UK embarked on the most ambitious programme of whole of government outcomes performance management under the Blair Government (1997–2007). The key mechanism within the government's toolkit was the Public Service Agreement (PSA) framework, which was used to establish explicit outcome targets for all departments, which then trickled down to the various arm's-length bodies that operate under the auspices of each department. Overall, the PSA regime provided an important example of steering at a distance as a form of political leadership. However, the British experience also exposed several constraints that impeded the effectiveness of the framework, such as institutional barriers to joint working; the political challenges of imposing a meaningful sanctions and rewards regime; and the mismatch between short-term electoral incentives and long-term policy outcomes.[18] Most significantly, the outcomes were set from the top-down by the prime minister in consultation with the relevant ministers of state and key stakeholders. There was never an attempt to design a national dialogue to facilitate broad-based support for the outcomes in question and subject them to ongoing review.

Improving the Public Service Experience

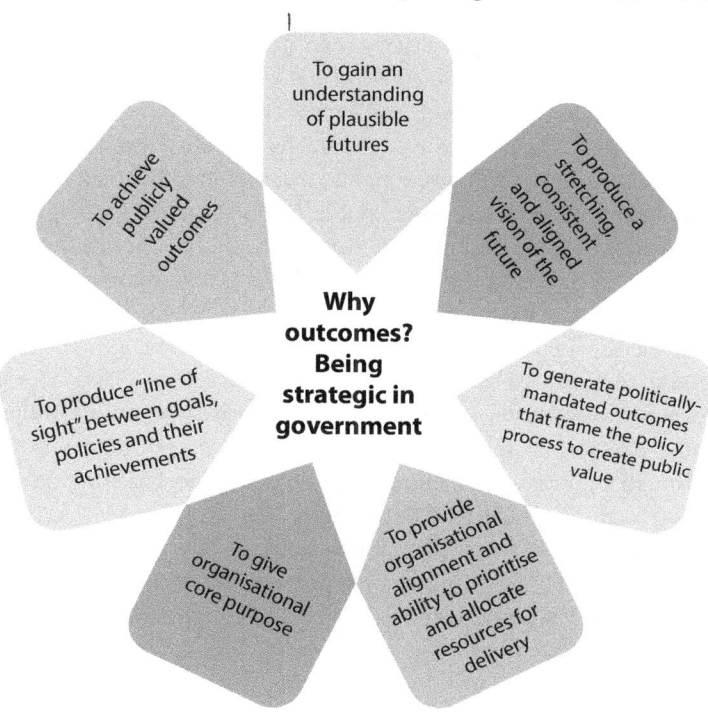

Figure 11.2 Why outcomes? Being strategic in government.

Petals around center "Why outcomes? Being strategic in government":
- To gain an understanding of plausible futures
- To produce a stretching, consistent and aligned vision of the future
- To generate politically-mandated outcomes that frame the policy process to create public value
- To provide organisational alignment and ability to prioritise and allocate resources for delivery
- To give organisational core purpose
- To produce "line of sight" between goals, policies and their achievements
- To achieve publicly valued outcomes

Participatory governance systems should be legally constituted to identify and review progress on the achievement of publicly valued outcomes

This design principle may appear ambitious, but there are already a significant number of countries that engage in the measurement of well-being outcomes that have emerged through legal processes. Laws such as the Scottish Community Empowerment Act 2015, the French 2015-411 law (also known as the 'Sas' law after its main author, the Member of Parliament Eva Sas) and the Italian Budget Law which entered into force in 2016, all place a duty on government to regularly report on a set of well-being indicators.[19] For example, in Scotland there is a duty on Scottish Ministers to consult on, develop and publish a new set of National Outcomes for Scotland, and to review them at least every five years. The outcomes themselves are then ultimately for the government of the day to achieve.[20]

In New Zealand, the government has embedded well-being measurement in the Public Finance Act 1989.[21] This includes requirements for: (i) the government to set out how its well-being objectives, along with its fiscal objectives, will guide its budget decisions; and (ii) the Treasury to report on well-being indicators, alongside macroeconomic and fiscal indicators. The New Zealand government also appears to have made significant progress in outcomes-driven performance management largely as a consequence of the

Whanau-ora programme in which services are co-designed with Māori citizens and their representatives around well-being outcomes and the diffusion of the outcomes approach to other agencies such as health, youth and families and sports.[22]

In Wales, the Future Generations Act 2015 targets all levels of the policy cycle. Informed by a large-scale twelve-month public consultation, the main provisions of the Act came into force in 2016 requiring all public bodies to place seven well-being goals at the centre of their decision-making. The Act can therefore be seen as a legally binding common purpose, overseen by the Future Generations Commissioner for Wales, who monitors and reports the extent to which the different public bodies are setting and reaching their well-being objectives, and reviewing them accordingly. The review is then published and shared with Welsh Ministers.[23] One key benefit of a legislative approach is that it provokes national debate, discussion and a degree of consensus forming; legislation cannot usually be passed if a majority of lawmakers do not support it, and proposals can be refined through a process of amendments to ensure broad-based support.

Other countries that have explicitly introduced well-being frameworks and indicators into their strategic development planning include Colombia (through 'Presidential Dashboards' developed by the Ministry for National Planning), Ecuador (via the policy goals included in the Nationals Plans for Buen Vivir, carried out by the Ministry of Planning), Paraguay (which has adopted the Social Global Happiness and Wellbeing Policy Report 2019 146 147 Progress Index as a well-being monitoring tool in its National Development Plan 2030) and Slovenia (in the Slovenian National Development Strategy 2030, adopted by the Slovenian Government in 2017).[24]

The Scottish National Performance Framework is a further example of clarifying the government's strategic objectives through a wide-ranging set of well-being, inclusiveness and sustainability indicators.[25] In Finland, the strategic debate in government is supported by the Strategic Government Programme Indicators, which use a variety of data including well-being metrics, a selection of which is presented during government sessions every fortnight.[26] To some extent, the 2030 Sustainable Development Goals and targets, which were adopted by all United Nations member states in September 2015, can also be seen as a form of development planning and performance monitoring, organized around a set of multidimensional well-being objectives with specific targets and indicators.

Outcomes setting provides a unique opportunity to create a strategic focus for public value creation and citizen-centric governance at the national scale. However, its authenticity requires engagement beyond the usual technocratic suspects. In Slovenia, for example, stakeholders and citizens were invited to shape the Slovenian National Development Strategy 2030, both in the initial stages (e.g. participating in situational analysis and horizon scanning) all the way through to assessing the draft strategy in a series of surveys and topical debates towards the end of the process.[27] Outcomes setting also provides the opportunity for integrating representative democracy with participatory democracy through the creation of participatory governance systems that bring politicians and citizens together to deliberate on the fundamental issues of the day.

In 2020, there were calls for the 2030 Sustainable Development Goals and targets to be used as the basis for post-Covid-19 recovery planning given that they were adopted by all United Nations member states in September 2015.[28] This would provide a fantastic opportunity for national dialogue on what is essentially an outcomes-setting process. Drawing on the successful Irish model described in Chapter 5, assemblies could be created consisting of a one-third, two-thirds mix of politicians and randomly selected lay citizens supported by experts, and chaired by a trusted intermediary, to ensure governmental follow-through. Participants should be free from political constraints. A plurality of viewpoints and engagement methods should be used to increase the range of perspectives that contribute to the assembly's recommendations facilitated through quality process design. Representation must be inclusive, equal and diverse and give voice to the majority of citizens. The final recommendations should be transmitted to the legislature for scrutiny and ratification.

Above all, the notion of citizen participation should be accepted as a founding value of democratic governance and public value creation. Recognition that there is more to democracy than voting and that post-pandemic recovery calls for a new way based on engagement with those most affected.

Public value creation is value-driven

Officials working in the public realm should have a strong idea of *why* they are working in the public domain. Mere service is not enough. A sense of how to serve most effectively, a sense of how to support political leaders in achievement of their goals, a sense of how those goals can themselves be shaped in a way that best creates public value, all these attributes are not simply desirable qualities in our public officials: they are the fundamental duty of public officials. Hence public value management requires both new values and practices and in certain instances the rediscovery of old ones, for example, the notion of public service. Five elements of a new public service ethos should be adopted by all providers of public services:

1. A citizen-centred performance culture: a strong commitment to service for individuals and the community reflected in responsive service delivery and reinforced by training, support and systems to ensure a sustainable citizen-centred service culture and continuous improvement.
2. A commitment to accountability: an emphasis on open access to information both to individuals and to groups of interested citizens with strong public accountability to the electorate at large.
3. A capacity to support universal access: recognition of a special responsibility to support the rights of all service users in an environment where their choice of service is restricted.
4. Responsible employment practices: well-trained, well-managed and well-motivated staff that act professionally and are fairly rewarded.

5. Contribution to community well-being: a recognition of the need to work in partnership with others across the public, private and voluntary sectors to contribute to the promotion of community well-being and to meet the needs of individuals.

This list may well have its deficiencies, but the essential observation remains that management for public value requires that all those involved in delivery share certain ethical values and commitments.[29]

Evaluating the democratic performance of a public service in an era of citizen-centric governance

What does liberal democracy require of a public service? Box 11.1 presents the key criteria for evaluation, noting the centrality of whether the public service is sufficiently accountable to government, the parliament and the public, representative of the people and the diversity of its national cultures, and in touch with, the needs and aspirations of everyday citizens.

In conclusion – towards authentic public value creation

This chapter has argued that the transformation of our public services is a key component of democratic renewal because it is the performance (supply) of government that matters most in orienting the outlooks of citizens, together with commitment to procedural fairness and equality. We termed this condition of trusted government *performance legitimacy* and argued that it was best achieved through the search for public value and the practices of public value management. However, we noted that thus far attempts to adopt a public value approach have been thwarted by a lack of strategic government, insufficient focus on publicly valued outcomes and the use of inappropriate engagement methods to determine public value. We therefore presented seven design principles to inform authentic public value management practice.

In summary, the role of public organizations at all levels should be circumscribed by the search for publicly valued outcomes and a commitment to a public service ethos. Decision centres in governance structures should include a balance of forces in decision-making (public service panels, political representatives, technical support). Public managers should be neural arbiters of public value but subject to shared accountability mechanisms through the application of a co-governance model. A participatory learning-based approach should be adopted to the challenge of public service delivery at all levels of governance and stages of the policy process. These principles would help to bring the politics back into policy deliberation and operational delivery at a time when the public standing of governmental institutions has reached its nadir. They would help to foster collaborative problem-solving, and reflexive public organizations committed to delivering public value. And they would enable the transformation of our public services into a functional component of democratic governance.

Box 11.1 Criteria for evaluating the democratic performance of public services

1. Services provision and implementation, and the regulation of social and economic activities, should be mandated by democratically elected officials as far as possible.
2. Public managers should establish intelligent performance indicators linked directly to politically mandated long-term outcomes with citizens and stakeholders. Monitoring systems should be designed to identify movements towards or away from achieving these objectives.
3. Public managers should design appropriate participatory governance systems in their sphere of operations with citizens and stakeholders and relevant elected officials that link to different decision points in the policy process. These include strategic direction (reassessment of the evidence base and co-production of appropriate outcomes), service design and the monitoring of service delivery and learning (deliberation, distillation and diffusion of better practice).
4. Policy-making should be deliberative, carefully considering the interests of all relevant actors.
5. The management of public sector programmes and services should be impartially conducted within administrators' legally available powers.
6. All citizens should have full and equal access to government and the services and goods to which they are entitled, and their rights should be protected in decision-making, and 'due process' rules followed in adjudicating their cases.
7. Wherever 'para-state' organizations (NGOs or private contractors) deliver services, public value standards (action within the law, equal treatment and access, respect for human rights and freedom from corruption) should apply.
8. Public services, contracting and regulation should be free from corruption, with swift action taken against evidence of possible offences.
9. The public service should recruit and promote staff on merit, having due regard to combatting wider societal discrimination that may exist on grounds of race, ethnicity, gender, disability or other factors.
10. The public service should ideally be a 'representative bureaucracy' whose social make-up reflects the population being served. with recruitment biases addressed on the basis of ethnicity, gender and disability.
11. Government services should be efficient, effective and deliver 'value for money' with agency performance appropriately documented in public documents.
12. Organizational work plans should be subject to annual review with effective reporting systems both to politicians and to the public operated through the principle of shared data for shared learning.

13. Procedures for complaints and citizen redress should be easy to access and use, and agencies should operate them in transparent and responsive ways, fulfilling 'freedom of information' requirements.
14. The public service and the political executive have complementary roles with the former providing the stable, non-partisan stewardship component and the latter the dynamic political element, and with mutual check and balance functions.

CHAPTER 12
REPRESENTATIVE DEMOCRACY AND CRISIS MANAGEMENT

Coping with crisis has become a new normal in democratic politics.[1] Terrorist attacks, natural disasters, the collapse of banks, cyberattacks and pandemics – all of these events are an integral part of the twenty-first-century experience of democracies. The impact of Covid-19 stands out during 2020/2021, and it provides one of the most sustained experiences of crisis for all nations. Covid-19 has been the cause of millions of direct deaths and substantial indirect effects, with denied or delayed disease prevention, loss of jobs and income, draconian restrictions on freedom of movement and disruption of social networks.[2] Responding to the crisis created by Covid-19 has led to interventions in social and economic life more disruptive and radical than anything that has normally been part of political decision-making within peacetime. The question that this chapter addresses is: how do democracies fare in the context of a crisis? We argue that to save democracy we are going to have to reflect on how to crisis-proof its operation.

There are reasons to think that some of the practices of democracy are more difficult in the context of a crisis. Firstly, the normal, time-consuming nature of democratic decision-making does not always fit comfortably with a context where rapid decisions in an uncertain environment are required, as they generally are in a crisis. Executive decision-making may come more to the fore, leaving the more reflective and representative elements of democracy less able to exercise oversight or judgement.[3] Secondly, citizens may find the threats they face create fear and to relieve that psychological pressure they may be more willing to follow or support political leaders without question or without engaging in the scrutiny and challenge that would normally be an integral part of democratic oversight. Citizens may feel the pressure to support their countries' leaders (rightly or wrongly) in the middle of a crisis and more generally they may abandon reasoned judgement for choices made through emotion or affect. Thirdly, responding to a crisis may involve value calls (where to put resources, how to weigh different risks) which are the normal business of democracy. But meeting the demands of a crisis is also likely to involve the need for expertise or knowledge to a greater degree. During the Covid-19 crisis the demand for expertise was expressed through repeated calls for decision-makers to 'follow the science'. Various branches of science have played a more direct role in influencing policy-making in response to Covid-19. As noted in Chapter 9, some democratic theorists are nervous that experts claim too much authority and squeeze out other voices in decision-making.[4] Such concerns expose what can be a difficult relationship between expertise and democracy and lead us to ask how that relationship could be effectively managed.

Saving Democracy

These three concerns – abnormal pressures on governing institutions, increased citizen anxiety and the lionization of expertise – are explored in this chapter. Before exploring our three main concerns, the opening section asks a broader question still: do democracies perform better than authoritarian regimes in responding to crisis? We will also explore criteria for evaluating democratic performance during and after crisis.

Does democracy help or hinder in a crisis?

As the Covid-19 pandemic unfolded in the early months of 2020 there was a question that soon came to be posed. Will democracies fare better or worse than authoritarian systems in managing the crisis? There are two conventional wisdoms at play here. The first is that democracies are best placed to meet a range of societal challenges and that would appear to be the case in terms of responding to a pandemic that required significant engagement between government and citizens. This conventional wisdom is well-summarized by the idea that

> ... high-income countries in the Western world, with their open societies and democratic institutions ... (would) ... be well placed to fight the pandemic, and that effective public action would flourish where there is accountability and open debate. This expectation is rooted in the fact that such governments have better incentives to assess health risks and the capacity to undertake policy initiatives needed to halt the spread of the disease.'[5]

The second conventional wisdom is that authoritarian systems might have some advantages in providing the rapid action and strong compliance from citizens that a pandemic or another crisis might demand. Some point to how China, although initially at the epicentre of Covid-19, has managed to come through the situation in a way that places it and other East Asian countries at an advantage. While Western democracies continued to wrestle with the virus throughout the latter months of 2020, China was already getting its economy back on track.[6]

In the main, there is a sense that democracies did struggle compared to other systems. Timothy Besley and Sacha Dray suggest that in terms of numbers of Covid-related deaths, wider impacts of the economy and the severity of lockdowns, 'high-income countries and those with more individual freedoms have generally fared worse, not better, than countries without civil liberties and/or with lower incomes'.[7]

Yet they are quick to argue that the situation is nuanced with some democracies performing relatively well and some authoritarian regimes relatively badly. Others[8] suggest that democracies have some advantages in a crisis (such as the ability to bring people along and the open sharing of information) as do authoritarian regimes (in terms of the ability to take rapid action). And both systems have disadvantages. In the case of democracies, the devolved nature of power can slow and confuse action and decision. With respect to authoritarian regimes the lack of free sharing of information or knowledge can have a negative impact. Indeed, this concern has become part of a blame game with China's initial slowness in acknowledging Covid-19 helping, it is claimed, helping to ensure the global spread of the virus. Still others are confident that in the final analysis regime type will not be the deciding factor in getting to a more effective response to Covid-19 but instead what will count is strong state capacity, trust in government and fellow citizens and good leadership.[9] A failure on any of these fronts would count potentially against success.

All these assessments of success might depend on when in the timeline of the pandemic the question is asked. Australia was, in the judgement of its citizens, compared to those of Italy, the UK and the United States, viewed to have successfully managed the pandemic at the mid-2020 point. But it is far from clear that the relative judgements would be the same at the mid-2021 point, with the relative success of the vaccine programmes in the United States and the UK, compared to Australia.[10] The position is sufficiently fluid and uncertain that it would seem wise to conclude that there is no clear evidence to support the argument that democracies struggled more than authoritarian systems because of features of their systems.

Yet democracies do face a variety of pressures in dealing with pandemics that are unique to their systems. The organization of elections has been disrupted, and as a result different types of campaigning in keeping with social distancing measures and greater use of postal voting have been required. This difficulty in turn has created a political opportunity at least in the case of the US presidential election for renewed vigour in claims of fraud rather obviously from the candidate who lost. There are coping mechanisms that can be adopted to make elections happen (and be fair) but there may be extra costs and additional work involved for those who organize elections.[11]

The free flow of information or more particularly misinformation through the social media is an issue of concern. Rumours about where the virus originated, what protective measures worked and the safety and efficacy of vaccines were all the focus of misinformation in democracies.[12] Some argue, again as part of an international blame game, that the situation was deliberately exploited by China and Russia to destabilize democratic regimes and others called on the major social media companies to take more responsibility for what is shared on their platforms.[13] The concern calls for a response:

The proliferation of homegrown and foreign sources of fake news engenders distrust toward democratic institutions and disruptive behavior that is particularly harmful during a pandemic. Democracies should work together to foster an ecosystem of reliable information, in partnership with tech companies, governments, and civil society.[14]

Again, the argument is not that democracy cannot cope but that it has to adapt.

But in what ways should it adapt? Reaching for more participation from citizens is a common theme, especially in response to the impact of Covid-19.[15] Democratic reformers argue that participation will capture the diversity of experiences of those coping with the impact of the pandemic which is better than decision-making by closed groups of experts, politicians and public administrators. It will improve the legitimacy of decision-making in a way that distrusted politicians cannot. The argument is that 'when people can see that decisions reflect their lives and interests; trust and acceptance follow'.[16] In general terms, many (including ourselves) might support these arguments but there seems limited evidence that lack of trust (in the absence of citizen participation) was an issue in the context of the management of Covid-19. There is some emerging evidence that where participatory culture and practices existed before the pandemic, they were better placed to respond.[17] However, trust is likely to be a key issue in the recovery phase when there is greater contestation over the distribution of resources which may heighten historical and regional social, political and economic antagonisms.

In practice, in most liberal democracies organized public deliberation played little part in at least the immediate policy response to the Covid-19 pandemic. Although civic action was prominent, such that neighbour helping neighbour, as well as various forms of volunteering, provided an embrace of mutual support, delivering food, medicines and social care to those who needed help. Many vaccination programmes also involved an army of volunteers to ensure that large-scale immunization could be delivered. Yet in the absence of direct participation or citizen deliberation trust did not decline. In most countries, a large majority of citizens have shown strong support for both lockdown restrictions and vaccine take-up. In the UK, for example, careful research tracking people's movements has shown that about 90 per cent of the population not only agreed with but followed lockdown restrictions.[18] Acceptance of quite draconian policy measures has emerged from citizens without much in the way of public participation or organized deliberation. In some countries, a degree of non-compliance or vaccine hesitancy appears to have been stimulated deliberately or inadvertently by the negative or confused messaging from political elites. Lack of participation was not a driver of distrust but rather poor or confusing messaging from elites.

In the immediate drama of a crisis, citizen deliberation and participation might appear to be a low priority. But in the later stages of crisis management – reflecting on accountabilities and drawing lessons for the future – the case for citizen engagement comes back to the fore. As public inquiries are slowly launched to explore what went right and what went wrong, the option of drawing citizens into the discussion is one that if not taken up will happen without invitation.[19] The argument that Covid-19 could have been managed more successfully if there had been more public participation and debate might be difficult to sustain, given the whirlwind of uncertainty and the need for rapid decisions that characterize a crisis. But there can be little doubt that at some point the public will have their say. In those reflections they might like to consider how best to limit the creep of executive power, the difficulties of organizing public debate in a period of high anxiety and how to get the best out of the experts that are afforded a greater role in finding solutions. These are the issues we now turn to consider.

Do governments behave differently in a crisis?

In many respects it is not surprising that democracies are knocked out of their stride by crises. A threat so extreme and substantial makes a governance system operate outside its comfort zone and can reveal both problems within the governing institutions, in the processes of governing and in the relationship between the government and citizens and does so in an environment of uncertainty, threat and time constraints. As the authors of the key text on the politics of crisis management comment: 'crises provide real-world stress tests to the resilience of political systems'.[20] A stress test pushes systems to deal with issues that force them to operate in extreme rather than normal conditions. As Arjen Boin and colleagues observe, crises

> ... surprise in various ways; they are fundamentally ambiguous, even messy. So much happens in such a short time, so many problems appear simultaneously or in rapid succession, so many people do not know what to think and whom or what to trust, that a generalized sense of uncertainty emerges. These are unique events that defy conventional approaches to planning.[21]

A crisis does provide a stress test for political systems. In medicine, one example of a stress test is when the performance of the heart is measured while the patient is exercising and making the heart work extremely hard. A stress test for a banking system asks how the system would cope when things start to go wrong. In engineering a stress test might judge just how much load or structural pressure a bridge could withstand. So, what do we mean by a stress test for a democracy? Our answer is that the standard way of policy-making, often and evocatively described as 'muddling through', is not sustainable and viable in the context of a crisis.

To understand why a crisis provides the momentum for a stress test it is useful to provide a portrait of the style of decision-making characteristic of democratic governance. Charles Lindblom describes the process of making policy in one of the most cited articles in the history of political studies as the 'science of muddling through'.[22] In the publicly presented image of policy-making, a problem is identified, and a solution found to answer that problem. In practice there are disagreements over what the problem is and what the solution might be. As Charles Lindblom notes:

> The test of a "good" policy is typically that various analysts find themselves directly agreeing on a policy (without their agreeing that it is the most appropriate means to an agreed objective).[23]

Various policy-makers and influencers can back the policy for different reasons. The administrator may lend their support because it gives their department more money to spend. For the organized interest, their endorsement could protect their members against more negative changes. For elected representatives, their support could be premised on the idea that their constituency might gain investment. In short, agreement comes not because all are convinced the policy will solve the problem but rather all are persuaded that there is something in the policy that matches their interests or values. The policy process is thereby simplified as not searching for the best but the acceptable. Searching for options is drastically limited in that the aim is not to find the best or perfect solution and so alternative potential policies are neglected. But equally it is problematic in that negative possible outcomes are overlooked, and some important values are abandoned.

How do democracies survive this process of muddling through? In part it is because nothing is finally resolved, and all the participants know it is possible to come back and fight another day. Moreover, in the process of implementation some watering down, or subtle changes can make a difference to how the policy works. Key players within the governance system can ignore or bypass new rules. Others negotiate hard to get something more acceptable to them. Some implement the rules in one way, and some in another. People say to elected leaders: 'You are in charge, why don't you decide and then make it happen?' The process of mutual adjustment that is central to decision-making in any complex system of democratic governance means that it is difficult and often close to impossible to deliver on that request. The making of policy inevitably involves compromise and lacks the coherence that might be given by overarching central direction.

There is therefore a contradiction between the naive concept of democracy that is often in the public shorthand description and the reality of the way that the governmental process works in practice. The public may be told to vote for a certain leader and they will be in charge and do as you ask (or suffer the consequences). The reality is of a messy, differentiated governance system where there is a great deal of 'mutual adjustment' among the leading politicians, bureaucrats, other elected representatives and organized interests. Goals may be set by leaders but what emerges is much more of a tangled web.

This 'normal' state of affairs comes into sharp focus in the context of a crisis. In a crisis, citizens look to leaders to deal with the threats caused by the crisis and the standard operating style of governance of muddling through seems a poor fit and the executive arm of government as opposed to the representative arm tends to take a stronger role. A crisis involves threat, uncertainty and demands urgency. It provides a context better suited at least initially to action by the executive rather than representative arms of democracies. And even within the executive there may be a narrowing of the range of actors involved in key decisions. Of course, even these changes do not mean that muddling through is avoided, as every public inquiry after a crisis tends to show.[24]

Do citizens behave differently in a crisis?

The propensity for citizens to lend their support to leaders during periods of crisis is well-documented. The Covid-19 pandemic, for example, did not disappoint in this respect. At least in the initial stages of the pandemic's spread, surveys revealed a parallel surge in support for incumbent leaders.[25] Leaders in a large number of countries enjoyed an increase in public confidence. The approval rating of Giuseppe Conte, prime minister of Italy, the country worst hit at that point in terms of deaths, hit 71 per cent in March

2020 – 27 points higher than the previous month. German Chancellor Angela Merkel saw her approval rise to 79 per cent. The prime ministers of Canada and Australia, Justin Trudeau and Scott Morrison, respectively, saw similar surges in popularity during the early weeks of the pandemic hitting their countries. So did, although to a more modest level, the UK prime minister, Boris Johnson.

This tendency to rush to support leaders is often described as the 'rally-round-the-flag' effect.[26] The underlying idea is that there is a rush of patriotic fervour to a nation under threat, with the key beneficiary being the national leader as an embodiment of the nation. Rallies of support are driven by an increasing 'affective' commitment to the nation and its leader. Marc Hetherington and Michael Nelson argue that the support for the leader reflects their position as the 'ceremonial leader of the nation and the living symbol of national unity' and 'lies in the emotions the role arouses in citizens'.[27] With these observations in mind, they speculate that constitutional systems such as presidencies, where the leader is both a politician and a formal chief of state, are more likely to be beneficiaries of rallies, rather than 'a partisan political leader in the manner of, for example, the British prime minister'. The US presidency is seen as highly likely to be endowed with these qualities of underlying emotion or affective support and so highly prone to rally effects. Ironically, in the case of Covid-19, President Trump in 2020 received a virtually indetectable boost, reflecting perhaps that the rally effect demands some sense from the public that the leader is demonstrating leadership.

For John Mueller, a 'rally-round-the-flag' impact must involve an event which is international, involves the country and particularly the leader directly and is 'specific, dramatic, and sharply focused'.[28] The logic of these conditions is simply that the given event must be one that is existential to the health of the country, that is not borne from internal disagreement or conflict (e.g. riots), and that is sudden and dramatic enough to have focused public attention. This latter qualification is perhaps the most important, since there are many international existential threats which involve leaders but are of low salience and unfold over extended time periods, such as climate change. The coronavirus pandemic fits Mueller's definition: it is global in scope and significance, directly involves national governments and leaders in the response, and dominates the public agenda worldwide. As a major public health outbreak, the pandemic is qualitatively different to other rallying events such as terror attacks, war and other international conflicts, not to mention presenting distinct challenges in terms of its governance.

Beyond a rush to patriotism, the severity of the threat faced can impact the outlook of citizens, making them more information hungry and more anxious and fearful. In experimental work conducted by Bethany Albertson and Shana Kushner Gadarian involving induced threats (the arrival of a pandemic was the issue chosen), trust in leaders and government also increased due to the heightened perception of threat.[29] How does this work? The authors go on to explain that anxiety in various forms can emerge from a threat. First, there is the direct threat to your own well-being which can be anxiety-inducing. Then there is the anxiety of wanting to take back control, to do something about the situation and that in turn can encourage people to search for information but also put their faith in people, including political leaders, who appear to be offering solutions. In a crisis, people pay more attention to information and more generally to politics. They are also more prone to be trusting of political actors and institutions who they think can help resolve the crisis and more supportive of public policies that will deliver security, even if those policies deny previously cherished rights. The situation is complex. The threat from a new virus and the need to take significant new precautions to maximize personal safety – as experienced during the first waves of Covid-19 – would seem to be a logical driver of these two shifts in behaviour. Covid-19 presents a crisis directly experienced by the vast majority of people at least in terms of the impact of lockdowns and other public health policies. The crisis is also a powerful shared experience, stimulating information exchange and debate with others: narratives of what it is like on the frontline touches most households through connections with health and social care workers, communication with relatives, co-workers or friends unfortunate enough to catch the disease bring home its impact. Thus, although political elites may seek to influence Covid-19 responses, their vertical cues to frame public opinion are operating alongside a range of widely distributed horizontal cues.

Anxiety is an unpleasant feeling, and individuals are therefore 'motivated to regulate this emotion through strategies that restore a sense of security and affective balance'.[30] Threat can lead to an anxiety response and that in turn can trigger attempts to regulate that emotion by placing greater trust in those who might be seen as resolving the crisis. These are coping mechanisms that give people back a sense of control in the context of a serious threat. And it has implications for politics. Citizens seek to learn more but tend to focus on the most threatening information. They look to governmental leaders to take action that will remedy or mollify their fears and are more willing to contemplate interventions that restrict freedom. Problems that lie outside the individuals' capacity to cope can stimulate anxiety, an unwanted emotional state, and a core coping mechanism is an increased tendency to trust government in the hope it can offer protection from the threat. In addition, the perception of leader competence may be affected by the presence or absence of critical challenge in the early or later days of the crisis. Hetherington and Nelson note how sometimes a crisis means opposition actors and media become uncritical and even supportive of the government, leaving little room for citizens to 'read, see, or hear'.[31]

There are normative reasons to welcome a boost in support for political leaders in times of crisis. During a period of danger, it might be considered a social gain as strong leadership and support for unusual levels of government intervention can help resolve the problem. In the case of any crisis, including a pandemic, greater cooperation between government, citizens, business and voluntary organizations is also likely to help. Even if the support for leadership is driven by affect or emotion, the process should be a positive one since emotions are an embedded feature of human nature and they can stimulate the drive to learn, encourage, reflect and steer action. As George Marcus and colleagues argue, affective intelligence and the mobilization of the mind's surveillance system 'signals novelty of threat in the environment and indicates the need to reassess routine beliefs and preferences'.[32] Their view is that emotion and anxiety can break voters out of their habitual positions and enable them to seek new information and reformulate their political stance.

Others are concerned that surges in support for leaders and trust in government pose challenges. Jennifer Merolla and Elizabeth Zechmeister argue that citizens, when faced with a threatening crisis, are not stimulated by their anxiety to seek new information and cues. Instead, anxiety stimulates 'coping strategies' that 'reflect psychological processes that lie outside the realm of overt and rational calculations'.[33] These are strategies designed to relieve anxiety rather than improve their political judgement. Projecting qualities on to a leader reflects a desire to find a saviour rather than a rational calculation and may lead to citizens pinning their hopes on an unqualified politician and sits uncomfortably with the idea of the critical democratic citizen. A surge in support for leaders in this respect reflects a psychological coping mechanism and helps people feel better – but it does not improve the political judgement of their leaders. Worse, these coping mechanisms of blaming others and deifying leaders could undermine the fabric of a democratic civic culture that demands tolerance of others and critical political judgement. It may make citizens more susceptible to being manipulated by political elites that seek to exploit their anxiety. People may also become more distrustful or intolerant of others or more hostile towards other communities or nations. In the context of Covid-19, there have been several reports of increased antagonism towards Chinese or 'Chinese-looking' people in many countries.[34]

These behavioural observations about increased anxiety leading to negative outlooks are insightful and there is evidence for their impact. Yet research and experience also suggest that many citizens do not lose their capacity for reason or critical judgement in a crisis. Citizens can oppose wars or too heavy-handed responses to terrorist attacks. Above all, the competence and outcomes of the government's actions matter. A threat is recognized as a cause for concern by a citizen, but if the government is perceived as not able or willing to address it then support for the government and its leaders will ebb. This phenomenon happened precisely in the context of the Covid-19 pandemic, as illustrated in Figure 12.1.

If we then examine public opinion again with the success of the vaccine programme in the early months of 2021 in the UK, we can observe public opinion again moving to reflect that situation. Lived experience matters. Above all voters are more trusting of political actors viewed to be dealing with any threat effectively or expertly but express less trust for those perceived to be acting incompetently. The public may be more in the driving seat than typically assumed in the 'rally-round-the-flag' literature and the focus on the impact of anxiety. Despite an extremely emotive event, and one which evokes considerable, albeit unevenly distributed anxiety, competence still matters in determining trust in both leaders and government. Whilst affective mechanisms do play a substantial role, we would be remiss to sideline people's judgement of how our governors are handling the crisis: a judgement which is likely to grow in importance as threat fades and people begin to reflect on what governments did well and what they did wrong. Governments that have attempted to rely on framing the crisis and public messaging instead of competent performance may be surprised that they are not rewarded in the medium or long term. In times of crisis, it appears that many citizens do not lose their heads but use them.

Saving Democracy

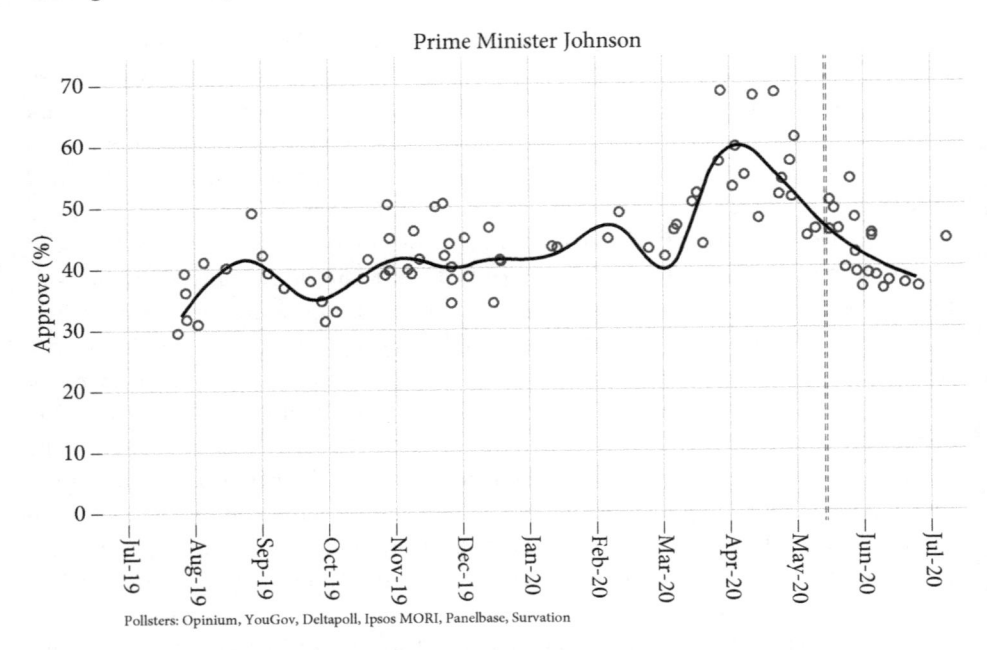

Figure 12.1 The rise and fall of support for British Prime Minister Boris Johnson during Covid-19.

Is there an enhanced role for experts in crisis management?

Experts play a major role in decision-making in normal times, but at times of crisis expert and scientific knowledge about an issue or topic can have even greater influence. If an earthquake or flooding has occurred, then it would seem appropriate to seek advice from those with technical knowledge about how to respond effectively. But there is much research that shows that evidence produced through expert knowledge is not automatically used to drive public policy in times of non-crisis. Indeed, it is sometimes a source of great annoyance to scientists that their advice is either not asked for or when proffered is ignored or subject to bargaining as comprises become the order of the political day. As noted earlier in the context of Covid-19, the mantra of 'following the science' was often claimed by leaders and there is little doubt that experts in various areas played a major role in shaping the response to the pandemic. Medical experts including virologists, epidemiologists, public health scholars and statisticians were instrumental in suggesting policies to counteract the spread of coronavirus, including many restrictions on social and economic life that had a major impact. They have also guided the development of vaccine response at a pace and level previously thought to be impossible both in their roles as vaccine developers and regulators.

As Covid-19 raced across the globe, the leaders of almost every country were forced to rely on their health experts to advise them on the sudden threat. Of course, the degree of that reliance and the nature of the leader's relationship with their advisers varied. US

President Donald Trump notoriously fought with the health professionals, as he sought to downplay the virus. In contrast, in many other democracies governments were at pains from the start to stress policy prescriptions were evidence-based, driven by the expert advice. Not only has the health advice been pivotal to the crafting of policy responses, but elected leaders have used the presence of their health officials – in person, regularly at the news conferences of the prime minister and premiers – to buttress their political authority.

Why do experts become more important in the context of a crisis? Again, the nature of a crisis provides part of the answer. Experts get dragged into more direct contact with the policy dialogue to a greater degree because time pressures and a high degree of uncertainty about what to do make their involvement more attractive to policymakers. And as noted earlier, a crisis is likely to demand a degree of knowledge and understanding built up through years of training and professional practice that are not available to elected leaders or for that matter citizens. Responding effectively to a crisis demands quick and ready access to expertise.

A further factor of significance is that experts help to win public approval and trust of the measures undertaken. In the context of Covid-19 expert advice has been used to justify lockdowns and other restrictive measures. It was used to design packages of economic support. It was key to promoting both the efficacy and safety of vaccines. Experts became a tool in meeting and overcoming another feature of a crisis, namely, the tendency towards fear and anxiety among the public. There appears to be a connection between whether citizens judge political leaders as taking on board advice from leaders and their sense that their leader is handling a crisis well or badly.

As Table 12.1 indicates, Giuseppe Conte from Italy and Scott Morrison from Australia got higher ratings compared to leaders in the UK and United States for their handling of the Covid-19 crisis in May and June of 2020. And both these leaders were seen as taking the trouble to work with expert advice. The then leader of the United States was seen as the worst performer in terms of the management of Covid-19 and the least likely to take expert advice. The case of the UK prime minister, Boris Johnson, does not so clearly follow the pattern. Although his performance was considered poor in relative terms, he was seen to be listening to experts. It's just that they turned out to be the wrong experts! The joint report from the House of Commons' Science and Technology Committee and Health and Social Care Committee published in October 2021 found that some government initiatives were examples of global best practice but that others represented 'serious mistakes'. For example, the UK's pandemic planning was based too narrowly on a flu model that had failed to learn the lessons from the SARS, MERS and Ebola epidemics, which meant that its Covid planning was worse than in other countries.[35]

This suggests that for a political leader listening to experts is not a magic bullet in a crisis but on balance it does help promote a sense that the crisis is being managed as well as it could be. There is a complication in the role played by experts reflected in the well-recognized phenomenon: not all experts agree. In many democracies, the lack of agreement between experts was exposed several times during the Covid-19 crisis, from

Saving Democracy

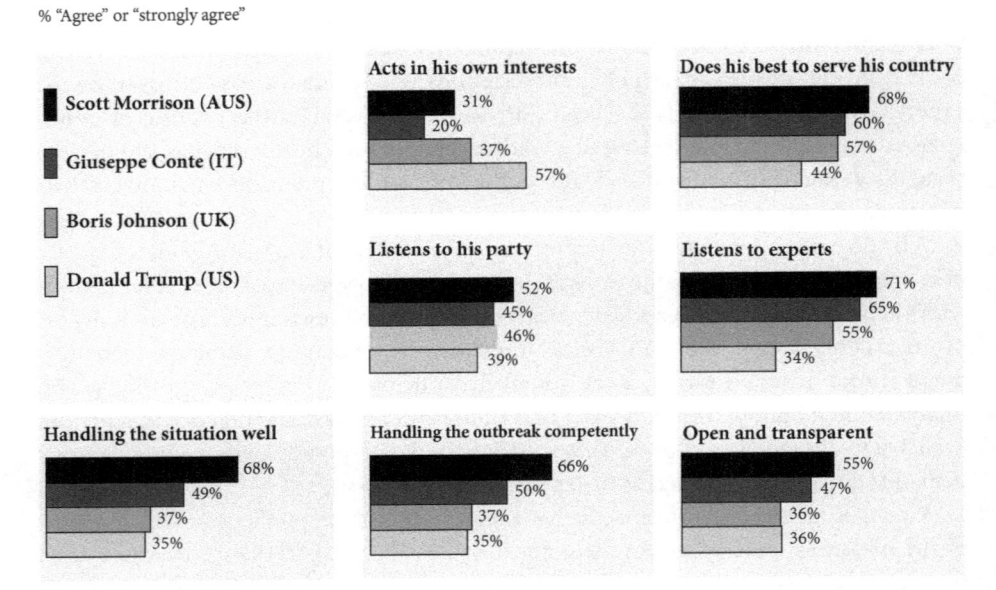

% "Agree" or "strongly agree"

- Scott Morrison (AUS)
- Giuseppe Conte (IT)
- Boris Johnson (UK)
- Donald Trump (US)

Acts in his own interests
- 31%
- 20%
- 37%
- 57%

Does his best to serve his country
- 68%
- 60%
- 57%
- 44%

Listens to his party
- 52%
- 45%
- 46%
- 39%

Listens to experts
- 71%
- 65%
- 55%
- 34%

Handling the situation well
- 68%
- 49%
- 37%
- 35%

Handling the outbreak competently
- 66%
- 50%
- 37%
- 35%

Open and transparent
- 55%
- 47%
- 36%
- 36%

Base: 1,134 adults in Italy 21-22 may 2020, 1,061 adults in Australia 28 May –15 June 2020, 1,167 adults in the UK 18-19 May 2020, 1,150 adults in the USA 19-23 May 2020

Figure 12.2 Perceptions of political leadership during the Covid-19 crisis.

Source: adapted from Will Jennings, Viktor Valgardsson, Gerry Stoker, Dan Devine, Jenn Gaskell and Mark Evans,: *Political Trust and the COVID-19 Crisis – pushing populism to the backburner? A study of public opinion in Australia, Italy, the UK and the USA* (Canberra; Democracy 25/IGPA/MoAD/Trustgov, 2020).

the early stages of the response with shifting advice about the wearing of face masks to the later stages over the effectiveness of different vaccines for different age groups. There were even greater and sustained differences between experts that pushed a version of herd immunity arguing for allowing non-vulnerable groups to catch the virus and those that argued for lockdowns and strict social isolation because the virus was both contagious and adverse enough in its effects that healthcare systems would be overwhelmed if the spread of infection was not contained. The latter group, with the high-profile exception of Sweden, won that argument in most countries. There were other differences over the way that Covid-19 contact tracing should operate and over international border closures and quarantine rules. Differences among experts ran alongside a sustained desire to take on board expert advice from both political leaders and citizens.[36]

It is interesting more generally to understand the particular appeal to legitimacy by experts.[37] It is different to that of political leaders that claim that their election and prospective accountability in future elections give them legitimacy by making them responsive to public opinion. For experts, their legitimacy is built on their unique knowledge and their claims that the application of that knowledge brings beneficial results. Experts ask people to support them because they have the competence to solve social and economic problems. In contrast to elected leaders, experts argue that they are not beholden to special interests, they are neutral and they hold themselves responsible by providing their advice for the benefit of all. Experts make a set of powerful claims to citizens: unique knowledge, selfless behaviour and a capacity to produce solutions that work for the benefit of all. These claims, if they are to be believed, provide the basis for the support that citizens afford expert advice.

There is a degree of inbuilt animosity to both bureaucracy and experts among the advocates of democratic innovation. Not without good reason since both can be a barrier to public engagement. A challenge for future democratic reform is to combine competing legitimacy claims from citizen engagement, elected representatives and experts and technocrats. Citizens can accommodate the legitimacy claims of all three groups. A detailed empirical study of nine European countries by Eri E. Bertsou and Daniele Caramani shows a solid block of 13 per cent of people who offer a strong commitment to decision-making by technocrats, with only marginally higher percentages displaying a strong commitment to government through popular participation (16 per cent) or party representatives (17 per cent).[38] The argument made here is not to support technocratic government but to emphasize that for many citizens it is the mix that matters.

The greater prominence given to expertise in the context of crisis brings to the fore wider questions for democracy. Democracies must improve the space for experts in politics because their expertise is needed to enlighten decision-making, but its impact needs to be cautiously managed. This challenge is so important that we have devoted much of three chapters to it.[39] Experts can of course be wrong; they can offer technocratic solutions that hide value judgements or provide a useful shield for elected leaders trying to avoid blame or responsibility for unpopular decisions. But they also bring something to democracy that is unique and needed in a complex and challenging world. They can illuminate and expand our understanding of issues and they can also help to find solutions that work in response to intractable and threatening problems. Our societies work through a range of specialist knowledge networks, and the experience of a crisis that cries out for an informed and evidenced-based response suggests that in the wider operation of democracy, we need to find further space for expertise to perform its crucial work.

Evaluating the quality of democracy during crisis

How are we best evaluating the quality of democracy during and after crisis? A set of criteria are presented in Box 12.1. Covid-19 has brought into sharp focus how much different national cultures value human life, particularly vulnerable and elderly citizens. In a democratic society this should be a matter of social equality and nothing else. It is therefore imperative that emergency and recovery budgets reflect the priorities and needs of hardest-hit communities, communicating with the public effectively throughout the crisis and equipping legislative actors and civil society organizations with tools to hold the government accountable in the delivery of relief and recovery funds.

Saving Democracy

We have already observed how important it is for governments to retain high levels of public trust in times of crisis management. Public trust is also critically important for pandemic recovery. Without it, the confidence necessary to build an effective and sustained recovery is in peril. Citizens and public and private institutions need to trust the government to support more government intervention that makes a difference. For those democracies that have lost the trust of their citizens what can be done to reverse the trend? The Organisation for Economic Cooperation and Development (OECD) has provided some timely guidelines that suggest the need for greater community engagement.[40] This can be achieved by the government taking the following steps: proactively releasing timely information on vaccination strategies, forms of delivery and accomplishments in a user-friendly format, providing transparent and coherent public communication to address misinformation and what is known as the 'infodemic' and engaging the public when developing vaccination strategies.

But the public also needs to have its say. At the start of the pandemic, co-designing strategies with citizens was a low priority. But in the later stages of crisis management when behavioural change – in the current context, to facilitate vaccine take-up – became critical to containing the virus, you ignore the views of citizens at your peril. Moreover, in the recovery stage when it is time to reflect on the government response, take accountability for missteps and draw lessons for the future, citizen engagement becomes even more important. As inquiries are eventually launched to explore what went right and what went wrong with the coronavirus response, the public must be a central voice in the discussion. As we have seen in Chapter 5 there are models for how to do this such as the citizen's assemblies that have been formed in France and the UK to push for greater action on climate change in the post-Covid global recovery.

There is no way of knowing if Covid-19 could have been managed more successfully if there had been more public participation and debate from the start, given the whirlwind of uncertainty and the need for rapid decisions to tackle a crisis. However, important nationwide discussions now need to be had on how best to limit the creep of executive power, how to better facilitate public debate in a period of high anxiety and how to get the best out of the experts. We have also witnessed examples of democratic backsliding during Covid-19 which will need to be identified and addressed such as the suspension of elections in particular countries, the erosion of civil liberties due to the withdrawal of certain individual rights during lockdown and increased state surveillance through the use of smartphone location tracking, and social media monitoring. Most significantly, the power and prestige of parliaments around the globe have largely taken a backseat to the executive in times of crisis management and will need to reassert themselves in the recovery process.

What is certain is that democratic elections around the world will be won or lost on which party or parties are best able to forge a national consensus on a post-Covid-19 recovery plan. This is not a mere matter of economics but about what type of society we want to live in, the values that should drive it and the form of democracy which will best protect us in a turbulent and uncertain world.

In conclusion – 'Never waste a good crisis!'

'Never waste a good crisis' is a saying that is sometimes (incorrectly) attributed to Winston Churchill but indicates that a crisis can expose learning opportunities as well as impose constraints. It is in that spirit we approach this chapter: how can democracies improve their response to crisis? No political system is likely to be perfectly designed for dealing with a crisis, but democracies are more resilient than some critics suggest.[41] Yet they need to do more to adapt their practices to cope with what unfortunately is likely to be a common and repeated. Yet they need to do more to adapt their practices to cope with what unfortunately is likely to be a common and repeated experience of the twenty-first century: the impact of unexpected, threatening and troublesome events.

We need to prepare democracy for the reality of a regular experience of crisis. There are clearly coping mechanisms that work to some degree. Governments do lean on

Box 12.1 Criteria for evaluating democratic performance during and after crisis

1. The highest value should be placed on all human life reflected in the equitable distribution of public resources for stabilization and recovery.
2. High levels of public trust should be maintained throughout the crisis.
3. A participatory governance system should be established for both crisis management and recovery.
4. In the light of Covid-19, public managers should design appropriate participatory governance systems in their sphere of operations with citizens and stakeholders and relevant elected officials that link to different decision points in the policy process. These include strategic direction (reassessment of the evidence-base and co-production of appropriate outcomes), service design and the monitoring of service delivery and learning (deliberation, distillation and diffusion of better practice).
5. Recovery efforts should be deliberative, carefully considering the interests of all relevant actors and social groups.
6. The impact of Covid-19 on democratic institutions and processes should be carefully reviewed by an independent body and areas of backsliding identified and addressed.
7. All citizens should have full and equal access to government and the services and goods to which they are entitled, and their rights should be protected in decision-making, and 'due process' rules followed in adjudicating their cases.
8. Wherever 'para-state' organizations (NGOs or private contractors) deliver services, public value standards (action within the law, equal treatment and access, respect for human rights and freedom from corruption) should continue to apply.
9. Public services, contracting and regulation should be free from corruption, with swift action taken against evidence of possible offences.

leadership and executive decision-making more than in 'normal times' but the more representative and reflective branches of government can come into their own when it comes to learning lessons. The anxiety created by a crisis may lead citizens to place rather too much trust in leaders and rally to their support, becoming less critical. Yet the evidence is that support is never unconditional and is contingent on the leader acting effectively. Experts may become more prominent in decision-making in a crisis as their specialist knowledge is seen as the key to unlocking understanding and solutions but again there are checks and balances at play. In reflections on the Covid-19 crisis it will be essential to reflect on how to make sure that the principles and practices of democracy do not get lost as well as drawing more specific lessons about whether actions were taken in a timely, appropriate and effective manner. The issue for democracies is not just what worked in terms of beating the virus during one of the greatest crises of the twenty-first century but also what maintained the values of democracy and the adaptive practices that made a difference.

CHAPTER 13
FUTURE PROOFING DEMOCRACY

A common charge levelled against democracies is that the principles of justice informing their decisions are not chosen in John Rawls's terms 'behind a veil of ignorance' but prioritize the present over the future and are both partial and irrational. For some environmentalists, democracies are also seen as at fault for failing to deal with issues such as environmental change and global warming that require long-term policy-making. James Lovelock spoke for many when he argued:

Even the best democracies agree that when a major war approaches, democracy must be put on hold for the time being. I have a feeling that climate change may be an issue as severe as a war. It may be necessary to put democracy on hold for a while.[1]

Iñigo González-Ricoy and Axel Gosseries add to the list of areas of failure in long-term policy-making:

An excessive focus on the short term is especially problematic in policy domains with an extended timeframe, such as environmental sustainability, investment in blue-sky research, pension system reform, population control, or nuclear waste management. Since these are domains that typically require costly action in the short term (e.g. increasing taxes, cutting benefits, imposing regulatory burdens) with benefits only arriving in the long run, democratic institutions are too often tempted to pass such costs on to the next generations, thus failing to adopt the required policies.[2]

Democracies as political systems struggle to deliver long-term policy goals 'that require governments to arrange losses and gains in a particular temporal order: to impose social costs long before most benefits will arrive'.[3]

Beyond a practical concern that democracies may be neglecting vital issues that require long-term action is the idea that democracies are inherently and irredeemably victims of 'presentism', and as such normatively fail to match their concern with citizens in the here-and-now with a concern for citizens in the future. They are failing in the terms of public philosopher, Roman Krznaric, to act as 'good ancestors'. His deep moral concerns about neglecting our responsibilities for the future are expressed in a powerful way:

When Britain colonised Australia in the eighteenth and nineteenth centuries, it drew on a legal doctrine now known as terra nullius – 'nobody's land' – to justify

> its conquest and treatment of the indigenous population as if they didn't exist or have any claims on the land. Today our societal attitude is one of tempus nullius. The future is seen as 'nobody's time,' an unclaimed territory that is similarly devoid of inhabitants. Like the distant realms of empire, it is ours for the taking. Just as Indigenous Australians still struggle against the legacy of terra nullius, so too there is a struggle to be had against the doctrine of tempus nullius.[4]

The practical concerns about how to avoid an impending climate crisis when mixed with the moral imperative to act to save future populations encourage many to argue that the only way forward is to take decisions out of the control of democratic politics. The future demands less democracy. In contrast, this chapter argues that it is possible to future proof democracy and the future demands better democracy not less. We start by challenging the idea that democracies are inherently and irredeemably victims of 'presentism', always short term, driven by the demands of voters and the desire for politicians to get themselves re-elected by showing quick results.[5] Democracies in the last decades have performed better in focusing on inter-generational concerns than autocratic systems. Many of those who claim that democracies simply cannot do long-term policy-making build their case on over-exaggerated claims about the tendency of both citizens and politicians to always discount the future. There is no denying that pressures towards short-termism exist but there are balancing forces that also need to be considered.

Our argument is that there is hope and a prospect for reform of democracies. To tackle short-termism requires a better understanding of its causes. These concerns occupy the second section of the chapter. The causes of democratic myopia are complex as solutions are not easy to find and face several significant hurdles. But the path to reform is already being trodden, and the third section of the chapter outlines some of these reform practices and makes a general argument for those that encourage a different dynamic to democratic politics rather than seeking to limit its decision-making scope and influence. We need to tip the balance in democratic practice towards better regard for the future but in a way that allows for political disagreement and conflict. Whether you are eighteen or eighty years of age you have the same responsibility to act as a 'good ancestor' but how to act on that responsibility could be a legitimate matter of disagreement and should be the focus of democratic debate and political challenge.

Are democracies inherently myopic?

There are good reasons to argue that democracies need to learn to better balance short-term and long-term concerns, but it does not follow that democracies are inherently and irredeemably myopic in outlook. Too many of the arguments that democracies are short-termist operate with an overly simplistic model of democracy and the motivations of its actors. One of the most famous examples is offered in the work of William Nordhaus but is based on a stylized model of a representative democracy, a one-dimensional rational choice model which views politicians and voters as driven by self-interested calculation.

Voters will judge parties on their performance in delivering for them in the short run and incumbent politicians are therefore under irresistible pressure to deliver short-term gains or risk being voted out of office. As a result, democracies 'will make decisions biased against future generations'.[6] In terms of public spending a predictable pattern is 'policy, starting with relative austerity in early years and ending with the potlatch right before the elections'.[7]

The Nordhaus model has received serious attention and multiple developments but it is based on a 'rationality trap' where, given assumptions that actors have full information and act in a self-interested manner, there appears no way out of the social dilemma identified. They will be short term in their actions. To break from its grip is not too hard. All that needs to be done is recognize that democracy and people's motivations are more complicated than the model allows. Democracy is not just about individual citizens and politicians. It involves organized interests who may be willing to think and act long term in the right circumstances. Democracy is also a form of government that involves multiple agencies and actors who have roles that are tied into thinking long term. At one end of the spectrum there are future forecasting and planning units and at the other end, public institutions would not be recognizable without their three- or five- or ten-year plans or units that look forward to various potential scenarios over a longer-term time horizon, often decades ahead. As part of the regular business of government, issues are dealt with over different time horizons from policies aimed at fiscal sustainability or responsibility to those that are considered over a few years (e.g. tax benefits) or decades (e.g. pensions), to nuclear waste management policies, which may extend to several centuries.

Citizens themselves also have motivations that stretch beyond simple self-interest. People do think about collective concerns and also along moral or normative lines. Moreover, their reasoning is rarely fixed. As Michael McKenzie observes:

> *If individuals (or groups) have moderate but adjustable preferences for the near term, as opposed to strong and inflexible ones, some of the causes of short-termism in our political systems may be (more or less effectively) addressed through institutional design.*[8]

We are not denying the pressures to default to short-termism but suggest that they can be (and to a degree already are) countered. As Roman Krznaric comments:

> *... the capacity to think and plan over long timespans is wired into our brains and has enabled monumental feats such as the construction of London's sewers after the Great Stink of 1858, the public investment of Roosevelt's New Deal, and the dedicated struggles of anti-slavery campaigners and advocates for women's rights.*[9]

Politics in democracies is strewn with examples of how long-term thinking and action have made a difference with governments, civil servants and activists all contributing to the achievements of actions that may have involved some short-term sacrifice but delivered long-term benefits.

Saving Democracy

Beyond these sighting shots, it is vital to recognize that if autocratic government is the alternative to democracy then there is strong evidence to indicate it is not the panacea when it comes to addressing inter-generational justice. Putting democracy 'on hold' to tackle climate change, as James Lovelock proposes, does not guarantee success. Comparing nations and their political systems is an exercise fraught with difficulties. But one sophisticated attempt to do so is provided by Roman Krznaric in collaboration with Jamie McQuilkin. They develop an Intergenerational Solidarity Index (ISI) – a composite set of indicators of long-term policy practice in the environmental, social and economic realms. The results are startling:

> ... out of the countries with the 25 highest scores on the ISI, 21 of them – 84 per cent – are democracies. Out of the countries with the 25 lowest scores on the ISI, 21 are autocracies. Out of all 60 democracies, 77 per cent are long-term democracies, while out of all 62 autocracies, only 39 per cent are long-term autocracies. The average intergenerational solidarity score for democracies is 59 while the average for autocracies is just 42.[10]

The measures and methods used could be challenged but they are more sophisticated than cherry-picking examples of nations that do something long term such as China, Russia or even Singapore and using them as abstracted empirical cases to support eco-authoritarianism. Our starting assumption should be that 'autocracies tend towards short-termism, while democracies tend towards long-termism'.[11] The challenge then is to give greater institutional support to long-term thinking within democracies.

The drivers of short-termism in democracies

Democracies still have many factors that push them towards the short term, despite their capacity for long-term thinking and action. To address these pressures, it is important to understand the complexity of the dynamics involved. Expressed in an abstract manner there are at least three ways that people might prioritize the present over the future.[12] Firstly, people are not naturally inclined to defer their gratification and will often want benefits sooner rather than later. Our brains are to a degree hardwired to seek pleasure and if possible, avoid immediate pain. Both citizens and politicians often operate in this way and reactive practices are reflected in the very framework of democracy. After all 'democratic government is supposed to be responsive. To the extent that it transfers these psychological tendencies to the political process, it produces laws and policies that reflect this bias toward the present.'[13] While at the outset of this chapter, we questioned whether all motivation always follows this path, there seems little doubt that this might be a factor in the tendency towards short-termism.

A second driver of short-termism is that people choose the short term because they are far from certain that benefits will be delivered in the long term. Alan Jacobs and J. Scott Matthews used an experimental design to test responses among citizens to a range of long-term policy options and found that it is not so much impatience or a desire for immediate benefits that led to doubts about taking those options.[14] It was rather that citizens did not trust government and doubted its ability to deliver in the future, even if its commitment was genuine. Long-termism demands, then, what the political culture in many established democracies appears to conspicuously lack – public trust and faith in government to its promises and the competence to deal with the complexities of delivery for long-term policy-making. But as we shall see later in the chapter there are ways in which trust can be built and sustained. Governments may fail to do so but making a credible commitment to its achievement should be possible.

A final driver of short-termism is that citizens tend to discount the moral importance of future people because they lack a connection with them. Do I feed my family now or worry about generations to be born in fifty years? Or as Groucho Marx put it rather more sarcastically: 'what have future generations ever done for us?'[15] The concept of inter-territorial justice is perhaps easier to justify in the abstract than in the here and now. But some activists are rather good at promoting the idea. In December 2018, Greta Thunberg spoke to the United Nations Climate Change COP24 Conference in Katowice, Poland and argued:

The year 2078 I will celebrate my seventy-fifth birthday. If I have children, then maybe they will spend that day with me. Maybe they will ask about you. Maybe they will ask why you didn't do anything, while there was still time to act. You say you love your children above all else, and yet you are stealing their future in front of their very eyes.[16]

The idea of stewardship or being a 'good ancestor' is regularly repeated in human history. The absence of a moral connection to the future may drive short-termism but it is a connection that is not always absent.

The causes of short-termism which we have identified so far are mixed which in turn suggests that the solutions are also likely to be mixed. There is not a single change that will deliver greater long-term policy-making but rather several interventions. All the drivers of short-termism are in different ways built into, indeed, integral to democratic systems. If the focus is on immediate gratification that in part reflects that there are intense pressures in democracies to deliver. That is one of its strengths, but it does push the system towards short-termism. If the focus is on trusting governments to deliver in the long term there are sound reasons why citizens will be sceptical of the capacity of governments of the future to keep their promises. Scepticism about those who hold power is a classic justification and argument for democracy. Democracy exists because powerholders cannot be assumed to be trustworthy and not because they are trustworthy. Moreover, the moral commitment to the future may find itself challenged by other moral demands present in most democracies to tackle inequalities, create meaningful employment and work for citizens or invest in their education or health. The solutions that will work are about making sure that pressures for the future find matching institutional expression in the pressures for the present that are a defining feature of democracy. These include, for example, the electoral cycle, where politicians (if they want to get re-elected) must consider how best to represent themselves to voters.

Democracies require regular and competitive elections which tend to generate demands to deliver sooner rather than later. Special interest groups play a major part in all democracies as they are consulted about policies in their areas of interest. And at times those groups 'with considerable (or undue) political influence can use their influence to win concessions that distribute long-term costs to others and confer benefits on themselves'.[17] A powerful economic actor through directly funding a political party or an election campaign or through indirectly threatening to withdraw their job and wealth creating investment can push politics down the route of short-termism, and so lead to, for example, activities that could accelerate the threat of climate change. As they often have better organized lobby groups and supporters that are more willing to turn out and vote, the priorities of older generations regularly triumph over the needs of younger or unborn generations in democracies.

Finally, there is the complex issue of how democracies can hear from people who do not yet exist. Future generations cannot be present. Young people are often advanced as a surrogate voice for the future;[18] others advocate the idea of people or organized groups with a special care for the future, such as committed environmentalists,[19] speaking for future generations. But neither option is entirely convincing or likely to be viewed as always legitimate within democratic practice. After all what is being made is a claim to represent and that claim can be challenged. But legitimate political decisions typically require authorization and/or accountability by those very people whose interests are potentially affected and that fundamental democratic argument provides both a case for engaging citizens of the present and citizens of the future. A confounding issue is the assumption that future citizens will all hold the same views because they all share the same interests. But this is an unwarranted view, as Graham Smith has argued, because differences in 'social and economic power are expressed within and between future generations and any policy choice will have distributional impacts across each generation' and a result it cannot be assumed 'that future generations speak with one voice; rather it will involve balancing the variety of interests within and across future (and current) generations. Normative judgements are to be made'.[20] In addition, there are challenging issues over whether the future can be accurately predicted. A sour law of human prediction is that it is often wrong. A famous study by Philip Tetlock claims to show that the predictions of experts, especially famous ones, were no better than those made by random chance and although in later work he recognized the emergence of super-forecasters, their success in prediction was usually achieved over a time frame of less than a year.[21]

A strategy and practice of reform

Reforms that claim to future proof democracy have come to the fore in the last decade or so. A list is provided by Michael MacKenzie which does its utmost to capture the range and variety of options that are on offer.[22] His list provides the basis of the contents of Box 13.1. We support his list of reforms because they range in a broad sense over the input, throughput and output elements of a democratic system that aligns with the organizing principle of this book. We are not quite so positive about all the reforms he proposes, but do agree that combinations of these reforms could play a major role in shifting the balance in democracies towards long-term policy-making. The starting point is reforms aimed at making representative politics more forward-looking. We are maybe a little more sceptical than him about the prospects of success or even the legitimacy of the reforms proposed but we are sympathetic to the general principle of tweaking representative institutions to ensure that they take their responsibilities for the future more seriously. Some of the reforms, implemented in the right circumstances, have shown evidence of achievement.

The second reform driver is about different ways of allowing citizens to participate and express their commitment to long-term policy. MacKenzie is not alone in thinking that citizens given the appropriate opportunity can drive forward long-term policy-making. Graham Smith argues that deliberative mini-publics or citizens' assemblies (as they were described in Chapter 5) composed of randomly selected citizens who sift through evidence, reflect, deliberate and then come to a judgement 'outperform more traditional democratic institutions in orientating participants to consider long-term implications, often in areas where preferences are not well formed'.[23]

Random selection creates a diverse group of citizens especially if the group is selected using quota sampling so that the chosen citizens reflect the social and cognitive diversity of the population and as such are better placed to speak to a range of future interests and concerns. Moreover, because these citizens are randomly selected, they are less likely to be captured in their decision-making by powerful interests keen to defend their interests in the short run. Deliberation provides additional drivers towards long-termism because citizens in the mini-public can be made aware of intergenerational issues and spend time thinking about what their duty to the future is and what this could mean in terms of decision-making.

Finally, deliberation promotes 'slow thinking' in its participants unlike the more intuitive 'fast thinking' that tends to dominate when asked for a quick response to a survey question, for example.[24] 'Slow thinking' gives space for humans to show, as noted earlier in the chapter, their hardwired capacity to think and plan over long time horizons. This works best when positions are not too strongly formed and reflective of an established partisan divide before citizens start to deliberate. If positions are more fixed and antagonistic within the group then it may be that some participants will already be captured by powerful lobbies or unwilling to change their mind or listen to evidence that contradicts their previous positions.

The next set of reforms are about shifting governance practices. We would add to the suggestions from Michael MacKenzie that there is an argument for devolving power as a potential driver of long-term policy-making within democracies. Here we are siding again with Roman Krznaric who calls for 'a radical devolution of power away from nation-states'.[25] His argument is that big corporate interests and other vested interests are better at capturing national politics and that local politics is more open, sometimes,

Saving Democracy

Table 13.1 Reforms to improve long-term policy-making within democracies

Reform type and form	Key features	Likely impact
Representation		
Youth quotas	Reserved seats for young citizens to help them speak for future generations	Could be positive but young elected representatives may face pressures to deliver for the short-term and may focus on needs of the young rather than future generations
Representatives of the future	Elected positions for those who can speak for future generations	Selecting who can take on that role in a way seen as legitimate by most voters makes this proposal problematic
Longer electoral terms	Avoiding too frequent elections to encourage longer-term policy-making (some suggest terms of 15 years)	Could have positive effects but cannot address all the drivers of short-termism in politics and may well be regarded as too undermining of public accountability by most voters
Second chamber	Given role in scrutinizing legislation to protect future generations	Potentially valuable but if greater powers reside in first chamber short-term considerations may still dominate
Citizen participation		
Referendums	Public vote on issue set by government that 'binds' a way forward for the future	Some referendum defined as 'once in a generation opportunity' to set direction but changes in political context always mean that the vote can be revisited
Citizens initiatives	Public vote on issue framed by citizens' campaign for similar purpose	Again, can be agenda defining for the future but inevitably subject to being overthrown in the future
Citizens' assemblies	Evidence-driven and reflective judgement on issue of long-term policy by randomly elected citizens	Can show the capacity of citizens for engaging in long-term policy-making but may lack legitimacy
Governance procedures		
Devolve power	Letting regional and city government take more power and decisions given their tendency to think more long-term	The local level can allow for the building of long-term policies and long-term coalitions of support

Reform type and form	Key features	Likely impact
Sub-majority rules	Allows a minority (a third) in an elected assembly to block legislation until the next election	A proposal so open to abuse in conflict driven politics that it makes for a virtual non-starter
Posterity impact statements	Requiring legislation to demonstrate future positive influence	A useful challenge in defining policy but may collapse into a ritual tick box exercise
Administrative procedures		
Ombudsman for Future Generations	Independent body to advocate for the future	A powerful advocate limited by lack of power and legitimacy
Intergenerational trusts	Offers legally protected public money from being spent in current accounts and reserves them for decisions by future generations	Future generations may still make short-term decisions about how to spend the money reserved
Constitutional and legal		
Balanced budget clauses	Stops the practice of spending now and getting other generations to pay later	May be difficult to enforce as spending and taxation decisions move forward but also may be undesirable as long-term borrowing may be appropriate to meet some pressing spending needs in tune with the economic cycle or the demands of crises
General protections for future generations	Clauses put in constitution to insist that needs of future generations are considered in decision-making	May depend on how the clauses are interpreted by courts and standing of the courts compared to other political sources of power. May also be difficult to enforce
Environmental clauses	Clauses to protest the future environment	Will face similar constraints as general protection clauses

to a wider range of interests. Of course, it can be recognized as a counterargument that special interests can capture local or regional government and that local democracy is far from immune to corruption. We would argue that devolved government may have a particular role in promoting long-termism for the reason that it is an expression of dispersed but often relatively stable representative politics (because electoral competition is often more limited given the concentration of preferences and interests in different populations). Long-term policies and long-term coalitions of support especially around issues of economic development have been a feature of local politics for some time.

Local leaders can use a variety of strategies for reaching out to citizens and can appeal to local identity and community as a basis for a 'leap of faith' to trust commitments made about future benefits for potentially short-term costs. One advantage in this respect is that in most mature democracies devolved government tends to be seen by citizens as more trustworthy than central government.[26] Roman Krznaric's research based on the Intergenerational Solidarity Index shows that 'the more decentralised a government is in its decision-making, the better it performs in terms of long-term public policy'.[27] Hence a highly federalized country such as Switzerland scores well.

The next set of reforms in Box 13.1 are captured under the heading of 'administrative changes'. These provide some of the most thought-provoking and powerful examples of reforms. The idea of an Ombudsman for the Future has become a practice in several polities, including Hungary, Israel and Wales. These are independent bodies tasked with protecting the interests of future citizens using public argument and in some instances powers to delay actions by other government agencies if they fail to account for the future impact of their decision-making. They have had a mixed history with the Israeli office being abolished after one parliamentary term and the powers and status of the Hungarian body diminished. But they nevertheless offer an option for pushing democracies closer to including long-term thinking in their decision-making.

The independence of these ombudsman institutions is an asset in that they can be free from immediate political pressures and able to act without worrying too much about what their coalitions or supporters might think of their judgements. But there are difficulties and limits to how they can operate in the context of the wider cut and thrust of democratic politics. These institutions may claim to speak for the future, but that claim can be disputed not least as different interests may exist in the future as much as they do now. They may also lack legitimacy when engaged in a row with elected politicians or popular movements of citizens. Who are they to overrule the will of the people? Finally, they are vulnerable to changes in government and vacillations in political elite opinion particularly at times of broader political change in the aftermath of disruptive global events.

Here Graham Smith comes up with a suggestion that fits with our idea that sometimes the best reforms combine different elements of reform. In this case the independent body seeks to actively bolster its standing by engaging in extensive and deliberative public participation to both guide its decisions and give them greater legitimacy. He concludes that 'while public participation cannot fully overcome the challenges to legitimacy experienced' by these institutions for the future, 'it can potentially ameliorate these vulnerabilities in two related ways. First participation can enable more inclusive judgements about the interests of future generations. Second, participation can enhance the political standing of these institutions'.[28]

The idea of reserving funds for future generations to spend also provides a potentially powerful mechanism for future proofing democracy. The most prominent example of such an institution is the Government Pension Fund of Norway which comprises two investment funds owned by the Government of Norway.[29] The larger fund engages in global investment funded by the surplus revenues of the Norwegian production of oil and gas. It is the world's largest investment fund with over $1 trillion (in US dollars) in assets and is worth about US $200,000 for each Norwegian citizen. The smaller fund is limited to the narrower function of national insurance, underwriting pensions funding through investments in Scandinavian companies and property. As Michael MacKenzie explains, intergenerational trust funds fulfil at least three functions: (1) they save for the future a share of whatever wealth is created within current generations; (2) they therefore prevent funds being used solely for short-term objectives; and (3) they can reserve funds for investments that might match the immediate preferences of citizens but might be their choice in the future. In short, they can address 'three potential sources of short-termism: the absence of future generations, the political dynamics of short electoral cycles, and the immediate preferences of voters'.[30]

The final set of reforms come under the heading of 'constitutional and legal clauses'. There are considerable attractions in the idea that it might be possible to build into the political system constraints and rules that favour the future. They could provide a decision-making framework and be designed in such a way as to protect the future against the pressures of the present. As Roman Krznaric argues:

> *Law matters not just because it is a way to ring-fence the interests of futureholders and protect them from the short-termism of incumbent politicians, but because it acts as a reference point against which future generations commissioners and citizen assemblies can judge governments and hold them to account.*[31]

But even though there are a number of efforts and ideas on offer to capture the interests of future generations the biggest issue that he notes is the problem of making enforcement real. After all it proves hard enough to enforce the rights of those who are living so it might prove more difficult still to enforce the rights of future generations. There are difficulties of trying to change the world through words in legal and constitutional statements as they can be interpreted in different ways and pushed in different directions or even ignored by powerful interests.

Evaluation – embedding long-term thinking in government

What would a governmental system that mainstreams long-term thinking into its work plan with the aim of future proofing democracy look like? Here we draw upon the thoughts of Barry Quirk in his provocative book *Re-imagining Government – public leadership and management in challenging times*.[32] The book examines how democratic political systems work and how public decisions are made – and how they could be made better. Quirk argues that 'real solutions to public problems may be best found among the people who share the problem rather than from those working for government'. In search of public value, the most effective public leaders are those that establish the goals to be achieved, put managerial accountabilities in place; marshal the resources available to them, select the right operating strategies and 'attempt to inspire and motivate people to do their best'.[33] For Quirk, 'good governments centre their concerns on improving the life and capabilities of their citizens' but to achieve this they need to re-imagine

Saving Democracy

'how collective challenges are best addressed', 'how public interest questions are defined and determined' and how they can create common cause with their citizens.[34] As noted in Chapter 11, good governments and effective public managers understand that their purpose is driven by legitimacy concerns and that there is a democratic requirement for them to engage in public reason, deliberate publicly with citizens, explain their actions and set a course for the long term. The very act of making legitimate decisions in the public interest inevitably casts public managers as stewards of the long term. Of course, what is and what is not the public interest is contested and public servants do not have the sole right to determine what it is. Sometimes it may be laid down in legislation by the elected government of the day and it will be the duty of public servants to follow. However, the pathology of short-term imperative that bedevils elected governments places public servants in a unique position to say focused on the long term. Elected politicians come and go but public servants are permanent governors of the continuous realm of government.

Box 13.1 presents criteria for judging whether governments have embedded long-term thinking in government to future proof democracy, many of which we have already

Box 13.1 Criteria for evaluating whether governments have achieved a long-term decision culture

1. Long-term environmental, social and economic outcomes have been co-created with citizens through the establishment of a participatory governance system and are updated on a cyclical basis. See Chapter 11.
2. Representatives for the future, universities, integrity agencies, communities of practice, public broadcasters and public services are effective stewards of long-term thinking in the public interest. See Chapters 7–11.
3. The budgetary system incentivizes long-term thinking through long-term funding compacts in areas of key concern. Annual budget measures require reflection on their contribution to improving long-term outcomes. See Chapter 11.
4. Evidence-based practice informed by long-term modelling is mainstreamed in all forms of decision-making. See Chapters 9 and 11.
5. In their policy and service areas, public managers have established intelligent performance indicators linked directly to politically mandated long-term outcomes with citizens and stakeholders. Monitoring systems have been designed to identify movements towards or away from achieving these outcomes.
6. Public managers co-design appropriate participatory governance systems in their domains of interest.
7. A broad range of deliberative mechanisms with citizens and stakeholders exist for embedding long-term thinking through representation, different methods of citizen participation, legislative and administrative requirements and forms of constitutional protection. See Box 13.1.

considered in this and other chapters. We believe that the stewardship role in defence of the public interest cannot be confined to public servants and needs to be extended to other public institutions such as universities, integrity agencies, communities of practice (particularly professional associations) and publicly funded media to ensure that long-term thinking is culturally embedded whole of government and society. Moreover, the appointment of representatives for the future in elected assemblies, outlined above, could also provide guardianship of the public interest to think long term.

Nor do we believe that this stewardship role gives public servants licence to depart from government policy and cease to serve the government of the day. Public servants have a crucial brokering role in future proofing democracy which begins with the co-creation of publicly valued outcomes updated on a cyclical basis in the light of new and compelling evidence and is inculcated in a value-based decision-making culture, incentivized in the budgetary process and protected by various guardians of the public interest.

In conclusion – governing for the long term

There is no compelling argument or evidence to support the idea that democracies cannot be future-proofed. The idea that is often mooted that only autocratic governments can plan and act in the interests of the future is not supported by the evidence. Equally there is no easy way to ensure that the balance of pressures in democracies is more tilted towards the future and away from the present. Yet in this chapter we have outlined a wide range of reform strategies and argue that a mix of them could make a difference.

Democracy is a messy practice, but it can be made a better practice. Future proofing democracy is an exercise in politics as much as morals. The response of citizens remains central to any politics of the long term. Citizens can, quite reasonably, have no strong views on some issues and are therefore willing to concede decision-making authority to others as long as decisions appear to be being made in the public interest or more particularly are not being usurped by self-interested politicians or organized interests. The hurdle, therefore, that advocates of the long term have to get over is not to win every argument or get all citizens to agree, it is to increase the capacity of democracy to protect the future by getting enough citizens to go along with supporting long-term commitments, even when there may be some short-term pain.

In our better democracy, many citizens will not spend large amounts of effort in reasoning about the short- or long-term consequences of policy and instead rely on cues or heuristics to judge their support or otherwise to what is going on. Some citizens may be particularly likely to mobilize against changes in policy that are likely to impose losses on them in the short run but mobilization is often only a reluctant choice.

Under these conditions it is easy to imagine that there are a myriad of opportunities for political leaders, campaigners and political movements to approach citizens to gain their agreement or acquiescence, at least, to long-term policies demanding short-term sacrifices. Studies suggest that there are many strategies open to advocates of change, for managing pain and making the case for long-term delivery rather than short-term satisfaction.[35] Adapting work on how governments go about avoiding blame and inflicting loss suggests that three broad categories of persuasion might work.

1. Procedures can be changed to lower the visibility of the policy and thus playing on the inattentiveness of citizens.
2. Perceptions can be influenced. Obfuscation of the damaging implications of long-term policy changes is an option and is quite common, for example, in taxation policy.
3. The final option open to political leaders seeking to justify short-term losses for long-term gains involves manipulating pay-offs – a long-standing tradition in policy analysis in which benefits are redistributed to offset losses.[36]

One option here is to try to share the pain as widely as possible. Another is to concentrate on citizens who for some reason or another will struggle to fight back. A further option is to compensate those who might be particularly prone to protest or exempt them from some of the worst effects of the long-term policy.

It is important to recognize, of course, that just as proponents of long-term policies can use some of the strategies identified so too can opponents, using variations of the tactics to undermine long-term policy options. They can work hard to increase the visibility of the policy. They can take on proponents for change in the battle of perceptions. They can extend the scope and range of citizens that notice they are adversely affected by the policy. Above all, they can expose the manipulations by supporters of long-term policy for what they are. Nonetheless, long-term policy can take its chances in the contest of ideas, power and politics.

But this chapter also offers reforms that increase the chances that the political battle goes in favour of recognizing the legitimate concerns of future citizens. A world where there are consistent advocates for the future in elected assemblies, where citizens are regularly tasked with deliberating and judging on the best long-term options, where devolved government seeks consensus about the right strategies for its area for decades to come, where independent bodies speak up strongly and public backing is provided for future interests and where legal and constitutional protections for our role as 'good ancestors' are present. These reforms would enhance the prospects for long-term policy-making considerably. Future proofing democracy to tip democratic politics towards taking inter-generational justice and climate change more seriously is an achievable and realistic goal.

CHAPTER 14
IN CONCLUSION – RESTORING AND STRENGTHENING THE 'PROTECTIVE POWER' OF DEMOCRACY

When assessing issues of continuity and change in democratic culture, one of our favourite books to look back at is Gabriel Almond and Sidney Verba's *The Civic Culture*.[1] It is considered a seminal work because it was the first systematic survey of attitudes to politics in five different countries, including the UK and the United States. The book was first published in 1963 but the survey work on which its analysis was drawn was undertaken in 1959. The authors broadly concluded that in different ways the UK and the United States were exemplars of effective democratic cultures. Indeed, one key finding was that the citizens of those countries prided themselves on their political institutions, many times more than the other three countries surveyed: Germany, Mexico and Italy. Without being directly prompted to say so, '8 in 10' American respondents expressed pride in their country's political arrangements and '5 in 10' UK respondents also expressed pride. The figures for the other countries were less positive – '1 in 10' for Germany and Italy and '3 in 10' for Mexico. Given the analysis presented at the beginning of this book of the malaise that has impacted many democracies, it is hard to imagine that pride in political arrangements would be exhibited by many citizens in the UK and the United States today. Pride in the way your political systems work might have improved from the low base identified for Germany, Italy and Mexico but it would not be wise to imagine the majority of citizens of those countries spontaneously think of their political institutions and actors as a source of pride.

There is concerning evidence, some of which we have covered in this book, of the disconnect between government and citizen reflected in low levels of public trust in our key political institutions, the polarization of politics and erosion of public confidence in the capacity of governments (of whatever colour) to address public policy concerns. But our goal was not to add to the research that tells us that democracy is in trouble. The gap between reality and how citizens imagine their democracy has widened to such a degree that we need to pause, listen and reflect on whether democracy can adapt to the new realities of twenty-first-century governance. The motivation for writing this book has been a recognition that democracy needs to find ways to renew itself.

We are convinced that it is worth 'saving' democracy. The 'protective power of democracy', as Amartya Sen calls it, has withered away as the political class has become more disconnected from the citizenry it serves.[2] This includes

... first, the intrinsic importance of political participation and freedom in human life; second, the instrumental importance of political incentives in keeping governments responsible and accountable; and third, the constructive role of democracy in the formation of values and in the understanding of needs, rights, and duties.[3]

The protective power of democracy remains clear in principle, the challenge is to deliver it more effectively in practice. Most of the problems of democracy that we have encountered in this book stem from the persistence of inequality of one form or another that the political class has conspicuously failed to counter. In contrast, effective democracy is shown to be most firmly embedded in creating empowering political and socio-economic conditions that make people both capable and willing to engage in democratic practice as critical citizens. For citizens that have less interest in participating, they should be able to rest assured that their representatives will perform that role responsibly and legitimately.

We remain confident in the adaptive capacity of liberal democracy and its citizens to renew our democratic settlements, restore and strengthen the 'protective' power of democracy. With this aim in mind, we have presented a programme of reform which has targeted those areas of democratic governance which are most conspicuous in their failure to deliver representative and responsive government: interventions at the input stage to enable critical citizenship, interventions at the throughput stage to improve the quality and integrity of politics and interventions at the output stage to improve the capacity of politics to deliver for everyday citizens. Table 14.1 presents the constituent elements of the programme which we have built cumulatively throughout the book in response to the democratic challenges outlined in Table 1.1.

There have been some inevitable sins of omission in the construction of this reform project. Constitutions, for example, have historically played an important role in preserving the political and civil rights of the powerful but have struggled to extend those rights to the powerless – new groups of citizens defined by race, ethnicity or sexuality. By implication, the protective power of democracy has hitherto been used to preserve the power of established elites. We argue, however, that constitutions even in countries with bills of rights remain notoriously difficult to change which is why they have not been a focus of our attention.[4] The key to changing the constitutional foundations of liberal democracies lies in changing the nature of democratic politics first, forcing through a new constitutional settlement and thereby extending the protective power of democracy to new groups of citizens, or old groups of citizens, as in the case of Indigenous Australians.

We hope that the reforms we suggest enhancing input, throughput and output legitimacy will help to restore the 'protective power of democracy' for marginalized groups. Although they will need to be adapted to meet the specific needs of particular groups with the recognition that historic or intergenerational sources of marginalization cannot be rectified overnight.[5] The current plight of Indigenous Australians, for example, provides a classic case of the culture of democratic complacency that bedevils the contented political class.[6] In this specific context, it would be up to Indigenous Australians to decide the best pathways to reform but the creation of a culturally

Table 14.1 Saving democracy

Inputs: responsiveness to citizen concerns and the framing of political demands to enable critical citizenship

Challenge	Reform
An unequal political community reflects and reproduces social inequality.	Build and embed 'fit for purpose' participatory governance systems that recognize the intrinsic democratic value of public participation, integrate representative and participatory instruments of democracy, match engagement methods to engagement purposes, build on respected institutions and reach out and empower disaffected citizens. See Table 3.1.
Better information and education about politics should be provided for all citizens through publicly funded adult education and be embedded in high school and first year university curriculum. This reform should include building the capacity of citizens to discern and refute fake news. Publicly funded universities should be mandated to provide independent, evidence-based fact-checking services in their areas of expertise. Integrity agencies should also play a fundamental role in enhancing the political literacy of the citizenry through active public engagement.
Lack of citizen voice and opportunity to engage effectively in politics.	Give citizens more say in (1) strategic decision-making, (2) policy design, (3) policy delivery and (4) policy learning at all levels of government through various direct, deliberative, user design and digital democratic methods. The criminal jury system should be used to populate public sector juries and panels. Ensure an appropriate balance of political, citizen, stakeholder and expert representation.
Enhance the role of local democracy through the implementation of the concept of subsidiarity – that central authority should have a subsidiary function and only perform those tasks that can't be performed at the local level – and legislate for the corresponding increase in local decision-making. See Figure 4.1.

Throughputs: enhancing the accountability, transparency and efficiency of decision-making processes

Challenge	Reform
Representative assemblies do their politics in ways that many citizens find alienating or pointless.	Reform parliamentary practices to make them more open and accessible to citizens and more consistent with modern working practices. For example, the availability of creches and gyms, flexible working patterns, parental paid leave, sociable procedural time, enabling voting and engagement from home through digital technology, and match breaks in political activities to school holidays. See Table 7.2. Make politics more transparent so that it is easier to follow. All publicly funded institutions, including assemblies, should list the decisions that they have taken in accessible language on their websites and identify whether those decisions are in keeping or depart from the existing evidence. Implement the recommendations of *The Good Parliament* (see pp. 83–86).
Improve the connection between people and parliament by initiating a range of opportunities for citizen engagement through upgrading linkage (outreach to seek the views of citizens), campaigning (encouraging e-Petitions to assemblies), scrutiny (committee work) and policy development roles (use of deliberative citizen assemblies and juries). See Tables 7.1 and 7.2.

Saving Democracy

Many groups do not see themselves represented in assemblies.	Make assemblies more representative of the diverse society it serves through ethnic, age and gender-based quotas in candidate recruitment. Lower the voting age to sixteen in line with the criminal justice systems in most democracies. Introduce Representatives of the Future, selected by sortition for each parliament to speak for future generations.
The public distrusts political parties and yet they remain pillars of mainstream democratic practice.	Loosen the power of political parties through the introduction of free votes in parliament and party democratization. Reduce constituency sizes to create single-member constituencies to encourage greater accountability of representatives to voters and better geographic representation. Finance the growth of new political parties. Place caps on political advertising and party donations.
The public distrust politicians partly due to bad behaviour in Parliament and partly due to lack of accountability to their constituencies.	All public office holders should be subject to the seven principles of public life enunciated by the Nolan Committee (see Box 8.1), closely monitored by a Parliamentary Integrity Committee with the purpose of ensuring effective implementation and monitoring of integrity reform. As consistent with modern working practices, politicians should be made accountable for their performance between elections through annual constituency reports (aligned with local election manifestos), and performance and integrity reviews. Integrity training, coaching and mentoring should be mandatory for all parliamentarians, but personal development plans should be co-designed with the target group to develop actionable training outcomes and ensure commitment. The power of recall should be available to electorates in the event of poor performance or parliamentary petition. These reforms would be given moral force through the creation of a parliamentary pledge that all parliamentarians should take on entering parliament to uphold the values of representative democracy.
The majority of democracies are showing 'little to no improvement' in tackling corruption.	Fostering integrity and preventing corruption in the public sector to support a level-playing field for businesses are essential to maintaining trust in government. The integrity of the lobbying system and the public sector consulting industry should be closely monitored using the OECD 'Principles for Transparency and Integrity in Lobbying'. Use behavioural insights to embed an integrity culture as suggested in Box 8.1 and Figure 8.2.
Decisions made with lack of evidence, forward thinking and public purpose cost legitimacy.	Introduce a *Foundations for Evidence-Based Policymaking Act* on the US model to embed an understanding of better evidence-based practice in policy formulation (see Box 9.3) but extend it to include provisions that all publicly funded new programme proposals or the recommissioning of programs should include an evidence health check. Use citizen assemblies and juries to consider long-term policy. To help future-proof democracy introduce General Protections for Future Generations, Posterity Impact Statements, Intergenerational Trusts, Environmental Clauses and an Ombudsman for Future Generations. The greater prominence given to expertise in the context of crisis brings to the fore wider questions for democracy. Democracies must improve the space for experts in politics because their expertise is needed to enlighten decision-making, but its impact needs to be cautiously managed. Integrate experts into the policy advisory system working alongside politicians, public servants, and (depending on the change opportunity, task or problem) stakeholders and citizens at different decision points in the policy process (policy development, new policy validation, evaluation and learning).

Cross-boundary and multilevel problems do not fit easily within the confines of democracies designed around nation states.	Ensure best practice collaborative governance with collaborative purpose, leadership and problem-solving to deliver publicly valued shared outcomes. See Figure 8.2.
Weak basis for shared political community due to polarization and 'truth decay'.	A delicate balance has to be struck between affording the media the freedoms it requires to perform its civil watchdog role and guaranteeing the public's right to know and ensuring that it performs its democratic role responsibly. On the supply side this will require less government 'spin' in political communication and the development of respectful working relationships between government and the media industry. On the demand side, this will require commitment to the democratic value of a free and responsible media, public interest journalism with professional ethical requirements of accuracy, fairness, truth-telling, impartiality and respect for persons. We would suggest that this was articulated in a public interest pledge and embedded in formal training and mentoring for new entrants to the profession.

The disturbing combination of toxic social media, news by algorithm, declining civic discourse and information being used as a weapon in a hyper partisan war of ideas have had serious implications for the quality of democratic practice. This requires legislating against the concentration of media ownership and the right to online anonymity (with exemptions for whistle-blowers and sharing and debating small 'l' liberal issues), funding public interest media through a renewed Fairness Doctrine, and building citizen capacity to address 'truth decay'. See reforms to civic education above. |

Outputs: the capacity of politics to deliver quality services and policy outcomes that are driven by agreed values and responsive to community needs

Challenge	Reform
Policy and interventions are failing at the design level without engagement from citizens and stakeholders.	The transformation of our public services is a key component of democratic renewal because it is the performance (supply) of government that matters most in orienting the outlooks of citizens, particularly in times of crisis, together with commitment to procedural fairness and equality. We termed this condition of trusted government, *performance legitimacy*, and argued that it was best achieved through the search for public value and the practices of public value management. This should involve a citizen-centred performance culture, co-design with target groups by default, digital-first service design for mainstream audiences, bespoke service design for vulnerable citizens, outcomes-driven public service production and the creation of participatory governance systems to identify and review progress on the achievement of publicly valued outcomes.

Making everyday bureaucracy better and delivering a service that is fair and respectful.	Improve government's standing by treating citizens in trust-earning ways demonstrating good performance, creating positive citizen experiences, institutionalizing citizen voice in public service production and communicating success stories.
Developing long-term governance capacity matters so that major issues such as climate change and other major crises can be addressed.	There is a strong argument for longer electoral terms and funding compacts for programmes aimed at addressing 'wicked problems'. The public service, as the continuous strand of governance, second chambers and regional and city governments (with important strategic roles in social and economic development) should have particular responsibilities for long-term stewardship. See Boxes 13.1 and 13.2. Introduce Representatives of the Future, selected by sortition for each parliament to speak for future generations.

appropriate participatory governance system to help map the way forward might be a good first step. Existing inequalities could be addressed through 'top-down' and 'bottom-up' empowerment strategies. The 'top-down' strategies – encompassing inputs, throughputs and outputs – could include constitutional recognition for the First Peoples of Australia, the replacement of the monarchy with an elected First Nations Head of State, and the establishment of a First Nations Parliament with a scrutiny and revising role to replace the widely recognized dysfunctional Senate with the role of safeguarding the rights of First Nations people and providing stewardship for the long term. The representation of First Nations people in the House of Representatives would need to be commensurable with the ability to protect their newly won constitutional authority.[7]

The 'bottom-up' strategies – also encompassing inputs, throughputs and outputs – could include the creation of participatory governance systems at every level of Australian governance to institutionalize First Nations citizen voice in the fabric of public policy decision-making and delivery including the principle of co-design by default. Drawing on best practice from international development, First Nations Community-driven Development Councils could be established in rural and regional Australia at the local level to drive 'strengths-based' social and economic development and education reform underpinned by world-class digital access and support.[8] This programme of reform would constitute a radical challenge to the established political order and would be resisted at every turn. But culturally embedded historic injustice requires a dramatic response.

We have also spent less time than we would have liked discussing how young citizens perceive and imagine democracy. Suffice to say that the reforms we suggest at the input stage to enable critical citizenship and extend the protective power of democracy are likely to benefit young citizens most.

Recognizing the complexity of the challenge

The framework we have used to steer the reform project via 'inputs, throughputs and outputs' is, we hope, a useful device for capturing our most important messages: reformers need to expand their horizons and not focus all their efforts on new ways to advance the quality and strength of inputs into the political system from citizens. Important as it is for citizens to 'have their say' better democratic practice is equally as powerful. We argue that the reform agenda needs to extend to changing how elected assemblies, political parties, governments and the media work and making partners in governance more effective at meeting the needs and aspirations of all citizens. This relatively straightforward message driven through the heuristic of viewing politics as a system should not be seen as an endorsement of the discredited idea that democracy is a conveyor belt where citizens demand, politicians respond and government delivers.

Systems theory has certainly moved away from the linear framing of inputs, throughputs and outputs.[9] Two features stand out. The first is recognition of the interaction between different parts of the system and the second interconnected feature is the way that different elements in the system respond and adapt to the behaviour of others. Citizens might adjust their demands for engagement, for example, if the throughputs of the political system worked in a way that would increase their chances of achieving influence. If decision-makers were confident in the capacity of the governance arrangements to deliver public services or complex programmes they might be more willing to take on board tougher tasks, targets and requests from citizens. More generally, if our goal is to move from a useful heuristic for broadening the horizons of reformers towards a way of understanding how to achieve reform, then it is necessary to have a more developed approach to systems thinking to hand. Fortunately, there is such an approach which goes under the label of 'complex adaptive systems'.

The idea of complex adaptive systems has a long and diverse history and multifaceted debates associated with it.[10] A system is complex and adaptive because it is driven by multiple interactions between different groups and individuals in an environment that is constantly changing. The environment in which actors operate has three features: uncertainty, difficulty and complexity. Uncertainty refers to the absence of perfect information. Difficulty reflects the influence of many variables on an issue and where there are several potential solutions to be found to resolve the problem but not necessarily one optimal solution. Complexity is reflected in the emergent and unpredictable nature of systems. What marks this variation of systems theory is that at its essence it is not about the behaviour of the system but rather the performance of agents – bounded, rational actors making decisions based on limited information and in interaction with each other. If any behaviour is rewarded or has positive outcomes, it becomes a guide for future responses. But, in addition, agents are capable of rule discovery by testing whether new behaviour brings greater reward. If the feedback is positive, then that behaviour will become a stronger rule. Eventually, rules can be combined to provide building blocks for more complex behaviours.

Saving Democracy

These characteristics of complex adaptive systems help to illuminate the way the political system operates and can regularly be observed. We will focus attention on the three core features. The first is threshold effects that are commonly observable within systems where something reaches a level or point at which larger processes of change start to happen rapidly; tipping points are a related concept. In campaigns for democratic reform, a point where the pressure for change becomes so great may emerge relatively rapidly, the issue for reformers is then to be ready to seize the moment. The second core feature of complex adaptive systems also explains why resistance to reform is often strong. The basic idea is that systems have emergent social traps where a shared set of behaviours are reinforced but weaken capacity among those agents for adapting to change.

Both ideas derive from a core idea in complex adaptive systems that niche behaviour clusters are common in diverse environmental settings as different agents develop different responses to the challenges they face. Sometimes these responses are sufficiently powerful that a niche behaviour spills out to the wider system with unpredictable consequences. On other occasions, the niche behaviour becomes a kind of social trap, where groups have developed an understanding of how the world works that in turn threatens to hold them back but gives them a powerful grip within their niche but uncertain impact on the wider system. In each of these cases, successful reform only becomes possible when groups abandon individual agendas in favour of a more collective approach.[11]

A third core feature of complex adaptive systems is the potential for a cascade effect where an unforeseen chain of events due to a small act in one part of the system leads to a major impact affecting all the system. Perhaps one example of this might be when a political party splits and some members drift away to form or support another party, which in turn has a major impact of the original party. A narrative that in many ways matches the way that the United Kingdom Independence Party moved from its fringe position to become a vehicle for those Conservative Party voters and members who favoured the UK leaving the EU to put pressure on the Conservative Party. This pressure arguably led to the Conservative Party to commit to a referendum on the issue which in turn led to the 2016 Brexit vote and its historic ramifications.

Several lessons for would-be democratic reformers emerge from these insights. The first is that the more recent versions of system theory support the basic contention of this book: that it is necessary for innovation in the political system to not only be focused on improving the inputs from citizens but also to push change in the way that representative politics works, how information is accessed and consumed in democracies and how service delivery and programmes can be delivered both within the context of an electoral cycle and over the longer term. The interaction and influence of different parts of the system on each other demand that intervention take place across the board. The second is that promoting reform requires a capacity to understand that resistance to reform is not only likely to be driven by those concerned about losing the power or control they have over decision-making but also by the various niche views and behaviours held by other groups. In short, getting successful reform may demand not only a demonstration of popular support or backing in party manifestos but it may also involve trying to address the concerns or attitudes of those who see the reform as a threat to their way of working rather than an opportunity to work in a different way. For example, in the discussion of the reform of Parliament in Chapter 7 a recognition of the wider and variety of roles that elected representatives might play in a democratic system could open opportunities for reform that would otherwise be missed.

The third lesson we would draw is that there is always hope. If a threshold or tipping point is reached what might have seemed an impossible change might suddenly become possible. The issue is being ready to seize that opportunity for change.

Leading reform

The solutions to the current malaise of democratic politics will vary from country to country. Our book aims to provide a sense of the breadth of reform options but choices about what to do need to reflect both an analysis of problems and the identification of reform preferences in different locations. We simply advise reformers to avoid two traps. The first trap is letting political elites be the sole arbiter of reforms. Why? The short answer is that democracy is an idea that relies on human practice and the evidence suggests that political elites tend to pick reform options which, whatever their merits, tend to be based on self-interest or the interests of their political parties rather than the health of democracy. On an individual level, politicians embrace reforms that enhance their autonomy from the party machine and on balance reject reforms that diminish their autonomy. Political parties tend to reject reforms that in any way diminish their autonomy.[12]

In a compelling review of some of the reforms of political systems in recent decades Shaun Bowler and Todd Donovan show how reforms are often undermined in the implementation process or indeed fatally flawed from inception.[13] Reforms are often selected with partisan advantage in mind and as a result can be self-defeating in terms of their impact in addressing democratic malaise. Bowler and Donovan's reform options are mostly focused on electoral reform or the use of referendums. But it appears that much the same sad lesson can be drawn from work of citizens' assemblies or other forms of participatory innovation. With the possible exception of the Irish Constitutional Convention, many of these reforms, while appearing to be endorsed in theory by political elites, can be ignored or undermined by those same forces in practice. As Ronald Van Crombrugge observes, a range of promising reforms in Belgium met exactly that fate:

> ... the 'types of minipublics that are most promising for a participatory conception of deliberative democracy, namely those that lend citizens a voice to criticise, contest and challenge the status quo, will face the most uphill struggle to become institutionalised'.[14]

Following Bowler and Donovan, he argues that reforms that are going to shift democratic practice require external pressure politics to push political elites into making the change.

Saving Democracy

Many of the reforms that we propose in this book to improve the health of democracy in some way diminish the power of political parties and politicians. There is of course a broader constitutional question here as to whether politicians should be a law unto themselves and have the power to decide their own powers, but it needs to be recognized that for most politicians accepting these reforms would be like turkeys celebrating Christmas.

The demand for reform is such that there is often the need for leadership to come from outside the world of existing political elites. There are many examples of non-governmental organizations or third sector campaigners who have led debates about reform, encouraged change in practice and achieved at least some partial success in forging change. The case of Charter 88 in the UK, which had some but not all of its programme of reforms implemented by the Labour governments from 1997 to 2010, provides one example.[15] By the end of the 1980s, the British Constitution was in crisis. Instead of being part of the context within which politics took place and was constrained, it had become an issue of major political salience on which social and political interests were deeply divided. Charter 88 (1988 to 2009) emerged in this reform space as an independent apolitical movement calling for 'greater democracy', 'just, open and accountable political institutions' and a democratic culture which 'protects individual rights, encourages responsibility and values the participation of every citizen'.[16] It began as an advertisement published on the anniversary of the 1688 Glorious Revolution in *The Guardian* and then the following week in *The Observer* and *The Independent*. The advertisement consisted of a petition outlining ten demands for the reform of the British constitution.[17] It was published in the context of low levels of public trust in government due to what Lord Leslie Scarman termed 'elective dictatorship and the erosion of civil liberties'.[18] It was, as one supporter remarked, 'a snowball that would become an avalanche'.[19] Within days of the publication of the advertisement, the Joseph Rowntrees Reform Trust invested $20 million to turn Charter 88 into an independent constitutional reform campaign group with a strong research capability – the Democratic Audit of the UK (which is still running at the London School of Economics and Political Science).[20] By 1997, all of the major UK political parties had been converted to aspects of constitutional reform and by 2000, eight out of Charter 88's ten demands had been implemented by the Labour Government under Tony Blair.[21]

Charter 88 was successful because it had the institutional capacity to respond to the three core features of complex adaptive systems outlined in the previous section. First, it was able to seize the moment when an unforeseen threshold effect for change emerged. This was largely a consequence of the historic fusion of social unrest caused by relative economic decline, the excessive centralization of the British State and the call by elites in the nations and regions of Britain for a decentralized polity and the erosion of civil liberties and increasing pressure through the European Union for the British government to address its poor human rights record. Above all, it became impossible for the Labour party in opposition to ignore the claims of the devolution and human rights lobbies even if it had wanted to. Constitutional reform provided Blair with a mobilizing theme for building a coalition of reform across the centre of the British political spectrum. This was the post-ideological 'space' in which the discourse of constitutional reform emerged.

Second, because Charter 88 was deliberately created and positioned as a post-ideological umbrella movement and resisted the temptation to prescribe particular types of reform – for example, the form of written constitution, bill of rights, national assembly, second chamber, freedom of information system or system of electoral reform – it was able to build a broad social and political network of supporter groups across the political spectrum and avoid the social traps associated with niche behaviour on specific areas of reform.

Third, Charter 88 also benefitted from a cascade effect where a reform in one part of the system leads to a major impact affecting all of the system. For example, the creation of a Scottish Parliament triggered the possibility of national assemblies in Northern Ireland and Wales and the need for regional democratic settlements. Once new political institutions are created a dynamic of institutional spill-over is created that becomes very difficult to roll back, as the Brexit example illustrates.

Our ideal would be for similar organizations to emerge or advance in all democracies. A civil society-led dynamic for reform that tries to put together a comprehensive package of reforms based on the many experiences of change noted in this book is the best way of reigniting the dynamic of saving democracy. In addition, the widely practised idea of an audit of democracy needs to be supplemented by an audit of reform progress. Rather than an audit of the failings of the system the analysis of reforms would highlight where positive reforms have occurred. As noted in this book, there are many examples of positive change and we need a mechanism to make sure they are more widely known. Moreover, an audit of democratic reform might help in terms of creating pressure for further change and igniting a virtual cycle of democratic renewal.

The second trap for reformers flows from one of the main themes of our book: namely it would be ill-advised to focus on reforms that place the onus of decision-making purely on the public. In an understandable reaction to the forces of resistance among elites it is probably fair to say that most advocates of democratic innovation have focused their thinking and efforts at renewed practice around new forms of citizen participation. We devote several chapters in our book to these reform ideas. But we share some of the scepticism of those scholars who argue that people might be discontented with politics but that does not mean that greater participation is necessarily the reform option they want.[22] The theoretical assumptions built into the argument for engagement are not necessarily borne out in studies of the way that people engage in practice. The advocates of engagement are prone to overestimate the extent and intensity of political engagement that most people desire or are even comfortable with.

Indeed, it may be that when citizens express support for greater democratic engagement, they are simply expressing frustration at a political system that does not work for them rather than demanding that they should run the show. In research in both the UK and Australia we have explored the democratic reform preferences that people support.[23] It is a challenging exercise because many of the reform options that we have considered in this book for example are not that well-known to members of the public. So, asking them about the changes they would like to see is best phrased in general terms. Broadly though the message from our research efforts is that the majority

Saving Democracy

of citizens would like to see reforms to the way that representative politics works and operates even more than new opportunities to directly engage themselves. Historically, reform decisions have been presented as a binary choice between those that strengthen the representative system of government and reforms that extend greater public participation. It is increasingly evident that citizens think that it is the mixture of reforms that restore and strengthen the protective power of democracy that will matter most in the next chapter of our democratic story. We agree with them.

POSTSCRIPT

We began writing *Saving Democracy* towards the end of 2018 in the context of the lowest reported levels of public trust and satisfaction with Australia and the UK's democratic arrangements set against a global democratic malaise, the rise of debased semi-democracies, the Brexit debacle and the general confusion associated with the Trump presidency. Democracy was under attack on a global scale and there was a pressing need for a book that provided an understanding of the political dynamics underpinning the pre-pandemic crisis and mapped out potential pathways to renewal. Then Covid-19 hit.

Unsurprisingly Covid-19 compelled us to rethink how we approached the book. The intrinsic value of democracy had not diminished but the challenges confronting democracies appeared starker and how democracy was being practised began to change as we wrote. We therefore decided to connect up with everyday citizens through a Facebook discussion group at https://www.democracy2025.gov.au/programs/save-democracy-post-covid-19.html which posed the question – how can we save democracy in a post-Covid-19 world?

The purpose of this international crowdsourcing experiment was to ensure that we were focusing on appropriate conceptual issues, drawing on the right areas of reform in terms of strengthening democratic practice and identifying credible pathways to reform. Knowledge of stellar international examples of democratic innovation during the pandemic was particularly welcomed. Over the following twelve months we posted draft chapters, invited comments, synthesized the commentary and posted a rejoinder on the lessons that we would draw for the subsequent redrafting of the chapter.

We were delighted with the feedback we received which has improved the book in at least three ways. It has sharpened our operational understanding of the concepts of 'democracy' and 'politics'; provided for a more nuanced understanding of deliberative, direct and digital democracy; and introduced us to a broader range of relevant reforms than originally envisaged. Participants were excited with the systems approach to politics that we developed, they recognized the difference between 'old' and 'new' power and its' implications for democratic politics, and they agreed with the global challenges to democracy that we identified. There were different views on the focus for reform. Participants felt that we were too kind to politicians and political parties, and too conservative on alternative forms of democratic representation through devices such as sortition. There was also cynicism with the capacity of existing democratic institutions to improve their own practices and connect up better with the citizenry.

We defend the representative role of politicians but think that it requires a serious redesign to address its dysfunctions and contradictions. We do not see sortition as

Saving Democracy

replacing representative democracy rather as a component of a broader participatory governance system where a variety of methods can be used to co-produce solutions to governance problems with citizens and stakeholders and bolster the legitimacy of public policy-making. We look to historical evidence as the basis of our optimism that democratic institutions can and do change for the better over time. However, we do share the concerns of our participants that although the protective power of democracy remains clear in principle, the challenge is to deliver it more effectively in practice. Most of the problems of democracy that we have encountered in this book stem from the persistence of inequality of one form or another that the political class has conspicuously failed to counter. We must all be more demanding of our politicians to take concerted action and willing to engage in democratic practice as critical citizens. After all, we largely get the democracy that we vote for.

We thank our eighty-three champions of democracy for their rich insights and hope that the final product, *Saving Democracy*, was worth the investment in time and thought.

Mark Evans and Gerry Stoker

NOTES

Chapter 1

1 For the key expositions see: Steven Levitsky and Daniel Ziblatt, *How Democracies Die* (New York: Crown, 2018) and Cass Sunstein (ed.), *Can It Happen Here?* (New York: HarperCollins, 2018). And for an earlier assessment see: Russell J. Dalton, *Democratic Challenges, Democratic Choices* (New York: Oxford University Press, 2004).

2 His full speech is available at https://www.ndtv.com/world-news/world-suffering-from-trust-deficit-disorder-united-nations-chief-antonio-guterres-1922131 [accessed 1 May 2020].

3 David Runciman, *How Democracy Ends* (London: Profile Books, 2018).

4 See, for example, recent annual reports by: Freedom House (https://freedomhouse.org/), the Economist Democracy Index (https://www.economist.com/graphic-detail/2020/01/22/global-democracy-has-another-bad-year), Reporters without Borders (https://rsf.org/en), the Electoral Integrity Project (https://www.electoralintegrityproject.com/), and the Varieties of Democracy project (https://www.v-dem.net/en/) [All accessed 7 May 2020].

5 For example, see: Larry Diamond and Marc F. Plattner (eds.), *Democracy in Decline?* (Baltimore: Johns Hopkins University Press, 2015); Joshua Kurlantzick, *Democracy in Retreat* (New Haven: Yale University Press, 2014); Edward Luce, *The Retreat of Western Liberalism* (Boston: Little Brown, 2017); Yascha Mounk, *The People vs. Democracy* (Boston: Harvard University Press, 2018); Levitsky and Ziblatt, *How Democracies Die*; and Sunstein, (ed.), *Can It Happen Here?*

6 Larry Diamond, *Ill Winds: Saving Democracy from Russian Rage, Chinese Ambition and American Complacency* (New York: Penguin Books, 2019), p. 11.

7 See: Robert Foa et al., *The Global Satisfaction with Democracy Report 2020*, https://www.bennettinstitute.cam.ac.uk/publications/global-satisfaction-democracy-report-2020/ [accessed 15 July 2020].

8 Ibid., p. 3.

9 Mohamed El-Erian, Nouriel Roubini and Paul Krugman debate the economic impact of Covid-19 at: https://www.businessinsider.com.au/unemployment-claims-millions-increase-economist-commentary-krugman-roubini-elerian-coronavirus-2020-3 [accessed 3 May 2020].

10 There is, however, greater contestation over the issue of how to manage economic recovery from the Great Cessation. Most economists believe that fiscal stimulus is the starting point but are then divided on the duration and size of stimulus required and the timing of the onset of public debt management or austerity measures. For a range of commentaries see: https://www.project-syndicate.org/commentary/coronavirus-greater-great-depression-by-nouriel-roubini-2020-03; https://fortune.com/2020/03/25/coronavirus-economy-worse-than-the-great-recession-2008/; and, https://www.nytimes.com/2020/04/01/business/economy/coronavirus-recession.html [all accessed 3 May 2020].

Notes

11 For evidence on all these positives see: Célia Belin and Giovanna de Maio, 'Democracy after Coronavirus: Five Challenges for the 2020s', *Foreign Policy*, August (2020).

12 Guanlan Mao, Maria Fernandes-Jesus, Evangelos Ntontis and John Drury, 'What Have We Learned so Far about COVID-19 Volunteering in the UK? A Rapid Review of the literature', *medRxiv*, November (2020).

13 See: Christian Welzel, *A Tale of Culture-Bound Regime Evolution: The Centennial Democratic Trend and Its Recent Reversal* (2017), https://www.v-dem.net/media/filer_public/2f/a7/2fa75734-24f4-4833-a343-547bc1264ab3/users_working_paper_11.pdf [accessed 7 May 2020].

14 Particularly prominent are: Archon Fung, *Empowered Participation Reinventing Urban Democracy* (New Jersey: Princeton University Press, 2004); Graham Smith, *Democratic Innovations* (Cambridge: Cambridge University Press, 2009); Brigitte Geissel and Marko Joas (eds.), *Participatory Democratic Innovations in Europe* (Opladen: Barbara Budrich, 2013); Ken Newton and Brigitte Geissel (eds.), *Evaluating Democratic Innovation* (Abingdon: Routledge/Taylor and Francis, 2012); and Stephen Elstrub and Oliver Escobar (eds.), *Handbook of Democratic Innovation and Governance* (Cheltenham: Edward Elgar, 2018).

15 See: Jane Mansbridge, James Bohman, Simone Chambers, Thomas Christiano, Archon Fung, John Parkinson, Dennis F. Thompson and Mark E. Warren, *A Systemic Approach to Deliberative Democracy* (Cambridge: Cambridge University Press, 2012) and John Parkinson, 'Deliberative Systems', in Mansbridge et al., *A Systemic Approach to Deliberative Democracy*, pp. 1–26.

16 The terms old and new power are developed by Henry Timms and Jeremy Heimans, *New Power: How It's Changing the 21st Century and Why You Need to Know* (London: Macmillan, 2018).

17 See: Vivien Lowndes, Lawrence Pratchett and Gerry Stoker, 'Diagnosing and Remedying the Failings of Official Participation Schemes: The CLEAR Framework', *Social Policy and Society*, 5, 2 (2006), pp. 281–91 and Andrea Cornwall, 'Unpacking Participation Models, Meanings and Practices', *Community Development Journal*, 43, 3 (2008), pp. 269–83.

18 This quotation is from one of the most respected theorists of democracy in the second half of the twentieth century Robert Dahl in *After the Revolution? Authority in a Good Society* (New Haven: Yale University Press, 1970), p. 4.

19 See: *Varieties of Democracy Project* at https://www.v-dem.net/en/ [accessed 7 May 2020].

20 A classification undertaken by Anna Lührmann, Marcus Tannenberg and Staffan I. Lindberg reported in 'Regimes of the World (RoW): Opening New Avenues for the Comparative Study of Political Regimes', *Politics and Governance*, 6, 1 (2018), pp. 60–77.

21 Amartya Sen, 'Democracy as a Universal Value', *Journal of Democracy*, 10, 3 (1999), pp. 3–17, p. 5.

22 See: Welzel, *A Tale of Culture-Bound Regime Evolution*.

23 Elizabeth Anderson, 'Democracy: Instrumental vs. Non-instrumental Value', in Thomas Christian and John Christman (eds.), *Contemporary Debates in Political Philosophy* (Oxford: Wiley-Blackwell, 2009), pp. 213–27.

24 On these arguments see the classics: Harold Lasswell, *Politics: Who Gets What, When, How Politics* (New York: Whittlesey House, 1936); John Rawls, *A Theory of Justice* (Boston: Harvard University Press, 1971); and Robert Dahl, *On Democracy* (New Haven: Yale University Press, 1998).

25 Timothy Besley and Masayuki Kudamatsu, 'Health and Democracy', *American Economic Review*, 96, 2 (2006), pp. 313–18, https://eprints.lse.ac.uk/33708/1/Health_and_democracy(lsero).pdf. [accessed 28 June 2021], p. 317.

Notes

26 Sen, 'Democracy as a Universal Value', p. 8.
27 Belin and de Maio, 'Democracy after Coronavirus: Five Challenges for the 2020s', p. 5.
28 Gabriel A. Almond, 'Comparative Political Systems', *The Journal of Politics*, 18, 3 (1956), pp. 391–409, p. 393.
29 David Easton, *A Systems Analysis of Political Life* (New York: John Wiley, 1965).
30 Vivien A. Schmidt, 'Democracy and Legitimacy in the European Union Revisited: Input, Output and "Throughput"', *Political Studies*, 61, 1 (2013), pp. 2–22.
31 Ibid., p. 7.
32 Bo Rothstein, 'The Chinese Paradox of High Growth and Low Quality of Government: The Cadre Organization Meets Max Weber', *Governance: An International Journal of Policy, Administration, and Institutions*, 28, 4 (2015), pp. 533–48.
33 Christian Welzel and Russell J. Dalton, 'From Allegiant to Assertive Citizens', in R. Dalton and C. Welzel (eds.), *The Civic Culture Transformed: From Allegiant to Assertive Citizens* (Cambridge: Cambridge University Press, 2017), pp. 282–306.
34 Russell J. Dalton, 'Cognitive Mobilisation and Partisan Dealignment in Advanced Industrial Democracies', *Journal of Politics*, 46, 1 (1984), pp. 264–84.
35 See: Pippa Norris (ed.), *Critical Citizens: Global Support for Democratic Governance* (Oxford: Oxford University Press, 1999).
36 Nick Clarke, Will Jennings, Jonathan Moss and Gerry Stoker, *The Good Politician: Folk Theories, Political Interaction and the Rise of Anti-Politics* (Cambridge: Cambridge University Press, 2019), p. 8.
37 Russell Dalton and Christian Welzel, *The Civic Culture Revisited: From Allegiant to Assertive Citizens* (Cambridge: Cambridge University Press, 2014), pp. 282–306.
38 Accessed 25 February 2019 from: https://data.oecd.org/inequality/income-inequality.htm.
39 John Kenneth Galbraith, *The Culture of Contentment* (New Jersey: Princeton University Press, 2017).
40 Cas Mudde, 'Populism: An Ideational Approach', in Cristóbal Rovira Kaltwasser, Paul Taggart, Paulina Ochoa Espejo and Pierre Ostiguy (eds.), *The Oxford Handbook of Populism* (Oxford: Oxford University Press, 2017), p. 4.
41 See: the Sortition Foundation, https://www.sortitionfoundation.org/ [accessed 15 June 2021] and the newDemocracy Foundation at https://www.newdemocracy.com.au/ [accessed 15 June 2021].
42 See: Carolyn Hendriks and Adrian Kay, 'From "Opening Up" to Democratic Renewal: Deepening Public Engagement in Legislative Committees', *Government and Opposition*, 54, 1 (2017), pp. 20–1.
43 Antonio Gramsci, *Letters from Prison*, volume 1 (New York: Columbia University Press, 1994).

Chapter 2

1 Joseph Schumpeter, *Capitalism, Socialism, and Democracy* (London: Allen and Unwin, 1962 [1942]), p. 262.
2 See: David Held, *Models of Democracy* (Stanford: Stanford University Press, 3rd edition, 2006), Chapter 5 for an extended review.

Notes

3   See: Patrice Duran, 'Max Weber and the Making of Politicians: A Sociology of Political Responsibility', *Max Weber Studies*, 9, 1 (2010), pp. 1–26.

4   Bryan Caplan, *The Myth of the Rational Voter: Why Democracies Choose Bad Policies* (New Jersey: Princeton University Press, 2007).

5   See: Peter John et al., *Nudge, Nudge, Think, Think: Experimenting with Ways to Change Citizen Behaviour* (London: Bloomsbury Academic, 2011).

6   Jason Brennan, *Against Democracy* (New Jersey: Princeton University Press, 2016). His views are captured in an interesting blog entitled 'Politics Makes Us Mean and Dumb', https://emotionresearcher.com/politics-makes-us-mean-and-dumb/ [accessed 15 July 2020].

7   James Kuklinski and Paul Quirk, 'Reconsidering the Rational Public: Cognition, Heuristics, and Mass Opinion', in Arthur Lupia, Matthew D. McCubbins and Samuel L. Popkin (eds.), *Elements of Reason: Cognition, Choice, and the Bounds of Rationality* (Cambridge: Cambridge University Press, 2000), pp. 153–82.

8   Christopher Achen and Larry Bartels, *Democracy for Realists: Why Elections Do Not Produce Responsive Government* (New Jersey: Princeton University Press, 2016), pp. 15–16.

9   For a relatively straightforward exposition of these ideas see: Gerd Gigerenzer, *Gut Feelings: The Intelligence of the Unconscious* (New York: Viking Press, 2007). And for developments in the argument see: Gerd Gigerenzer, *Adaptive Thinking* (Oxford: Oxford University Press, 2000); Gerd Gigerenzer, *Rationality for Mortals* (Oxford: Oxford University Press, 2008); and Gerd Gigerenzer, *Simply Rational* (Oxford: Oxford University Press, 2015).

10 Arthur Lupia, 'Shortcuts versus Encyclopaedias: Information and Voting Behavior in California Insurance Reform Elections', *American Political Science Review*, 88, 1 (1994), pp. 63–76.

11 Cindy D. Kam, 'The Psychological Veracity of Zaller's Model', *Critical Review*, 24, 4 (2012), pp. 545–67.

12 For an interesting discussion on this topic see: Ezra Klein and Marc Hethrington debate 'A New Theory for Why Republicans and Democrats See the World Differently', https://www.vox.com/policy-and-politics/2018/12/18/18139556/republicans-democrats-partisanship-ideologyphilosophy-psychology-marc-hetherington [accessed 15 July 2020].

13 George Marcus, W. Russell Neuman and Michael MacKuen, *Affective Intelligence and Political Judgment* (Chicago, IL: The University of Chicago Press, 2000).

14 Cindy D. Kam, 'When Duty Calls, Do Citizens Answer?' *Journal of Politics*, 69, 1 (2007), pp. 17–29, p. 17.

15 Herbert Simon, 'Invariants of Human Behaviour', *Annual Review of Psychology*, 41, (1990), pp. 1–19.

16 Ben Leruth and Gerry Stoker, 'Improving the Political Judgement of Citizens: Why the Task Environment Matters', 48, 3, (2020), pp. 381–96.

17 See: Nick Clarke, Will Jennings, Jonathan Moss and Gerry Stoker, 'Voter Decision-making in a Context of Low Political Trust: The 2016 UK EU Membership Referendum', *Political Studies*, May 2021, doi:10.1177/00323217211003419.

18 Ken Newton, 'Making Better Citizens', in Brigitte Geissel and Kenneth Newton (eds.), *Evaluating Democratic Innovations* (Abingdon: Routledge/Taylor and Francis, 2012), pp. 137–62, p. 155.

19 Isabel Hardman, *Why We Get the Wrong Politicians* (London: Atlantic Books, 2018).

20 Jennifer L. Lawless and Richard L. Fox, *Running from Office: Why Young Americans Are Turned Off Politics* (New York: Oxford University Press, 2015), p. 6.

Notes

21 Pippa Norris, *Passages to Power: Legislative Recruitment in Advanced Democracies* (Cambridge: Cambridge University Press, 1997), p. 5.

22 Nick Clarke, Will Jennings, Jonathan Moss and Gerry Stoker, *The Good Politician: Folk Theories, Political Interaction and the Rise of Anti-Politics* (Cambridge: Cambridge University Press, 2019), p. 214.

23 Ibid., p. 215.

24 Peter Allen and David Cutts, 'Women Are More Likely than Men to Blame Structural Factors for Women's Political Under-representation: Evidence from 27 Countries', *European Journal of Political Research*, 58 (2019), pp. 465–87.

25 John Gerring, Erzen Oncel, Kevin Morrison and Daniel Pemstein, 'Who Rules the World? A Portrait of the Global Leadership Class', *Perspectives on Politics*, 17, 4 (2019), pp. 1079–97.

26 Harold Lasswell was one of the first to make this argument in his book, *Power and Personality* (New York: W.W. Norton and Company, 1948).

27 Joseph A. Schlesinger, *Ambition and Politics: Political Careers in the United States* (Chicago: Rand McNally and Co, 1966).

28 Richard L. Fox and Jennifer L. Lawless, 'To Run or Not to Run for Office: Explaining Nascent Political Ambition', *American Journal of Political Science*, 49, 3 (2005), pp. 642–59.

29 James Weinberg, 'Who Wants to Be a Politician? Basic Human Values and Candidate Emergence in the United Kingdom', *British Journal of Political Science*, First View (2020), pp. 1–17, doi: https://doi.org/10.1017/S0007123419000814.

30 See: Michael Saward, *The Representative Claim* (Oxford: Oxford University Press, 2010).

31 Hardman, *Why We Get the Wrong Politicians*.

32 Ibid.

33 Clarke et al., *The Good Politician*.

34 For an analysis of nanotechnology and its way of working aimed at the general reader see: Sonia Contera, *Nano Comes To Life* (New Jersey: Princeton University Press, 2019).

35 Albert O. Hirschman was Professor of Social Science, Emeritus, at the Institute for Advanced Study in Princeton University. Here we focus on his views presented in his book *Exit, Voice, and Loyalty* (Boston: Harvard University Press, 1970).

36 Pippa Norris, *Democratic Deficit* (Cambridge: Cambridge University Press, 2011), Chapter 8.

37 Enrique Hernández, 'Europeans Views of Democracy: The Core Elements of Democracy', in Mónica Ferrín and Hanspeter Kriesi (eds.), *How Europeans View and Evaluate Democracy* (Oxford: Oxford University Press, 2016), p. 63.

38 See: Aidan Connaughton, Nicholas Kent and Shannon Schumacher, 'How People around the World See Democracy in 8 Charts (Pew Research Center, 2020)', https://www.pewresearch.org/fact-tank/2020/02/27/how-people-around-the-world-see-democracy-in-8-charts/ [accessed 9 July 2021].

39 Christian Welzel, 'A Tale of Culture-Bound Regime Evolution: The Centennial Democratic Trend and Its Recent Reversal', Users Working Paper Series, No. 11, (Gothenburg: The Varieties of Democracy Institute, University of Gothenberg, 2017), p. 30, https://www.v-dem.net/media/filer_public/2f/a7/2fa75734-24f4-4833-a343-547bc1264ab3/users_working_paper_11.pdf.

40 Ibid., p. 57.

Notes

Chapter 3

1. For a detailed assessment see: Wolfgang Merkel and Sascha Kneip (eds.), *Democracy and Crisis: Challenges in Turbulent Times* (Berlin: SpringerLink, 2019).
2. See: Pierre Rosanvallon, *Counter-Democracy: Politics in the Age of Distrust* (Cambridge: Cambridge University Press, 2008); and Merkel and Kneip, *Democracy and Crisis: Challenges in Turbulent Times*.
3. See: Involve, *People and Participation: How to Put the Citizens at the Heart of Decision-making* (London: Involve, 2005), https://www.involve.org.uk/resources/publications/practical-guidance/people-and-participation-how-put-citizens-heart-decision [accessed 5 July 2021]; and NESTA, *Our Futures, by the People, for the People* (London: NESTA, 2019), https://www.nesta.org.uk/report/our-futures-people-people/ [accessed 5 July 2021].
4. Marc Hetherington and Jason Husser, 'How Trust Matters: The Changing Political Relevance of Political Trust', *American Journal of Political Science*, 56, 2, (2012), pp. 312–25, p. 312.
5. For a detailed exposition see: John Parkinson, 'Deliberative Systems', in Andre Bächtiger, John S. Dryzek, Jane Mansbridge, and Mark Warren (eds.), *The Oxford Handbook of Deliberative Democracy* (Oxford: Oxford University Press, 2018), pp. 432–46.
6. For the seminal account see: Graham Smith, *Democratic Innovations* (Cambridge: Cambridge University Press, 2009).
7. See: Brian Head, 'Wicked Problems in Public Policy', *Public Policy*, 3, 2 (2008), pp. 101–18.
8. See: David Held, *Models of Democracy* (Cambridge: Cambridge University Press, 2006); and David Beetham, Edzia Carvalho, Todd Landman and Stuart Weir (eds.), *Assessing the Quality of Democracy: A Practical Guide* (Stockholm: International Institute for Democracy and Electoral Assistance, 2008).
9. See: Bob Goodin, *Innovating Democracy: Democratic Theory and Practice after the Deliberative Turn* (Oxford: Oxford University Press, 2008); and Carolyn Hendriks, *The Politics of Public Deliberation – Citizen Engagement and Interest Advocacy* (London: Palgrave Macmillan, 2011).
10. For a detailed exposition of this argument see: Claudia Chwalisz, *The Populist Signal: Why Politics and Democracy Need to Change* (London: Rowman and Littlefield International, 2015).
11. Pierre Rosanvallon's book *Counter-Democracy: Politics in the Age of Distrust* presents a detailed theorization of how to integrate representative and participatory forms of democracy.
12. See, for example, Andre Felicetti, Simon Niemeyer and Nicole Curato, 'Improving Deliberative Participation: Connecting Mini-Publics to Deliberative Systems', *European Political Science Review*, 8, 3 (2016), pp. 427–48; and John Parkinson, 'Deliberative Systems'.
13. For a review of three decades of research and practice see: Carole Pateman, 'Participatory Democracy Revisited', *Perspectives on Politics*, 10, 1 (2012), pp. 7–19.
14. For a detailed account of different methods of public participation see: Involve Organization, *People and Participation: How to Put the Citizens at the Heart of Decision-making*; and, NESTA, *Our Futures, by the People, for the People*.
15. See, for example, Sherry Arnstein's, 'A Ladder of Citizen Participation', *Journal of the American Institute of Planners*, 35, 4 (1969), pp. 216–24, p. 217.
16. See the International Association for Public Participation (IAP2) as an exception in this regard at https://www.iap2.org [accessed 21 June 2021].

Notes

17 Matt Qvortrup, *Direct Democracy: A Comparative Study of the Theory and Practice of Government by the People* (Manchester: Manchester University Press, 2013), p. 9.

18 Adapted from IAP2 at https://www.iap2.org [accessed 5 July 2021].

19 Jon Elster (ed.), *Deliberative Democracy* (Cambridge: Cambridge University Press, 1999), p. 1.

20 See: Nelson Dias, *Hope for Democracy: 30 Years of Participatory Budgeting Worldwide* (Oficina, 2018), https://www.oficina.org.pt/hopefordemocracy.html# [16 December 2019].

21 See: Citizens for Climate France, *Discover the 149 Propositions from the Citizens Convention*; and Climate Assembly UK, *Climate Assembly UK Members on Their Report*.

22 See: Mark Evans and Nina Terrey, 'Co-design with Citizens and Stakeholders', in Gerry Stoker and Mark Evans (eds.), *Evidence-based Policymaking in the Social Sciences: Methods That Matter* (Bristol: Policy Press, 2016), pp. 243–62; and John Boddy and Nina Terrey, *Design for a Better Future: A Guide to Designing in Complex Systems* (Abingdon: Routledge/Taylor and Francis, 2019).

23 NESTA, *Our Futures, by the People, for the People*, p. 15.

24 See, for example, Changefest and place-based change, https://changefest.com.au/ [accessed 5 July 2021].

25 See: Cities of Service, 'We Help City Leaders Engage Their Citizens to Build Stronger Communities', John Hopkins Krieger School of Arts and Science, citiesofservice.org/resource/crowdsourcing-a-constitution-mexico-city [accessed 22 June 2021].

26 For a full assessment see: Andrea Felicetti, Simon Niemeyer and Nicole Curato, 'Improving Deliberative Participation: Connecting Mini-publics to Deliberative Systems', *European Political Science Review*, 8, 3 (2016), pp. 427–48.

27 There are many outstanding resources for evaluating participatory modes of governance in practice but two are particularly useful. The *Participedia* project, led from the University of British Columbia and the Ash Center for Democratic Governance and Innovation at Harvard University crowdsource, catalogues and compares participatory political processes around the world contributing to public understanding of what works in democratic practice. See: https://participedia.net/ [accessed 5 July 2021]. Healthy Democracy, is a US-based nonpartisan nonprofit organization that designs and coordinates innovative deliberative democracy programmes. Healthy Democracy pioneered the Citizens' Initiative Review process. See https://healthydemocracy.org/ [accessed 5 July 2021].

Chapter 4

1 Pew Research Center, 'Globally, Broad Support for Representative and Direct Democracy', https://www.pewresearch.org/global/2017/10/16/globally-broad-support-for-representative-and-direct-democracy/ [accessed 5 July 2021].

2 Daniel Kahneman, *Thinking Fast and Slow* (New York: Macmillan, 2011).

3 See: Richard H. Thaler and Cass R. Sunstein, *Nudge: Improving Decisions about Health, Wealth, and Happiness* (New Haven, CT: Yale University Press, 2008).

4 John Haskell, *Direct Democracy or Representative Government? Dispelling the Populist Myth* (Boulder, CO: Westview Press, 2001).

5 Daniel Lewis, *Direct Democracy and Minority Rights* (Abingdon: Routledge, 2013), p. 3.

Notes

6   David Altman, *Direct Democracy Worldwide* (Cambridge: Cambridge University Press, 2011).

7   For two broad ranging accounts of the recent use of referenda see: Altman, *Direct Democracy Worldwide*; and Matt Qvortrup, *Direct Democracy* (Manchester: Manchester University Press, 2013).

8   The following data is sourced from Ballotpedia, https://ballotpedia.org/2016_ballot_measures [accessed 5 July 2021].

9   An initiative, also known as a popular or citizens' initiative, is a means by which a petition signed by a certain minimum number of registered voters can force a government to choose to introduce a law or hold a vote in parliament in what is called an indirect initiative. The proposal is immediately put to a plebiscite or referendum. In an indirect initiative, a measure is first referred to the legislature, and then put to a popular vote only if not enacted by the legislature. In a direct initiative, a measure is put directly to a referendum.

10 He Beogang, 'Referenda as a Solution to the National-Identity/Boundary Question: An Empirical Assessment of the Theoretical Literature', *Alternatives*, 27, 1 (2002), p. 77.

11 Sveinung Arnesen, Troy Broderstad, Mikael Johannesson and Jonas Linde, 'Conditional Legitimacy: How Turnout, Majority Size, and Outcome Affect Perceptions of Legitimacy in European Union Membership Referendums', *European Union Politics*, 20, 2 (2019), pp. 176–97.

12 Altman, *Direct Democracy Worldwide*, p. 89.

13 See: Gregg Strauss, 'The Positive Right to Marry', *Virginia Law Review*, 102, 7 (2016), pp. 1691–766.

14 See: Benjamin Kentish, 'David Cameron Says EU Referendum Ended the Poisoning of British Politics', *The Independent*, 26 April 2017.

15 See: Ellie Forman Peck, 'The Brexit Referendum and the British Constitution', *The Economist*, 30 May 2019.

16 See: University College London, Constitution Unit, *Citizens' Assembly on Brexit*, https://www.ucl.ac.uk/constitution-unit/research/deliberative-democracy/citizens-assembly-brexit [accessed 5 July 2021].

17 This definition encompasses and develops various strategies of localism described by Paul Hildreth, 'What Is Localism and What Implications Do Different Models Have for Managing the Local Economy?' *Local Economy*, 26, 8 (2011), pp. 702–14, doi:10.1177/0269094211422215 and developed by Mark Evans, David Marsh and Gerry Stoker, "Understanding Localism", *Policy Studies*, 34, 4 (2013), pp. 401–7, doi: 10.1080/01442872.2013.822699.

18 Hildreth, 'What Is Localism and What Implications Do Different Models Have for Managing the Local Economy?'

19 Gerry Stoker, 'Was Local Governance Such a Good Idea? A Global Comparative Perspective', *Public Administration*, 89, 1 (2011), pp. 15–31.

20 Joe Penny, 'Between Coercion and Consent: The Politics of "Cooperative Governance" at a Time of "Austerity Localism"', *London, Urban Geography*, 38, 9 (2017), pp. 1352–73, doi:10.1080/02723638.2016.1235932.

21 Joseph S. Nye, 'Soft Power', *Foreign Policy*, 80 (1990), pp. 153–71.

22 Stoker, 'Was Local Governance Such a Good Idea? A Global Comparative Perspective'.

23 Evans et al., *Understanding Localism*.

24 Ibid.

25 For ungovernability and political overload arguments see: Anthony Birch, 'Overload, Ungovernability and Delegitimation: The Theories and the British Case', *British Journal of Political Science*, 14, 2 (1984), pp. 135–60.

26 In the aftermath of the UK parliamentary expenses scandal, a number of Members of Parliament involved in wrongdoing resigned as MPs following related court cases – for example, Eric Illsley, whose resignation caused the Barnsley Central by-election, 2011, and Denis MacShane, who caused the Rotherham by-election, 2012, were cases brought up by supporters of recall to allow voters to 'sack' MPs who break the rules. See: United Kingdom, Parliamentary Debates, House of Commons, 25 May 2010, vol 510, col 32; and United Kingdom, Parliamentary Debates, House of Commons, 1 March 2011, vol 524, cols 145–7.

27 This is distinct from the use of 'collective recall', a form of citizen-initiated election used in Switzerland, Germany and Japan.

28 We are not focussing here on the removal of members of Parliament by way of an early general election. For this issue see: Anne Twomey, 'The Recall of Members of Parliament and Citizens' Initiated Elections', *The University of New South Wales Law Journal*, 34, 1, (2011), pp. 41–69.

29 UK House of Commons, PRC, 'Right to Recall MPs', PCRC Report June, 2012, https://publications.parliament.uk/pa/cm201213/cmselect/cmpolcon/373/373.pdf. [accessed 8 April 2020].

30 Twomey, 'The Recall of Members of Parliament and Citizens' Initiated Elections', p. 70.

31 See: Helge Larsen, 'Directly Elected Mayors – Democratic Renewal or Constitutional Confusion?' in Janice Caulfield and Helge Larsen (eds.), *Local Government at the Millenium* (Urban Research International: VS Verlag für Sozialwissenschaften, Wiesbaden, 2013), pp. 111–33.

32 See: Deepti Bhatnagar, Rathore Animesh, Moreno Torres and Magui Kanungo, *Participatory Budgeting in Brazil: Empowerment Case Studies* (Washington, DC: World Bank, 2003), http://documents.worldbank.org/curated/en/2003/01/11297674/participatory-budgeting-brazil [accessed 10 November 2021].

33 See, for example, Involve, 'Participatory Budgeting', https://www.involve.org.uk/resources/methods/participatory-budgeting [accessed 10 November 2021].

34 See: Nelson Dias, Sahsil Enríquez and Simone Júlio, *The World Atlas of Participatory Budgeting* (Washington, DC: Officini, 2019), https://www.pbatlas.net/index.html [accessed 10 November 2021].

35 Department for Communities and Local Government (UK), *Communities in the Driving Seat: A Study of Participatory Budgeting in England*, https://assets.publishing.service.gov.uk/government/uploads/system/uploads/attachment_data/file/6152/19932231.pdf [accessed 5 July 2021].

36 For insights into the participatory budgets in England during the global financial crisis and their problems see: https://www.involve.org.uk/sites/default/files/field/attachemnt/Participatory-budgeting-and-t...-for-Arts-Council-England.pdf [accessed 5 July 2021].

37 Peter Yeung, 'How Paris's Participatory Budget Is Reinvigorating Democracy', *City Monitor*, 8 January 2021, https://citymonitor.ai/government/civic-engagement/how-paris-participatory-budget-is-reinvigorating-democracy [accessed 18 November 2021].

38 Porto Alegre City Government, *Participatory Budget*, https://www2.portoalegre.rs.gov.br/op/ [accessed 18 November 2021].

Notes

39 UIC Great Cities Institute, *Participatory Budgeting in Chicago*, http://www.pbchicago.org/pb-in-chicago.html [accessed 18 November 2021].

40 International Observatory on Participatory Democracy, *Seoul's Participatory Budgeting*, https://oidp.net/en/practice.php?id=1302 [accessed 18 November 2021].

41 Ernesto Ganuza and Francisco Francés, 'The Participants Print in the Participatory Budget: Overview on the Spanish Experiments', in Nelson Dias (ed.), *Hope for Democracy: 25 Years of Participatory Budgeting Worldwide* (São Brás de Alportel: Loco Association, 2014), pp. 301–12, https://www.researchgate.net/publication/326446155_20_Years_of_Participatory_Budgeting_in_Spain [accessed 18 November 2021].

42 Edward Paice, 'The Booklovers, the Mayors and the Citizens: Participatory Budgeting in Yaoundé', *Environment and Urbanization* (London: Africa Research Institute, 2014), https://www.environmentandurbanization.org/booklovers-mayors-and-citizens-participatory-budgeting-yaound%C3%A9-cameroon [accessed 18 November 2021].

43 Glasgow City Council, Participatory Budgeting Framework, https://www.glasgow.gov.uk/index.aspx?articleid=24597 [accessed 18 November 2021]. And for a recent evaluation see: Chris Harkins, 'An Evaluation of Glasgow City Participatory Budgeting Pilot Wards 2018–19', Glasgow Centre for Population Health, October 2019, https://www.gcph.co.uk/assets/0000/7721/An_evaluation_of_Glasgow_City_participatory_budgeting_pilot_wards_2018-19.pdf [accessed 18 November 2021].

44 Yeung, 'How Paris's Participatory Budget Is Reinvigorating Democracy'.

45 Gianpaolo Baiocchi and Ernesto Ganuza, 'Participatory Budgeting as if Emancipation Mattered', *Politics & Society*, 42, 1 (2014), pp. 29–50; Archon Fung, 'Putting the Public Back into Governance: The Challenges of Citizen Participation and Its Future', *Public Administration Review*, 75, 4 (2015), pp. 513–22.

46 Francesca Manes-Rossi, Isabel Brusca, Rebecca Levy Orelli, Peter C. Lorson and Ellen Haustein, 'Features and Drivers of Citizen Participation: Insights from Participatory Budgeting in Three European Cities', *Public Management Review*, (2021), doi: 10.1080/14719037.2021.1963821, [accessed 18 November 2021].

47 For an alternative approach see: Stephan Kyburz and Stephan Schlegel, '8 Principles of Direct Democracy', https://www.cgdev.org/blog/8-principles-direct-democracy [accessed 5 July 2021].

48 See: Michael J. Koplow, 'After Erdogan's Referendum Victory Turkey's Polarization Will Only Deepen', *Foreign Affairs*, 16 April (2017); and Matt Qvortrup, 'The Rise of Referendums: Demystifying Direct Democracy', *Journal of Democracy*, 28, 3 (2017), pp. 141–52.

49 Tony Benn MP, Farewell speech in the UK House of Commons, Hansard, 22 March 2001, https://publications.parliament.uk/pa/cm200001/cmhansrd/vo010322/debtext/10322-13.htm [accessed 5 July 2021].

Chapter 5

1 John Dryzek and Simon Niemeyer, 'What Is Deliberative Democracy?', https://deldem.weblogs.anu.edu.au/2012/02/15/what-is-deliberative-democracy/ [accessed 22 June 2021].

2 This issue is addressed by Carolyn Hendriks, John Dryzek and Christian Hunold in 'Turning Up the Heat: Partisanship in Deliberative Innovation', *Political Studies*, 55, 2 (2007), pp. 362–83 and by Carolyn Hendriks in *The Politics of Public Deliberation – Citizen Engagement and Interest Advocacy* (London: Palgrave Macmillan, 2011).

Notes

3   For a detailed appraisal see: Selen Ercan, 'Deliberative Democracy', in Denis C. Phillips (ed.), *Encyclopedia of Educational Theory and Philosophy* (Thousand Oaks, CA: Sage Publications, 2014), pp. 214–16.

4   For the full report see: Houses of the Oireachtas, *Report of the Joint Committee on the Eighth Amendment of the Constitution* (2017), https://data.oireachtas.ie/ie/oireachtas/committee/dail/32/joint_committee_on_the_eighth_amendment_of_the_constitution/reports/2017/2017-12-20_report-of-the-joint-committee-on-the-eighth-amendment-of-the-constitution_en.pdf. [accessed 5 July 2021].

5   For further detail on America Speaks methodology see: http://ncdd.org/rc/item/tag/21st-century-town-meeting/ [accessed 22 June 2021].

6   For a discussion on the legacy of America Speaks see: https://www.democracyfund.org/blog/entry/farewell-to-americaspeaks [accessed 22 June 2021]; and Abigail Williamson, *The Role of Citizen Participation in Legitimating the Unified New Orleans Plan* (Boston: Kennedy School of Government, Harvard University, 2007), http://www.fisherwilliamson.com/downloads/APPAM.UNOP%20Paper.pdf. [accessed 22 June 2021].

7   See the following insightful blog by Joe Goldman for an overview of America Speaks achievements: https://www.democracyfund.org/blog/entry/farewell-to-americaspeaks [accessed 22 June 2021].

8   '*My administration is committed to creating an unprecedented level of openness in Government. We will work together to ensure the public trust and establish a system of transparency, public participation, and collaboration. Openness will strengthen our democracy and promote efficiency and effectiveness in Government* (President Obama, 21 January 2009)', Obama Archives, https://obamawhitehouse.archives.gov/open [accessed 22 June 2021].

9   See: Danish Board of Technology (DBT), 'About DBT', http://www.tekno.dk/about-dbt-foundation/?lang=en [accessed 6 July 2021].

10 As an independent body of government, the DBT received an annual subsidy from the Danish Parliament to allow them to carry out their research. In addition to this, '[t]he Ministry of Research is the supervising authority for the Board and the Parliament's Research Committee is the Board's steady liaison to the Parliament'. As part of its work, the DBT submits an annual paper to Parliament. As these ties demonstrate, the Foundation primarily influences policy debate through its direct relationship with the Parliament and the government. See 'Profile of the Danish Board of Technology', https://tekno.dk/ [accessed 6 July 2021].

11 For detailed assessments see: Edna Einsiedel et al., 'Publics at the Technology Table: The Consensus Conference in Denmark, Canada, and Australia', *Public Understanding of Science*, 10, 1 (2001), pp. 83–98; and John Dryzek and Aviezer Tucker, 'Deliberative Innovation to Different Effect: Consensus Conferences in Denmark, France, and the United States', *Public Administration Review*, 68, 5 (2008), pp. 864–76.

12 See, for example, Anders Blok, 'Experts on Public Trial: On Democratizing Expertise through a Danish Consensus Conference', *Public Understanding of Science*, 16, 2 (2007), pp. 163–82.

13 In 2010, the Danish Board of Technology won the Jim Creighton Award which is awarded by the International Association for Public Participation.

14 Appreciative Inquiry (AI) is a similar approach for creating a vision and planning to achieve it. AI does this through understanding and appreciating the past, as a basis for imagining the future. See: Archon Fung, 'Varieties of Participation in Complex Governance', *Public Administration Review*, 66 (2006), Special Issue on Collaborative Public Management, pp. 66–75.

Notes

15 For further information see: Anna Lenhart, Joseph Paki and Alana Podolsky, *Consensus Conference on Autonomous Vehicles: Case Study* (Michigan: University of Michigan, 2018), https://deepblue.lib.umich.edu/handle/2027.42/146527 [accessed 6 July 2021].

16 Tom Ritchey, 'Wicked Problems', *Acta Morphologica Generalis*, 2, 1 (2013), pp. 1–8, http://www.swemorph.com/pdf/wp.pdf. [accessed 6 July 2021]. For a discussion, see: Martin Carcasson, 'Tackling Wicked Problems through Deliberative Engagement', *National Civic Review*, 105, 1 (2016), pp. 44–7, doi:10.1002/ncr.21258.

17 Ipsos, 'Two thirds of Citizens Around the World Agree Climate Change Is as Serious a Crisis as Coronavirus', 22 April 2020, https://www.ipsos.com/en/two-thirds-citizens-around-world-agree-climate-change-serious-crisis-coronavirus [accessed 6 July 2021].

18 For further detail see: Climate Assembly UK, 'About Citizens' Assemblies', https://www.climateassembly.uk/about/citizens-assemblies/ [accessed 6 July 2021].

19 Fiona Harvey, 'Thousands of Britons Invited to Climate Crisis Citizens' Assembly', *The Guardian*, 2 November 2019, https://www.theguardian.com/environment/2019/nov/02/thousands-britons-invited-take-part-climate-crisis-citizens-assembly [accessed 6 July 2021].

20 Involve's 'Citizens' Assembly Tracker' provides an excellent tool for 'keeping track of where citizens' assemblies and juries are taking place around the UK and on what topics'. See https://www.involve.org.uk/citizens-assembly-tracker [accessed 18 November 2021].

21 See: Graham Smith, 'Citizens Assemblies: How to Bring the Wisdom of the Public to Bear on the Climate Emergency', *The Conversation*, 27 June 2020, https://theconversation.com/citizens-assemblies-how-to-bring-the-wisdom-of-the-public-to-bear-on-the-climate-emergency-119117 [accessed 6 July 2021].

22 See: Climate Assembly UK, 'About Citizens' Assemblies', and Mathilde Bouyé, 'How Can Citizens Contribute to a Sustainable Recovery? Early Lessons from the French Citizens' Assembly', https://www.wri.org/blog/2020/05/sustainable-recovery-french-citizens-assembly [accessed 6 July 2021].

23 Planning Cells in Germany operate in a broadly similar way with a number of deliberating groups running in parallel in a longer, multiple stage process. See: Peter Dienel, 'Planning Cells: The German Experience', in Usman Khan (ed.), *Participation beyond the Ballot Box: European Case Studies in State-Citizen Political Dialogue* (London: UCL Press, 1995), pp. 88–100.

24 See: Healthy Democracy, 'Citizens' Initiative Review', https://healthydemocracy.org/cir/ [accessed 6 July 2021].

25 For further detail see: MosaicLab, 'Case Study: Jury Shapes Democracy in Geelong', https://www.mosaiclab.com.au/news-all-posts/2016/12/7/case-study-geelong-citizen-jury [accessed 6 July 2021].

26 For further information on the work of Mosaiclab see: https://www.mosaiclab.com.au [accessed 6 July 2021].

27 Nicole Moore, *Co-design and Deliberative Engagement: What Works*, Democracy 2025 Report No. 3. (Canberra: Museum of Australian Democracy/Institute for Governance, 2019), https://www.democracy2025.gov.au/documents/Democracy2025-report3.pdf. [accessed 6 July 2021].

28 See: Robert Goodin and John Dryzek 'Deliberative Impacts: The Macro-Political Uptake of Mini-Publics', *Politics and Society*, 34, 2 (2006), pp. 219–44.

Notes

Chapter 6

1. See, for example, Howard Rheingold, *The Virtual Community* (Reading, MA: Addison Wesley, 1993) and in critique Matthew Hindman, *The Myth of Digital Democracy* (New Jersey: Princeton University Press, 2008); and Jan van Dijk, 'Digital Democracy: Vision and Reality', in Ig Snellen, Marcel Thaens and Wim van de Donk (eds.), *Public Administration in the Information Age Revisited* (Amsterdam: IOS Books, 2012), pp. 49–62.
2. For different conceptual nomenclature see: Stephen Coleman and Deen Freelon, *Handbook of Digital Politics* (Cheltenham: Edward Elgar Publishing, 2015).
3. For this and other dilemmas see: Mark Franklin, *Digital Dilemmas: Power, Resistance, and the Internet* (Oxford: Oxford University Press, 2013).
4. One of the seminal accounts in this regard is W. Lance Bennett and Alexandra Segerberg, *The Logic of Connective Action: Digital Media and the Personalization of Contentious Politics* (Cambridge: Cambridge University Press, 2013).
5. David Karpf concludes with this observation in his book *Analytic Activism: Digital Listening and the New olitical Strategy* (Oxford: Oxford University Press, 2016).
6. This section builds on collaborative work on the notion of digital era governance with Patrick Dunleavy. See, for example, Patrick Dunleavy and Mark Evans, 'Digital Transformation', in Mark Evans, Michelle Grattan and Brendan McCaffrie (eds.), *From Turnbull to Morrison: Trust Divide* (Melbourne: Melbourne University Press, 2019), pp. 242–55. In turn, Patrick's collaboration with Helen Margetts is also critical to the development of these ideas. See: Helen Margetts and Patrick Dunleavy, 'The Second Wave of Digital Era Governance: A Quasi Paradign for Government on the Web', *Philosophical Transactions of the Royal Society*, 371 (2013), pp. 1–17.
7. See: Christopher Politt, 'Technological Change: A Central Yet Neglected Feature of Public Administration', *Journal of Public Administration and Policy*, 3 (2011), pp. 31–53; and Margetts and Dunleavy, 'The Second Wave of Digital Era Governance: A Quasi Paradign for Government on the Web'.
8. UN E-Government Surveys, *2020 United Nation E-Government Survey* (New York: United Nations, 2020), https://www.un.org/development/desa/publications/publication/2020-united-nations-e-government-survey [accessed 7 July 2021].
9. In terms of its application to public service production, Moore's Law is based on the observation that over time outputs in high productivity sectors get cheaper to produce and outputs in low productivity sectors get relatively more expensive. Given that the production of public services tends to be featured by low productivity and is labour-intensive, the relative price of public services rises over time. Digital services can potentially reverse the trend.
10. There are, of course, groups of citizens marginalized from this process of change. Management of the coronavirus demonstrated the increasing digital divide between citizens on a global scale. See: Gregory Porumbescu, 'The Digital Divide Leaves Millions at a Disadvantage during the Coronavirus Pandemic', *The Conversation*, 18 March 2020, https://theconversation.com/the-digital-divide-leaves-millions-at-a-disadvantage-during-the-coronavirus-pandemic-133608 [accessed 7 July 2021].
11. Gerry Stoker and Mark Evans (eds.), *Evidence-based Policy Making and the Social Sciences: Methods That Matter* (Bristol: Policy Press, 2016); and Nicole Moore and Mark Evans, 'It's All in the Practice: Towards Quality Co-design', in Tony Bovaird and Elke Loeffler (eds.),

Notes

Palgrave Handbook of Co-production of Public Services and Outcomes (London: Palgrave Macmillan, 2020), pp. 387–408.

12 Richard Buchanan, 'Design Research and the New Learning', *Design Issues*, 17, 4 (2001), pp. 3–23.

13 See: Peter John, 'Randomised Controlled Trials', in Gerry Stoker and Mark Evans (eds.), *Evidence-based Policy Making in the Social Sciences: Methods that Matter* (Bristol: Policy Press, 2016), pp. 69–82.

14 Matt Ryan, 'Qualitative Comparative Analysis for Reviewing Evidence and Making Decisions', in Gerry Stoker and Mark Evans (eds.), *Evidence-based Policy Making in the Social Sciences: Methods That Matter* (Bristol: Policy Press, 2016), pp. 83–102.

15 Nicole Moore, *Co-design and Deliberative Engagement: What Works*? Democracy 2025 Report No. 3. (Canberra: Museum of Australian Democracy and the Institute of Governance, 2019), https://www.democracy2025.gov.au/resources.html [accessed 7 July 2021], p. 25.

16 Patrick Dunleavy and Mark Evans, 'Digital Transformation'.

17 See: Adam Lewis, Simon Oliver et al., 'The Australian Geoscience Data Cube – Foundations and Lessons Learned', *Remote Sensing of Environment*, 202 (2017), pp. 276–92, doi.org/10.1016/j.rse.2017.03.015 [accessed 7 July 2021].

18 See: Australian Tax Office (ATO), *My Tax* (Canberra: ATO, 2020), https://www.ato.gov.au/Individuals/Lodging-your-tax-return/Lodge-online/ [accessed 7 July 2021]; and Stats New Zealand, *Integrated Data Infrastructure* (Wellington, Stats New Zealand, 2020), https://www.stats.govt.nz/integrated-data/integrated-data-infrastructure/ [accessed 7 July 2021].

19 Most interviewees referred to the Estonian example as a source of emulation but recognized that it wasn't the most exportable example given the country's state of development and different base-line for change.

20 For further information see: GOVTECH Singapore, *eGov Masterplans* (Singapore: GOVTECH, 2016), https://www.tech.gov.sg/media/corporate-publications/egov-masterplans [accessed 7 July 2021].

21 See: Human Rights Watch, *World Report 2019* (New York: Human Rights Watch, 2019), https://www.hrw.org/world-report/2019/country-chapters/singapore [accessed 7 July 2021].

22 See: Australian Commonwealth Ombudsman, *Centrelink's Automated Debt Raising and Recovery System: Implementation Report April 2019* (Canberra: Commonwealth Ombudsman, 2019), https://www.ombudsman.gov.au/__data/assets/pdf_file/0025/98314/April-2019-Centrelinks-Automated-Debt-Raising-and-Recovery-System.pdf [accessed 7 July 2021]; and Commonwealth of Australia Senate Report, *Census: Issues of Trust* (Canberra: Australian Parliament House, 2016), https://www.aph.gov.au/Parliamentary_Business/Committees/Senate/Economics/2016Census/Report [accessed 7 July 2021].

23 Luke Henriques-Gomes, 'Robodebt: Court Approves $1.8bn Settlement for Victims of Government's "shameful" Failure', *The Guardian*, 11 June 2021, https://www.theguardian.com/australia-news/2021/jun/11/robodebt-court-approves-18bn-settlement-for-victims-of-governments-shameful-failure [accessed 11 November 2021].

24 For further information see: Stephen Easton, 'Nadia: The Curious Case of the Digital Missing Person', *The Mandarin*, https://www.themandarin.com.au/106473-nadia-the-curious-case-of-the-digital-missing-person/ [accessed 7 July 2021].

25 Remarkably data.gov receives 20 million page views annually. See: https://www.data.gov/ [accessed 7 July 2021].

Notes

26 See: https://www.congress.gov/bill/115th-congress/house-bill/4174/text#toc-H8E449FBAEFA34E45A6F1F20EFB13ED95 [accessed 7 July 2021].

27 See: eBird, *About eBird* (Ithaca, NY: eBird, 2021), https://ebird.org/about [accessed 7 July 2021] and CSIROscope, *It's a Bird...It's a Plane...It's Citizen Science* (Canberra: CSIRO, 2019), https://blog.csiro.au/its-a-bird-its-a-plane-its-citizen-science/ [accessed 7 July 2021].

28 See: Volunteer Science, *Create Your Own Online Lab* (Boston: Volunteer Science, 2021), https://volunteerscience.com/researchers/ [accessed 7 July 2021].

29 See: Ryan O'Hare, 'Citizen-science Project Measures Impact of Coronavirus Pandemic on Mental Health', *Medical press*, 11 May 2020, https://medicalxpress.com/news/2020-05-citizen-science-impact-coronavirus-pandemic-mental.html [accessed 7 July 2021].

30 See: Brian Burke, *Gamify: How Gamification Motivates People to Do Extraordinary Things* (Brookline, MA: Bibliomotion, 2014).

31 See: Peter John et al., *Nudge, Nudge, Think, Think: Experimenting with Ways to Change Civic Behaviour* (London: Bloomsbury Academic, 2011).

32 See: NESTA, *Our Futures, by the People, for the People* (London: NESTA, 2019), https://www.nesta.org.uk/report/our-futures-people-people/ [accessed 5 July 2021].

33 Bennett and Segerberg, *The Logic of Connective Action*.

34 See: The *Participedia* project (https://participedia.net/); and *Healthy Democracy* (https://healthydemocracy.org/) for a broad range of examples from around the world [both sources accessed 7 July 2021].

35 See the interview with Paolo Gerbaudo at Pluto Books, https://www.plutobooks.com/blog/momentum-labour-online-digital-activism-social-media-party/ and with Open Democracy, https://www.opendemocracy.net/en/digitaliberties/digital-parties-on-rise-mass-politics-for-era-of-platforms/ [both sources accessed 7 July 2021].

36 See: Jörg Schatzmann, René Schäfer and Frederik Eichelbaum, 'Foresight 2.0 – Definition, Overview and Evaluation', *European Journal of Futures Research*, 1, 1 (2013), pp. 1–15.

37 See: Viewpoint, *Learninghub*, https://www.vpthub.com [accessed 5 July 2021].

38 See: Mark Evans, Gerry Stoker and Max Halupka, *Democracy 100: You Can Make a Difference: Towards a Charter for Australian Democracy* (Canberra: Museum of Australian Democracy and the Institute of Governance, 2017), https://www.democracy2025.gov.au/resources.html [accessed 5 July 2021].

39 National Issues Forums, *With the People*, https://www.nifi.org/ [accessed 5 July 2021].

40 Sinia Royo, Vicente Pina and Jaime Garcia-Rayado, 'Decide Madrid: A Critical Analysis of an Award-winning e-Participation Initiative', *Sustainability*, 12, 4 (2020), 1674, p. 7.

41 Consul is an organization which provides free software for citizen participation. The programme was awarded a United Nations Public Service Award, http://consulproject.org/en/ [accessed 5 July 2021].

42 *Better Reykjavik* is an open online consultation forum, https://reykjavik.is/en/better-reykjavik-0 [accessed 5 July 2021].

43 Royo, Pina and Garcia-Rayado, 'Decide Madrid', pp. 18–19.

44 Ibid.

45 Ibid.

46 For a useful evaluation framework see: Vivien Lowndes, Lawrence Pratchett and Gerry Stoker, 'Diagnosing and Remedying the Failings of Official Participation Schemes: The CLEAR Framework', *Social Policy and Society*, 5, 2 (2006), pp. 281–91.

Notes

47 W. Lance Bennett and Alexandra Segerberg, *The Logic of Connective Action*.
48 See, for example, the pioneers of the Citizens' Initiative Review process *Healthy Democracy*.

Chapter 7

1 David Beetham, 'Do Parliaments Have a Future?' in Sonia Alonso, John Keane and Wolfgang Merkel (eds.), *The Future of Representative Democracy* (Cambridge: Cambridge University Press, 2011), pp. 124–43, p. 124.

2 John Keane, 'Monitory Democracy?' in Sonia Alonso, John Keane and Wolfgang Merkel (eds.), *The Future of Representative Democracy* (Cambridge: Cambridge University Press, 2011), pp. 212–35.

3 A review of the evidence from the World Values Survey shows that a key trend across a wide range of political regimes is loss of trust in parliaments and parties. See TrustGov.net [accessed 7 July 2021].

4 We shall use these terms interchangeably in this chapter noting the difference in primary and secondary legislative powers afforded to these different institutions of representative democracy.

5 Inter-Parliamentary Union, *Women in National Parliaments*, http://archive.ipu.org/wmn-e/world.htm [accessed 7 July 2021].

6 Peter Allen, *The Political Class* (Oxford: Oxford University Press, 2018), pp. 25–7.

7 The evidence in support of these observations is Australian and UK based at present. See Mark Evans, Max Halupka and Gerry Stoker, 'Trust and Democracy in Australia', in Mark Evans, Michelle Grattan and Brendan McCaffrie (eds.), *From Turnbull to Morrison: Trust Divide* (Melbourne: Melbourne University Press, 2019), pp. 17–35; and Nick Clarke, Will Jennings, Jonathan Moss and Gerry Stoker, *The Good Politician: Folk Theories, Political Interaction and the Rise of Anti-Politics* (Cambridge: Cambridge University Press, 2019).

8 We also examine the attributes of the good politician in Chapters 2 and 8.

9 See: Anthony King and Ivor Crewe, *The Blunders of Our Governments* (London: Oneworld, 2013); and Will Jennings, Martin Lodge and Matt Ryan, 'Comparing Blunders in Government', *European Journal of Political Research*, 57, 1 (2018), pp. 238–58.

10 See: Lu Hong and Scott E. Page, 'Groups of Diverse Problem Solvers Can Outperform Groups of High-ability Problem Solvers', *Proceedings of the National Academy of Science*, 101, 46 (2004), pp. 16385–9; and Scott Page, *Diversity and Complexity* (New Jersey: Princeton University Press, 2011).

11 Many of these arguments are marshalled effectively by Jane Mansbridge in 'Should Blacks Represent Blacks and Women Represent Women? A Contingent "Yes"', *Journal of Politics*, 61, 3 (1999), pp. 628–57.

12 On descriptive representation see: Claudine Gay, 'Spirals of Trust? The Effect of Descriptive Representation on the Relationship between Citizens and Their Government', *American Journal of Political Science*, 46, 4 (2020), pp. 717–32; and Jonathan Homola, 'The Effects of Women's Descriptive Representation on Government Behaviour', *Legislative Studies Quarterly* (2021), https://doi.org/10.1111/lsq.12330 [accessed 7 July 2021].

13 See: Anne Philips, 2012, 'Representation and Inclusion'.

14 For the differences between 'descriptive' and 'substantive' representation see: Kenneth Lowande, Melinda Ritchie and Erinn Lauterbach, 'Descriptive and Substantive

Notes

Representation in Congress: Evidence from 80,000 Congressional Inquiries', *American Journal of Political Science*, 63, 3 (2019), pp. 644–59.

15 The key distinction was developed by Pippa Norris and Joni Lovenduski, *Political Recruitment: Gender, Race and Class in the British Parliament* (Cambridge: Cambridge University Press, 1995).

16 Peter Allen and David Cutts, 'An Analysis of Political Ambition in Britain', *Political Quarterly*, 89, 1 (2018), pp. 73–81.

17 See: Richard Fox and Jennifer Lawless, 'To Run or Not to Run for Office: Explaining Nascent Political Ambition', *American Journal of Political Science*, 49, 3 (2005), pp. 642–59.

18 Isabel Hardman, *Why We Get the Wrong Politicians* (London: Atlantic Books, 2018).

19 Allen, *The Political Class*, p. 93.

20 Ibid., p. 14.

21 See: Sarah Childs, *The Good Parliament* (Bristol: University of Bristol, 2016), https://researchbriefings.files.parliament.uk/documents/CDP-2016-0201/CDP-2016-0201.pdf [accessed 7 July 2021].

22 See: Gerry Stoker, 'Women in Politics: Who Set the House Rules?' *Broad Agenda*, 21 November 2017, https://www.broadagenda.com.au/2017/women-in-politics-who-set-the-house-rules/ [accessed 7 July 2021].

23 See: Sarah Childs, 'A Female Prime Minister Is Not Enough, Britain Needs a Representative Parliament Too', University of Bristol Media Release, 6 July 2016, http://www.bristol.ac.uk/news/2016/july/female-prime-minister.html [accessed 7 July 2021].

24 See: Allen, *The Political Class*, pp. 98–104 for a review of the evidence and arguments.

25 See: GOVLAB, 'Belgium Sortition Models', https://congress.crowd.law/case-belgian-sortition-models.html [accessed 18 November 2021].

26 Rachel Reeves, *Women of Westminster: The MPs That Changed Politics* (London: Bloomsbury, 2020). See: also Rachel Reeves, 'The Women of Westminster and How They Have Transformed Politics beyond Recognition', *LSE Blog*, https://blogs.lse.ac.uk/politicsandpolicy/the-women-of-westminster/ [accessed 7 July 2021]; and Claire Devlin and Robert Elgie, 'The Effect of Increased Women's Representation in Parliament: The Case of Rwanda', *Parliamentary Affairs*, 61, 2 (2008), pp. 237–54.

27 Cristina Leston-Bandeira, 'Parliamentary Petitions and Public Engagement: An Empirical Analysis of the Role of E-petitions', *Policy & Politics*, 47, 3 (2019), pp. 415–36.

28 Carolyn Hendriks, 'Coupling Citizens and Elites in Deliberative Systems: The Role of Institutional Design', *European Journal of Political Research*, 55, 1 (2016), pp. 43–60, p. 44.

29 Leston-Bandeira, 'Parliamentary Petitions and Public Engagement', p. 420.

30 Ibid., p. 432.

31 See: Involve, *Innovations for Select Committee Engagement* (London: Involve, 2017), https://www.involve.org.uk/resources/publications/practical-guidance/innovations-select-committee-engagement [accessed 7 July 2021], p. 40.

32 Ibid.

33 Carolyn Hendriks and Adrian Kay, 'From "Opening Up" to Democratic Renewal: Deepening Public Engagement in Legislative Committees', *Government and Opposition*, 54, 1 (2017), pp. 20–1.

34 Clive Betts MP and Dr. Sarah Wollaston MP, 'How a Citizens' Assembly Helped Select Committees Find Social Care Consensus', *Hansard Society Blog*, 10 October 2018,

Notes

https://www.hansardsociety.org.uk/blog/how-a-citizens-assembly-helped-select-committees-find-social-care-consensus [accessed 7 July 2021].

35 See, for example, the audit criteria developed by the Democratic Audit of the United Kingdom based at the London School of Economics and Political Science, https://www.democraticaudit.com/ [accessed 7 July 2021].

36 See: Vivien Lowndes, Lawrence Pratchett and Gerry Stoker, 'Diagnosing and Remedying the Failings of Official Participation Schemes: The CLEAR Framework', *Social Policy and Society*, 5, 2 (2006), pp. 281–91.

Chapter 8

1 James D. Long, 'Why Trump's Challenges to Democracy Will Be a Big Problem for Biden', *The Conversation*, 11 January 2021, https://theconversation.com/why-trumps-challenges-to-democracy-will-be-a-big-problem-for-biden-152218 [accessed 7 July 2021].

2 Australia is currently bucking the international trend due to positive perceptions of the Federal Government's management of Covid-19. See: Edelman Trust Barometer 2021, https://www.edelman.com/trust/2021-trust-barometer [accessed 7 July 2021]; and Will Jennings, Viktor Valgardsson, Gerry Stoker, Dan Devine, Jenn Gaskell and Mark Evans, Democracy 2025 Report No 8: *Political Trust and the COVID-19 Crisis – Pushing Populism to the Backburner? A Study of Public Opinion in Australia, Italy, the UK and the USA* (Canberra: IGPA/MoAD/Trustgov, 2020), https://www.democracy2025.gov.au/resources.html [accessed 7 July 2021].

3 See: Bo Rothstein, *The Quality of Government: Corruption, Social Trust, and Inequality in International Perspective* (Chicago: University of Chicago Press, 2011); and Jennings et al., *Political Trust and the COVID-19 Crisis*. Although it is important to note that there is strong evidence to demonstrate that a higher prevalence of postmaterialist values induces more corruption disapproval, and especially among postmaterialists themselves. See Maria Kravtsova, Aleksey Oshchepkov and Christian Welzel, 'Values and Corruption: Do Postmaterialists Justify Bribery?' *Journal of Cross-cultural Psychology*, 48, 2 (2017), pp. 225–42.

4 See: Transparency International, *CPI 2019 Global Highlights*, https://www.transparency.org/en/news/cpi-2019-global-highlights [accessed 7 July 2021].

5 Amongst the established democracies, New Zealand (87) and Denmark (87), followed by Finland (86), Singapore (85), Sweden (85), Switzerland (85), Norway (84) and Germany (80) come in the top tier. Australia (77), Canada (77), the UK (77), United States (69), France 69 and Spain (62), occupy spots in the second tier. With a score of 53, Italy increased by 11 points since 2012, while Greece (48) increased by 12 points during the same period. Both countries experienced institutional improvements, including the passage of anti-corruption laws and the creation of anti-corruption agencies in both countries.

6 For a discussion see: Nicholas Allen, 'A New Ethical World of British MPs?' *The Journal of Legislative Studies*, 14, 3 (2008), pp. 297–314.

7 See: OECD, *The OECD Integrity Framework* (Paris: OECD), http://www.oecd.org/gov/44462729.pdf [accessed 7 July 2021].

8 Kenneth Kernaghan, 'Promoting Public Service Ethics: The Codification Option', in Richard Chapman (ed.), *Ethics in Public Service* (Edinburgh: Edinburgh University Press, 1993), p. 16.

9   For a discussion see: Mark Evans, 'Beyond the Integrity Paradox – Towards "Good Enough" Governance?' *Policy Studies*, 33, 1 (2012), pp. 97–113.

10 See: Merrilee Grindle, 'Good Enough Governance: Poverty Reduction and Reform in Developing Countries', *Governance*, 17, 4 (2004), pp. 525–48.

11 See: Brian Head, 'Wicked Problems in Public Policy', *Public Policy*, 3, 2 (2008), pp. 101–18; A.J. Brown and John Uhr, 'Integrity Systems: Conceiving, Describing, Assessing', *2004 Australasian Political Studies Association Conference*, https://citeseerx.ist.psu.edu/viewdoc/download?doi=10.1.1.572.1745&rep=rep1&type=pdf [accessed 7 July 2021].

12 See: Integrity Action, http://integrityaction.org/corruption [accessed 7 July 2021].

13 Brown and Uhr, 'Integrity Systems: Conceiving, Describing, Assessing', p. 3.

14 Ian Thynne, 'Institutional Maturity and Challenges for Integrity Bodies', *Policy Studies*, 33, 1 (2012), pp. 37–47, p. 37.

15 John Dewey, *Democracy and Education: An Introduction to the Philosophy of Education* (New York: Free Press, 1966 [1916]).

16 Harold D. Lasswell, *Politics: Who Gets What, When, How* (New York: Whittlesey House, 1936), pp. ix and 264. See also David Easton, *A Framework for Political Analysis* (New York: John Wiley, 1965). For a contemporary application, see: Rein Taagepera and Matt Qvortrup, 'Who Gets What, When, How – Through Which Electoral System?' *European Political Science*, 11 (2012), pp. 244–58.

17 Joseph Stiglitz, *The Price of Inequality: How Today's Divided Society Endangers Our Future* (New York: W.W. Norton and Co, 2012).

18 See: Andre Gratto, Bryan Preston and Thor Snilsberg, *Mitigating Corruption in New Public Management*. Conference paper presented to Professor Mildred Warner, *Privatization and Devolution CRP 612* (Ithaca, NY: Cornell University), http://s3.amazonaws.com/mildredwarner.org/attachments/000/000/318/original/b0c039c239111fc1728c18b7b3e685f1 [accessed 7 July 2021].

19 Mark Bevir, *Democratic Governance* (New Jersey: Princeton University Press, 2010).

20 Richard S. Katz and Peter Mair, 'Changing Models of Party Organization and Party Democracy: The Emergence of the Cartel Party', *Party Politics*, 1 (2014), pp. 5–18.

21 Decca Aitkenhead, 'Interview with Andy Burnham: We've Lost the Art of Thinking Bigger'. *The Guardian*, 9 August 2013, https://www.theguardian.com/theguardian/2013/aug/09/andy-burnham-interview-thinking-bigger [accessed 7 July 2021].

22 See: Soeren Henn, 'The Further Rise of the Career Politician', *British Politics*, 13 (2018), pp. 524–53.

23 Kellogg, *Varieties of Democracy Project*, https://www.v-dem.net/en/about/ [accessed 4 March 2021].

24 See: Sonia Alonso, John Keane and Wolfgang Merkel (eds.), *The Future of Representative Democracy* (Cambridge: Cambridge University Press, 2011), pp. 124–43; Florence Faucher, 'New Forms of Political Participation: Changing Demands or Changing Opportunities to Participate in Political Parties', *Comparative European Politics*, 13 (2015), pp. 405–29; and, Paolo Gerbaudo, *The Digital Party* (London: Pluto Books, 2019).

25 OECD, *Behavioural Insights for Public Integrity: Harnessing the Human Factor to Counter Corruption: The Dynamics of Moral Decision-making* (Paris: OECD, 2018), https://www.oecd.org/gov/ethics/behavioural-insights-for-public-integrity-9789264297067-en.htm [accessed 7 July 2021].

Notes

26 See: Daniel Kahneman, *Thinking, Fast and Slow* (New York: Macmillan, 2011); and Richard H. Thaler and Cass R. Sunstein, *Nudge: Improving Decisions about Health, Wealth, and Happiness* (New Haven, CT: Yale University Press, 2008).

27 See: Peter John, *How Far to Nudge?: Assessing Behavioural Public Policy* (Cheltenham: Edward Elgar, 2018).

28 Brigitte C. Madrian (2014), 'Applying Insights from Behavioural Economics to Policy Design', *Annual Review of Economics*, 6 (2014), pp. 663–88.

29 Susannah Hume, Peter John, Michael Sanders and Emma Stockdale, *Nudge in the Time of Coronavirus: The Compliance to Behavioural Messages during Crisis* (20 March 2021), http://dx.doi.org/10.2139/ssrn.3644165 [accessed 7 July 2021].

30 David Halpern and Michael Sanders, 'Nudging by Government: Progress, Impact, and Lessons Learned', *Behavioral Science & Policy*, 2, 2 (2016), pp. 52–65.

31 See: OECD, *Behavioural Insights and Public Policy: Lessons from around the World* (Paris: OECD, 2017); and OECD, *Behavioural Insights for Public Integrity*.

32 OECD, *A Nudge in the Right Direction: Applying Behavioural Insights to Public Integrity* (Paris: OECD, 2018), https://oecdonthelevel.com/2018/03/12/a-nudge-in-the-right-direction-applying-behavioural-insights-to-public-integrity/ [accessed 7 July 2021].

33 OECD, *Behavioural Insights for Public Integrity*, Executive summary.

34 See: David Halpern, *Inside the Nudge Unit* (London: Penguin Random House, 2015).

35 For an example, see: Mark Evans, Gerry Stoker and Max Halupka, *Democracy 100: You Can Make a Difference: Towards a Charter for Australian Democracy*.

36 Behavioural Insights Unit, Mindspace, (London: BI), https://www.bi.team/publications/mindspace/ [accessed 7 July 2021].

37 Nolan Committee on Standards in Public Life (UK), *The Seven Principles of Public Life*, https://www.gov.uk/government/publications/the-7-principles-of-public-life [accessed 7 July 2021].

38 Ibid.

Chapter 9

1 James March and Johan Olsen, *Democratic Governance* (New York: Free Press, 1995), p. 178.

2 Taner Edis, 'A Revolt against Expertise: Pseudoscience, Right-wing Populism, and Post-truth Politics', *Disputatio*, 9, 13 (2020), pp. 1–29.

3 See: Ruth Lightbody and Jennifer J. Roberts, 'Experts: The Politics of Evidence and Expertise in Democratic Innovation', in Stephen Elstub and Oliver Escobar (eds.), *Handbook of Democratic Innovation and Governance* (Cheltenham: Edward Elgar, 2019), pp. 225–40.

4 For evidence on this point see: Eri E. Bertsou and Daniele Caramani, 2021, 'People Haven't Had Enough of Experts: Technocratic Attitudes among Citizens in Nine European Democracies.'

5 For a development of these arguments see: Eri Bertsou and Daniele Caramani, *The Technocratic Challenge to Democracy* (London: Routledge/Taylor and Francis, 2020).

6 Edward Page, 'Bureaucrats and Expertise: Elucidating a Problematic Relationship in Three Tableaux and Six Jurisdictions', *Sociologie du Travail*, 52, 2 (2010), pp. 255–73.

Notes

7   Tom Nichols, *The Death of Expertise. The Campaign against Established Knowledge and Why It Matters* (Oxford: Oxford University Press, 2017).

8   See: Shannon Jenkins, 2020, 'Big Four Consultancy Firms Receive $640mn a Year to Perform "day-to-day" Public Service Jobs', *The Mandarin*, 17 June 2020, https://www.themandarin.com.au/135197-big-four-consultancy-firms-receive-640mn-a-year-to-perform-day-to-day-public-service-jobs/ [accessed 8 July 2021].

9   Peter Haas, 'Epistemic Communities', in Daniel Bodansky, Jutta Brunnée and Ellen Hey (eds.), *The Oxford Handbook of International Environmental Law* (Oxford: Oxford University Press, 2012).

10 Ibid. See also: Roger Pielke, *The Honest Broker: Making Sense of Science in Policy and Politics* (Cambridge: Cambridge University Press, 2007).

11 See: Peter Self, *Administrative Theories and Politics* (London: George Allen & Unwin, 1977); and Alan Fenna and Linda Botterill, *Interrogating Public Policy Theory: A Political Values Perspective* (Cheltenham: Edward Elgar, 2019).

12 Self, *Administrative Theories and Politics*, p. 207.

13 For the British and US cases see: John Clarke and Janet Newman, '"People in This Country Have Had Enough of Experts": Brexit and the Paradoxes of Populism', *Critical Policy Studies*, 11, 1 (2017), pp. 101–16; and Eric Merkley, 'Anti-Intellectualism, Populism, and Motivated Resistance to Expert Consensus', *Public Opinion Quarterly*, 84, 1 (2020), pp. 24–48.

14 Nichols, *The Death of Expertise*, p. 3.

15 Quoted in Michael Deacon, 'Michael Gove's Guide to Britain's Greatest Enemy… the Experts', *Telegraph Online*, June 2016, https://www.telegraph.co.uk/news/2016/06/10/michael-goves-guide-to-britains-greatest-enemy-the-experts/ [accessed 8 July 2021].

16 James Traub, 'First, They Came for the Experts', *Foreign Policy*, 7 July 2016. See also: Stephen Cushion and Justin Lewis, 'Impartiality, Statistical Tit-for-tats and the Construction of Balance: UK Television News Reporting of the 2016 EU Referendum Campaign', *European Journal of Communication*, 32, 3 (2017), pp. 208–23.

17 Wellcome Global Monitor Report 2018, https://wellcome.org/reports/wellcome-global-monitor/2018 [accessed 8 July 2021].

18 See: 3M, *State of Science Index 2021*, https://www.3m.com/3M/en_US/state-of-science-index-survey/ [accessed 8 July 2021].

19 See: Cas Mudde, 'The Populist Zeitgeist', *Government and Opposition*, 39, 4 (2004), pp. 542–63.

20 Eric Merkley and Peter Loewen, 'Anti-intellectualism and the Mass Public's Response to the COVID-19 Pandemic', *Natural Human Behaviour* (2021), https://doi.org/10.1038/s41562-021-01112-w. [accessed 8 July 2021].

21 See: Gabriel Moore, Angela Todd and Sally Redman, *Strategies to Increase the Use of Evidence from Research in Population Health Policy and Programs: A Rapid Review* (Sydney: Sax Institute for NSW Health, 2009), https://www.health.nsw.gov.au/research/Documents/10-strategies-to-increase-research-use.pdf [accessed 8 July 2021].

22 See: Mark Evans, 'The Art of Prescription: Theory and Practice in Public Administration Research', *Public Policy and Administration*, 84, 2 (2007), pp. 128–52; Jonathan Lomas, 'The in-between World of Knowledge Brokering', *BMJ*, 334 (2007), pp. 129–32; and, for a more recent account, Trish Mercer, Russell Ayres, Brian Head and John Wanna (eds.), *Learning Policy, Doing Policy* (Canberra: ANU Press, 2021).

Notes

23 Peter Saunders and James Walter (eds.), *Ideas and Influence: Social Science and Public Policy in Australia* (Sydney: UNSW Press, 2005), p. 13.

24 Carol H. Weiss, 'Policy Research in the Context of Diffuse Decision Making', *The Journal of Higher Education*, 53, 6 (1982), pp. 619–39.

25 Nancy Cartwright and Jeremy Hardie, *Evidence-based Policy: A Practical Guide to Doing It Better* (Oxford: Oxford University Press, 2012), p. 12.

26 Institute of Public Affairs (IPA), *Evidence Based Policy Research Project: 20 Case Studies* (Sydney: new Democracy Foundation/IPA, 2018), https://apo.org.au/sites/default/files/resource-files/2019-11/apo-nid268021.pdf. [accessed 8 July 2021].

27 Institute of Public Affairs, *Evidence Based Policy Research Project*, pp. 4–5.

28 Ibid.

29 This is also termed the OPEN Government Data Act, Pub.L. pp. 115–435.

30 See: Robert Hahn, 'Building Upon Foundations for Evidence-based Policy', *Science*, 364 (2019), 6440, pp. 534–5, p. 534.

31 Moore, Todd and Redman, *Strategies to Increase the Use of Evidence from Research in Population Health Policy and Programs*, p. 7.

32 Danielle Campbell, Donald Braedon, Gabriel Moore and Deborah Frew, 'Evidence Check: Knowledge Brokering to Commission Research Review for Policy', *Evidence and Policy*, 7, 1 (2011), pp. 97–107.

33 See: Lomas, 'The in-between World of Knowledge Brokering'.

34 Chris Ansell and Alison Gash, 'Collaborative Governance in Theory and Practice', *Journal of Public Administration Research and Theory*, 18, 4 (2008), pp. 543–71, p. 544.

35 As Keith Provan and Patrick Kenis observe, the term 'network governance' is closely associated with collaborative governance but is broader in scope as it captures: '…groups of three or more legally autonomous organizations that work together to achieve not only their own goals but also a collective goal'. See: Provan and Kenis, 'Modes of Network Governance: Structure, Management, and Effectiveness', *Journal of Public Administration Research and Theory*, 18, 2 (2007), pp. 229–52, p. 231.

36 See: John Butcher and David Gilchrist, *Collaboration for Impact: Lessons from the Field* (Canberra: ANZSOG/ANU Press, 2020).

37 See: Kirk Emerson and Tina Nabatchi, 'Evaluating the Productivity of Collaborative Governance Regimes: A Performance Matrix', *Public Performance & Management Review*, 38, 4 (2015), pp. 717–47. In this article, Emerson and Nabatchi develop a performance matrix to assess the productivity of collaborative governance – this is a useful tool which ensures a comprehensive review of three units of analysis (participant organizations, the collaboration itself and target goals) and tests three performance levels (actions, outcomes and adaption).

38 See: Mark B. Brown, 'Expertise and Deliberative Democracy', in Stephen Elstub and Peter Mclaverty (eds.), *Deliberative Democracy: Issues and Cases* (Edinburgh: Edinburgh University Press), pp. 50–68; and Frank Fischer, *Democracy and Expertise* (Oxford: Oxford University Press, 2009).

39 See: Jakob Trischler, Timo Ditrich and Sharyn Rundle-Thiele, 'Co-design: From expert- to User-driven Ideas in Public Service Design', *Public Management Review*, 21, 11 (2019), pp. 1595–619.

40 See: John Boddy and Nina Terrey, *Design for a Better Future: A Guide to Designing in Complex Systems* (Abingdon: Routledge/Taylor and Francis, 2019).

Notes

41 See: Jennifer Kavanagh and Michael Rich, *Truth Decay: An Initial Exploration of the Diminishing Role of Facts and Analysis in American Public Life* (Santa Monica, CA: RAND Corporation, 2018), https://www.rand.org/content/dam/rand/pubs/research_reports/RR2300/RR2314/RAND_RR2314.pdf [accessed 7 July 2021].

42 In recent national elections, Finland urged voters to think about fake news, with government-commissioned adverts encouraging them to choose independently.

Chapter 10

1 See: UNESCO, *World Press Freedom Day*, https://en.unesco.org/commemorations/worldpressfreedomday [accessed 28 May 2021].

2 Ibid.

3 Margaret Scammell and Holli Semetko (eds.), *The Media, Journalism and Democracy* (Aldershot: Ashgate, 2000), pp. xi–xii.

4 See: John Street, *Mass Media, Politics and Democracy* (London: Palgrave Macmillan, 2010); and Dennis McQuail, *McQuail's Mass Communication Theory* (London: Sage Publications, 2005).

5 Nael Jebril, Václav Štětka and Matthew Loveless, 'Media and Democratization: What Is Known about the Role of the Mass Media in Transitions to Democracy?' *Reuters Institute for the Study of Journalism*, University of Oxford, 9 October 2013, https://www.politics.ox.ac.uk/news/media-and-democratisation-what-is-known-about-the-role-of-mass-media-in-transitions-to-democracy.html [accessed 7 July 2021].

6 Matthew Loveless, 'Understanding Media Socialization in Democratizing Countries: Mobilization and Malaise in Central and Eastern Europe', *Comparative Politics*, 42, 4 (2010), pp. 457–74, p. 470.

7 For the key sources see: Glenn Greewald, 'Edward Snowden: The Whistleblower behind the NSA Surveillance Revelations', *The Guardian*, 11 June 2013, https://www.theguardian.com/world/2013/jun/09/edward-snowden-nsa-whistleblower-surveillance [accessed 28 May 2021]; and Reuters, 'NSA Surveillance Exposed by Snowden Was Illegal, Court Rules Seven Years On', *The Guardian*, 3 September 2020. Retrieved 21 June 2021 from: https://www.theguardian.com/us-news/2020/sep/03/edward-snowden-nsa-surveillance-guardian-court-rules [accessed 28 May 2021].

8 Reporters without Borders, *The 2021 World Press Freedom Index* evaluates press freedom in 180 countries and territories annually. See: https://rsf.org/en/ranking [accessed 7 July 2021].

9 *Edelman Trust Barometer 2021*.

10 Ibid.

11 For key sources see: Hal Berghel, 'New Perspectives on (Anti)Social Media', *Computer*, 53, 3 (2020), pp. 77–82; Roger McNamee, *Zucked: Waking up to the Facebook Catastrophe* (Baltimore, MD: Penguin, 2019); and Christopher Wylie, *Mindf*ck: Cambridge Analytica and the Plot to Break America* (New York: Random House, 2019).

12 Reporters without Borders, *Information and Democracy Commission*, https://rsf.org/en/christophe-deloire [accessed 7 July 2021].

13 Graeme Turner, 'The Media and Democracy in the Digital Age: Is This What We Had in Mind?' *Media International Australia*, 168, 1 (2018), pp. 3–14.

Notes

14 See: Derek Wilding, Peter Fray, Sacha Molitorisz and Elaine McKewon, *The Impact of Digital Platforms on News and Journalistic Content*, Centre for Media Transition (Sydney: University of Technology, NSW, 2018).

15 Jennifer Kavanagh and Michael Rich, *Truth Decay: An Initial Exploration of the Diminishing Role of Facts and Analysis in American Public Life* (Santa Monica, CA: RAND Corporation, 2018), https://www.rand.org/content/dam/rand/pubs/research_reports/RR2300/RR2314/RAND_RR2314.pdf [accessed 7 July 2021].

16 See: Globescan, 'New Global Poll Documents the Pandemic's Impact on Inequality', 10 September 2020, https://globescan.com/tag/bbc-world-service-survey/ [accessed 7 July 2021].

17 See: Associated Press, 'Not Just Russia: China and Iran May Target US Elections, Experts Say', *The Guardian*, 31 October 2019, https://www.theguardian.com/us-news/2019/oct/30/us-elections-2020-hacking-misinformation-russia-china-iran [accessed 7 July 2021].

18 These models are ideal types and do not necessarily describe specific industry sectors. See: Thomas Hess, 'What Is a Media Company? A Reconceptualization for the Online World', *The International Journal on Media Management*, 16 (2014), pp. 3–8; and Nobuko Kawashima, 'Changing Business Models in the Media Industries', *Media Industries*, 7, 1 (2020), https://quod.lib.umich.edu/m/mij/15031809.0007.105?view=text;rgn=main [accessed 3 May 2021].

19 Yochai Benkler, Robert Faris and Hal Roberts, *Network Propaganda: Manipulation, Disinformation, and Radicalization in American Politics* (Oxford/New York: Oxford University Press, 2018), p. 221.

20 Ibid., p. 5.

21 See: Karl Popper, Alan Ryan and Ernst Hans Gombrich, *The Open Society and Its Enemies* (New Jersey and Oxford: Princeton University Press, 2013).

22 Clive Hollick, 'Media Regulation and Democracy', *Index of Censorship*, 4/5 (1994), pp. 54–8.

23 For the Federal Communications Commission see: https://www.fcc.gov/media/radio/public-and-broadcasting#OTHERAPP [accessed 7 July 2021].

24 Kathleen Ann Ruane, 'Fairness Doctrine: History and Constitutional Issues, Congressional Research Service', 13 July 2011, https://digital.library.unt.edu/ark:/67531/metadc822082/ [accessed 7 July 2021].

25 The mandate of equal airtime for office seekers became federal law in 1959, when Congress amended the Communications Act.

26 Notably the decision had no impact on the rule that candidates for public office be offered equal airtime, since that had become law. It also left the editorial and personal-attack provisions, which remained in effect until 2000. See: Robert D. Hershey Jr., 'F.C.C. Votes Down Fairness Doctrine in a 4-0 Decision', *New York Times*, 5 August 1987, https://www.nytimes.com/1987/08/05/arts/fcc-votes-down-fairness-doctrine-in-a-4-0-decision.html [accessed 7 July 2021].

27 Dylan Matthews 'Everything You Need to Know about the Fairness Doctrine in One Post', *Washington Post*, 23 August 2011, https://www.washingtonpost.com/blogs/ezra-klein/post/everything-you-need-to-know-about-the-fairness-doctrine-in-one-post/2011/08/23/gIQAN8CXZJ_blog.html [accessed 7 July 2021].

28 Keach Hagey, 'Fairness Doctrine Fight Goes On', *Politico*, 16 January 2011, https://www.politico.com/story/2011/01/fairness-doctrine-fight-goes-on-047669 [accessed 7 July 2021].

29 Hollick, 'Media Regulation and Democracy', p. 58.

Notes

30   Ronald Hamowy (ed.), *The Encyclopaedia of Libertarianism* (Thousand Oaks, CA: Sage Publications, 2008), p. xxi.

31   See: Karina Rigby, 'Anonymity on the Internet Must Be Protected', *MIT Paper* (Fall 1995), http://groups.csail.mit.edu/mac/classes/6.805/student-papers/fall95-papers/rigby-anonymity.html [accessed 7 July 2021].

32   For contending views see: Adir Shiffman, 'Time to End the Age of Anonymity Online', *Financial Review*, 6 May 2019, https://www.afr.com/technology/time-to-end-the-age-of-anonymity-online-20190503-p51jyd [accessed 7 July 2021]; and Arthur D. Santana, 'Virtuous or Vitriolic', *Journalism Practice*, 8, 1 (2014), pp. 18–33, doi:10.1080/17512786.2013.813194.

33   The indicators have different importance and are assigned different weight in the model with the media freedom indicators having the highest weight along with the education indicators with reading literacy having the highest share among them. The e-participation and trust in people indicators have less weight relative to the other indicators.

34   See: Emma Charlton, 'Facts or Fakery? Finland Is Teaching Children How to Tell the Difference', *World Economic Forum*, 21 May 2019, https://www.weforum.org/agenda/2019/05/how-finland-is-fighting-fake-news-in-the-classroom/ [accessed 7 July 2021].

35   Ibid.

36   In the recent 2019 national elections, the Finland Government urged voters to think about fake news, with government-commissioned adverts encouraging them to choose independently.

37   See: Patrick Dunleavy (ed.), *The UK's Changing Democracy: The 2018 Democratic Audit* (London: LSE Press, 2018), https://www.democraticaudit.com/the-uks-changing-democracy-the-2018-democratic-audit/ [accessed 18 November 2021].

Chapter 11

1   See: Gerry Stoker and Mark Evans, Democracy 2025 Report No. 2. *What Lessons Can We Draw from International Experience for Bridging the Trust Divide?* (Canberra: IGPA/MoAD, 2018), https://www.democracy2025.gov.au/resources.html. [accessed 8 July 2021].

2   Christine Boswell, *Manufacturing Political Trust* (New York: Cambridge University Press, 2018).

3   Tom Tyler and Rick Trinkner, *Why Children Follow Rules* (Oxford: Oxford University Press, 2017). We have already seen in the throughputs section of the book that the problem of performance legitimacy extends to the construction of representative politics, the representativeness of those elected, the behaviour of politicians, the community-linking role of political parties, the funding of election campaigns and broadly the way that representative institutions work and operate in terms of their conduct of business and engagement with special interests and the general public.

4   See: Christopher Hood, 'Contemporary Management', *Public Policy and Administration*, 10, 2 (1995), pp. 104–17; and Guy Peters, 'What Works? The Antiphons of Administrative Reform', in B. G. Peters and D. J. Savoie (eds.), *Taking Stock: Assessing Public Sector Reforms* (Montreal: McGill-Queen's Press, 1998), pp. 78–107.

5   Peter Carroll and Richard Common (eds.), *Policy Transfer and Learning in Public Policy and Management* (Abingdon: Routledge, 2013).

Notes

6. Ibid.
7. Mark Moore, *Creating Public Value: Strategic Management in Government* (Cambridge, MA: Harvard University Press, 1995).
8. See: Francesca Gains and Gerry Stoker, 'Public Value Management in Parliamentary Democracies: Possibilities and Pitfalls', *Parliamentary Affairs*, 62, 3 (2009), pp. 438–55; Rod Rhodes and John Wanna, 'The Limits to Public Value, or Rescuing Responsible Government from the Platonic Guardians', *Australian Journal of Public Administration*, 66, 4 (2007), pp. 406–21. And for a more positive perspective see: John Alford and Owen Hughes, 'Public Value Pragmatism as the Next Phase of Public Management', *The American Review of Public Administration*, 38, 2 (2008), pp. 130–48.
9. Gains and Stoker, 'Public Value Management in Parliamentary Democracies', p. 2.
10. Mark Moore, *The Public Value Scorecard: A Rejoinder and an Alternative to Strategic Performance Management in Non-Profit Organizations by Robert Kaplan* (Harvard, MA: The Hauser Centre for Nonprofit Organisations, Harvard University, 2003).
11. Annette Boaz and William Solesbury, 'Strategy and Politics: The Example of the United Kingdom', in Thomas Fischer, Gregor Schmitz and Michael Seberich (eds.), *The Strategy of Politics* (Gütersloh Verlag: Bertelsmann Stiftung, 2007), p. 130.
12. Gerry Stoker, 'Public Value Management: A New Narrative for Networked Governance?' *American Review of Public Administration*, 36, 1 (2006), pp. 41–7.
13. See: Wouter van Dooren, Gert Bouckaert and John Halligan, *Performance Management in the Public Sector* (Abingdon: Routledge, 2015).
14. HM Treasury (UK), https://www.gov.uk/government/organisations/hm-treasury [accessed 8 July 2021].
15. Ministry of Social Development (New Zealand), https://www.msd.govt.nz/ [accessed 8 July 2021].
16. See: Karma Ura, Sabina Alkire and Tshoki Zangmo, *GNH and GNH Index* (Bhutan: Centre for Bhutan Studies, 2012), https://opendocs.ids.ac.uk/opendocs/bitstream/handle/20.500.12413/11798/Bhutan-Happiness.pdf?sequence=1 [accessed 8 July 2021].
17. See: Gwyn Bevan and Christopher Hood, 'What's Measured Is What Matters: Targets and Gaming in the English Public Health Care System', *Public Administration*, 84, 3 (2006), pp. 517–38.
18. Felicity Matthews, *Complexity, Fragmentation and Uncertainty: Government Capacity in an Evolving State* (Oxford: Oxford Scholarship On-line, 2013), doi:10.1093/acprof:oso/9780199585991.003.0004
19. Global Council for Happiness and Wellbeing, *Global Happiness and Wellbeing Report 2019*, http://www.happinesscouncil.org/report/2019/ [accessed 8 July 2021].
20. The Community Empowerment (Scotland) Act 2015 means the outcomes approach continues, regardless of the political party or parties in government.
21. New Zealand Treasury, *Embedding Wellbeing in the Public Sector*, https://www.treasury.govt.nz/information-and-services/nz-economy/higher-living-standards/embedding-wellbeing-public-sector [accessed 8 July 2021].
22. See: Kevin Brady, *What Is the State of Public Sector Reporting, and What Is It Saying about Public Sector Management?* (Wellington: Auditor-General, New Zealand, 2009), http://oag.govt.nz/speeches-and-papers/state-of-public-sector-reporting [accessed 8 July 2021].
23. See: Wales Government, *Well-being of Future Generations (Wales) Act 2015: The Essentials* (Cardiff: Wales Government, 2015), https://futuregenerations [accessed 8 July 2021]. These

Notes

goals are as follows: a prosperous Wales, a resilient Wales, a healthier Wales, a more equal Wales, a Wales of cohesive communities, a Wales of vibrant culture and thriving Welsh Language and a globally responsible Wales.

24 See: Slovenian Government, *Slovenian Development Strategy 2030* (Ljubljana: Slovenian Government, 2017), http://www.vlada.si/en/projects/slovenian_development_strategy_2030/; and Scottish Government, *Consultation Process Undertaken to Produce Draft National Outcomes for Scotland* (Edinburgh: Scottish Government, 2018), https://digitalpublications.parliament.scot/ResearchBriefings/Report/2018/4/12/National-Outcomes-Consultation-2018 [accessed 8 July 2021].

25 Scottish Government, *Scotland's National Performance Framework*.

26 *Global Happiness and Wellbeing Report 2019*.

27 *Slovenian Development Strategy 2030*.

28 See: Newsroom, 'Rebuilding from COVID-19 Requires Green Resilient, Inclusive Actions', *Modern Diplomacy*, 3 September 2020, https://moderndiplomacy.eu/2020/09/03/rebuilding-from-covid-19-requires-green-resilient-inclusive-actions/ [accessed 8 July 2021].

29 See: Rod Aldridge and Gerry Stoker, *Advancing a Public Service Ethos* (London: New Local Government Network, 2002).

Chapter 12

1 Jay Blumler and Stephen Coleman, 'After the Crisis, a "New Normal" for Democratic Citizenship?' *Javnost – The Public*, 28, 1 (2021), pp. 3–19.

2 For global Covid-19 data see: John Hopkins University, Coronavirus Resource Centre, https://coronavirus.jhu.edu/ [accessed 8 July 2021].

3 For reflections on this issue see: Wolfgang Merkel, 'Who Governs in Deep Crises? The Case of Germany', *Democratic Theory*, 7, 2 (2020), pp. 1–11.

4 Some democratic theorists are nervous that experts claim too much authority and squeeze out other voices in decision-making. See: Taner Edis, 'A Revolt against Expertise: Pseudoscience, Right-wing Populism, and Post-truth Politics', *Disputatio*, 9, 13 (2020), pp. 1–29.

5 Timothy Besley and Sacha Dray, 'Institutions, Trust and Responsiveness: Patterns of Government and Private Action during the COVID-19 Pandemic', *LSE Public Policy Review*, 1, 10 (2021), pp. 1–11.

6 Francis Fukuyama, 'The Pandemic and Political Order', *Foreign Affairs*, 99, 4 (2020), pp. 26–32.

7 Besley and Dray, 'Institutions, Trust and Responsiveness', p. 1.

8 David Stasavage, 2020, 'Democracy, Autocracy, and Emergency Threats: Lessons for COVID-19 From the Last Thousand Years', *International Organization*, 74, S1 (2020), E1–E17. doi:10.1017/S0020818320000338.

9 Francis Fukuyama, 'The Pandemic and Political Order'.

10 Will Jennings, Viktor Valgardsson, Gerry Stoker, Dan Devine, Jenn Gaskell and Mark Evans, Democracy 2025 Report No 8: *Political Trust and the COVID-19 Crisis – Pushing Populism to the Backburner? A Study of Public Opinion in Australia, Italy, the UK and the USA* (Canberra, IGPA/MoAD/Trustgov, 2020), https://www.democracy2025.gov.au/resources.html [accessed 7 July 2021].

Notes

11 Robert Krimmer, David Duenas-Cid and Iuliia Krivonosova, 'Debate: Safeguarding Democracy during Pandemics: Social Distancing, Postal, or Internet Voting – The Good, the Bad or the Ugly?' *Public Money & Management*, 41, 1 (2021), pp. 8–10, doi: 10.1080/09540962.2020.1766222.

12 See: Will Jennings et al., 'Lack of Trust, Conspiracy Beliefs, and Social Media Use Predict COVID-19 Vaccine Hesitancy', *Vaccines*, 9, 6 (2021), p. 593, https://doi.org/10.3390/vaccines9060593

13 Célia Belin and Giovanna de Maio, 'Democracy after Coronavirus: Five Challenges for the 2020s', *Foreign Policy*, August 2020, https://www.brookings.edu/wp-content/uploads/2020/08/FP_20200817_democracy_covid_belin_demaio.pdf., p. 5.

14 Ibid., p. 7.

15 See: Graham Smith, 'Why Participation and Deliberation Are Vital to the COVID-19 Response',; and 2020c, 'Time for More Democracy Not Less', *thebmjopinion*, 7 January 2021, https://www.involve.org.uk/resources/blog/opinion/why-participation-and-deliberation-are-vital-covid-19-response [accessed 8 July 2021].

16 Ibid.

17 See: Graham Smith and Tim Hughes, *Democracy in a Pandemic: Participation in Response to Crisis* (London: University of Westminster Press, 2021).

18 See: Stephen Reicher and John Drury, 'Pandemic fatigue? How Adherence to COVID-19 Regulations Has Been Misrepresented and Why it Matters', *the bmjopinion*, 7 January 2021, https://blogs.bmj.com/bmj/2021/01/07/pandemic-fatigue-how-adherence-to-covid-19-regulations-has-been-misrepresented-and-why-it-matters/ [accessed 8 July 2021].

19 Arjen Boin, Paul 'T Hart, Eric Stern and Bengst Sundelius, *The Politics of Crisis Management: Public Leadership under Pressure* (Cambridge: Cambridge University Press, 2nd edition, 2016).

20 Ibid., p. 3.

21 Ibid., p. 8.

22 Charles Lindblom, 'The Science of Muddling through', *Public Administration Review*, 19 (1959), pp. 79–88.

23 Ibid., p. 81.

24 For some initial commentary on the muddle inside the UK government during COVID-19 see: Jen Gaskell, Gerry Stoker, Will Jennings and Dan Devine, 'COVID-19 and the Blunders of Our Governments: Long-run System Failings Aggravated by Political Choices', *The Political Quarterly*, 91, 3 (2020), pp. 523–33.

25 Jennings, W., V. Valgardsson, G. Stoker, D. Davine, J. Gaskell, and M. Evans. 'Political Trust and the COVID-19 Crisis: Pushing Populism to the Backburner? A Study of Public Opinion in Australia, Italy, the UK and the USA, TrustGov Project', *Democracy 2025* (2020).

26 For a useful review of the literature see: Marc Hetherington and Michael Nelson, 'Anatomy of a Rally Effect: George W. Bush and the War on Terrorism', *Political Science and Politics*, 36, 1 (2003), pp. 37–42.

27 Ibid., p. 38.

28 John E. Mueller, 'Presidential Popularity from Truman to Johnson', *American Political Science Review*, 64, 1 (1970), pp. 18–34, p. 21.

29 Bethany Albertson and Shana Kushner Gadarian, *Anxious Politics: Democratic Citizenship in a Threatening World* (Cambridge: Cambridge University Press, 2015).

30 Ibid.

Notes

31 Hetherington and Nelson, 'Anatomy of a Rally Effect', p. 38.
32 George Marcus, Russell Neuman and Michael MacKuen, *Affective Intelligence and Political Judgment* (Chicago, IL: The University of Chicago Press, 2000), p. 126.
33 Jennifer Merolla and Elizabeth Zechmeister, *Democracy at Risk: How Terrorist Threats Affect the Public* (Chicago, IL: The University of Chicago Press, 2009), p. 10.
34 See, for example, Human Rights Watch, 'COVID-19 Fueling Anti-Asian Racism and Xenophobia Worldwide', 12 May 2020, https://www.hrw.org/news/2020/05/12/covid-19-fueling-anti-asian-racism-and-xenophobia-worldwide [accessed 8 July 2021].
35 UK House of Commons Health and Social Care, and Science and Technology Committees, Coronavirus: Lessons Learned to Date, 21 September 2021, https://committees.parliament.uk/publications/7496/documents/78687/default/ [accessed 18 November 2021].
36 Mark Evans and Michelle Grattan, 'Health Expertise and COVID-19 – Managing the Fear Factor', *Australian Quarterly*, 92, 2 (2021), pp. 20–8.
37 Eri E. Bertsou and Daniele Caramani, 'People Haven't Had Enough of Experts: Technocratic Attitudes among Citizens in Nine European Democracies', *American Journal of Political Science*, 2020, Online-First, https://doi.org/10.1111/ajps.12554 [accessed 9 July 2021].
38 Figures from Bertsou and Caramani, 'People Haven't Had Enough of Experts'.
39 See also Chapters 9 and 13.
40 See: OECD, Enhancing Public Trust in COVID-19 Vaccination: The Role of Governments, 10 May 2021, https://www.oecd.org/coronavirus/policy-responses/enhancing-public-trust-in-covid-19-vaccination-the-role-of-governments-eae0ec5a/ [accessed 18 November 2021].
41 See, for example, Michael Goodhart, 'Democracy, Globalization, and the Problem of the State', *Polity*, 33, 4 (2021), pp. 527–46.

Chapter 13

1 James Lovelock is quoted in Leo Hickman, 'James Lovelock: Humans Are Too Stupid to Prevent Climate Change', *The Guardian*, Monday 29 March 2010, http://www.theguardian.com/science/2010/mar/29/james-lovelock-climate-change [accessed 9 July 2021].
2 Iñigo González-Ricoy and Axel Gosseries (ed.), *Designing Institutions for Future Generations: An Introduction* (Oxford: Oxford University Press, 2016).
3 See: Alan Jacobs, 'The Politics of When: Redistribution, Investment and Policy Making for the Long Term', *British Journal of Political Science*, 38 (2008), pp. 193–220.
4 Roman Krznaric, *The Good Ancestor: How to Think Long Term in a Short-term World* (New York: Penguin, 2020), p. 8.
5 See: Dennis F. Thompson, 'Representing Future Generations: Political Presentism and Democratic Trusteeship', *Critical Review of International and Political Philosophy*, 13, 1 (2010), pp. 17–37.
6 William Nordhaus, *The Climate Casino* (New Haven: Yale University Press, 2018), p. 187.
7 Potlach is a festival of giving. See: Nordhaus, *The Climate Casino*, p. 188.
8 Michael K. MacKenzie, 'Institutional Design and Sources of Short-Termism', in Iñigo González-Ricoy and Axel Gosseries (ed.), *Designing Institutions for Future Generations: An Introduction* (Oxford: Oxford University Press, 2016), https://www.ies.be/files/Sustainability.pdf [accessed 9 July 2021].

Notes

9 Roman Krznaric, *The Good Ancestor*, p. 13.
10 Ibid., p. 123.
11 Ibid.
12 González-Ricoy and Gosseries (eds.), *Designing Institutions for Future Generations: An Introduction*.
13 Dennis F. Thompson, 'Representing Future Generations', p. 1.
14 See: Alan Jacobs and J. Scott Matthews, 'Why Do Citizens Discount the Future? Public Opinion and the Timing of Policy Consequences', *British Journal of Political Science*, 42 (2012), pp. 903–35.
15 See: AZ Quotes, *Groucho Marx Quotes*, https://www.azquotes.com/author/9562-Groucho_Marx [accessed 9 July 2021].
16 Greta Thunberg addressing the United Nations Climate Change COP24 Conference in Katowice, Poland, 5 December 2018, https://www.youtube.com/watch?v=VFkQSGyeCWg&feature=youtu.be [accessed 9 July 2021].
17 Michael K. MacKenzie, 'Institutional Design and Sources of Short-Termism'.
18 See, for example, Tom Bakker and Claes de Vreese, 'Good News for the Future? Young People, Internet Use, and Political Participation', *Communication Research*, 38, 4 (2011), pp. 451–70.
19 See, for example, Sir David Attenborough's work on climate action. See: https://www.youtube.com/watch?v=2PRJL07-WK0 [accessed 9 July 2021]. Attenborough engages with Thunberg at https://www.bbc.com/news/uk-england-bristol-54541947 [accessed 9 July 2021]. For organized interest groups, see: the work of Greenpeace https://www.greenpeace.org/international/ [accessed 9 July 2021] and Friends of the Earth International https://www.foei.org/ [accessed 9 July 2021].
20 See: Graham Smith, *Can Democracy Safeguard the Future?* (Cambridge: Cambridge Polity Press, 2021): and 'Enhancing the Legitimacy of Offices for Future Generations: The Case for Public Participation', *Political Studies*, 68 (4) (2019), pp. 996–1013.
21 Philip E. Tetlock, *Expert Political Judgment: How Good Is It? How Can We Know?* (New Haven: Princeton University Press, 2009): and *Superforecasting: The Art and Science of Prediction* (New Haven: Princeton University Press, 2015).
22 Michael K. MacKenzie, *Institutional Design and Sources of Short-Termism*.
23 Graham Smith, *Can Democracy Safeguard the Future?*
24 Daniel Kahneman, *Thinking, Fast and Slow* (New York: Macmillan, 2011).
25 Roman Krznaric, *The Good Ancestor*, p. 144.
26 See: Taye Beshi and Ranvinderjit Kaur, 'Public Trust in Local Government: Explaining the Role of Good Governance Practices', *Public Organization Review*, 20 (2020), pp. 337–50.
27 Roman Krznaric, *The Good Ancestor*, p. 124.
28 Graham Smith, *Can Democracy Safeguard the Future?*
29 See: Government of Norway, *The Government Pension Fund* (Oslo: Ministry of Finance), https://www.regjeringen.no/en/topics/the-economy/the-government-pension-fund/id1441/ [accessed 9 July 2021].
30 Michael K. MacKenzie, *Institutional Design and Sources of Short-Termism*.
31 Roman Krznaric, *The Good Ancestor*, p. 120.
32 Barry Quirk, *Re-imagining Government – Public Leadership and Management in Challenging Times* (London: Palgrave Macmillan, 2011).

Notes

33 Ibid., p. 8.
34 Ibid., p. 17.
35 Leslie Pal and R. Kent Weaver (eds.), *The Government Taketh Away: The Politics of Pain in the United States and Canada* (Washington: Georgetown University Press, 2003).
36 See, for example, Claudia Scott and Karen Baehler, *Adding Value to Policy Analysis and Advice* (Sydney: University New South Wales Press, 2010).

Chapter 14

1 Gabriel Almond and Sidney Verba, *The Civic Culture: Political Attitudes and Democracy in Five Nations* (New Jersey: Princeton University Press, 1963), pp. 101–22.
2 Amartya Sen, 'Democracy as a Universal Value', *Journal of Democracy*, 10, 3 (1999), pp. 3–17.
3 Ibid., p. 11.
4 Richard Albert, *Constitutional Amendments: Making, Breaking and Changing Constitutions* (Oxford: Oxford University Press, 2019).
5 Adam D. Vass Gal, *Generational Poverty: An Economic Look at the Culture of the Poor* (Delaware: Vernon Press, 2017).
6 Bridget Brennan, 'Indigenous Leaders Enraged as Advisory Board Referendum Is Rejected by Malcolm Turnbull', *ABC News*, 27 October 2017, https://www.abc.net.au/news/2017-10-27/indigenous-leaders-enraged-by-pms-referendum-rejection/9090762 [accessed 19 July 2021].
7 For two of the best recent accounts see: Megan Davis and Marcia Langton (eds.), *It's Our Country: Indigenous Arguments for Meaningful Constitutional Recognition and Reform* (Melbourne: Melbourne University Press, 2016); and Harry Hobbs, *Indigenous Aspirations and Structural Reform in Australia* (London: Bloomsbury Publishing, 2020). And for the Uluru Statement from the Heart which could form the core vision for a reform process see: Megan Davis, 'Uluru Statement from the Heart: And Remind Them That We Have Robbed Them?' The Henry Parkes Foundation 2018 Oration', in Mark Evans, Michelle Grattan, and Brendan McCaffrie (eds.), *From Turnbull to Morrison: Trust Divide* (Melbourne: Melbourne University Press, 2019), pp. 267–74.
8 See: Harry Hobbs, *Indigenous Aspirations and Structural Reform in Australia*.
9 These issues are explored in Gerry Stoker, 'Embracing Complexity: A Framework for Exploring Governance Resources', *Journal of Chinese Governance*, 4, 2 (2019), pp. 91–107.
10 This section draws on Stoker, 'Embracing Complexity: A Framework for Exploring Governance Resources', Scott E. Page, 'Uncertainty, Difficulty and Complexity', *Journal of Theoretical Politics*, 20, 2 (2008), pp. 115–49; and Scott E. Page, *Diversity and Complexity* (Princeton: Princeton University Press, 2011).
11 John Kania and Mark Kramer, 'Collective Impact', *Stanford Social Innovation Review*, Winter (2011), https://ssir.org/articles/entry/collective_impact [accessed 14 November 2021].
12 Mark Evans, Gerry Stoker and Max Halupka, Democracy 2025 Report No. 5: *How Australian Federal Politicians Would Like to Reform Their Democracy* (Canberra: IGPA/Democracy 2025, 2019), https://www.democracy2025.gov.au/resources.html. [accessed 7 July 2021].
13 Shaun Bowler and Todd Donovan, *The Limits to Electoral Reform* (Oxford: Oxford University Press, 2013).

Notes

14 Ronald van Crombrugge, 'The Derailed Promise of a Participatory Minipublic: The Citizens' Assembly Bill in Flanders', *Journal of Deliberative Democracy*, 16, 2 (2020), pp. 63–72.
15 David Erdos, 'Charter 88 and the Constitutional Reform Movement: A Retrospective', *Parliamentary Affairs*, 62, 4 (2009), pp. 537–51.
16 Evans, Mark, *Charter 88: A Successful Challenge to the British Political Tradition?* (Aldershot: Dartmouth, 1995), pp. xiv–xix.
17 Ibid., pp. 72–85.
18 Ibid., p. 21.
19 Ibid., p. xiv.
20 Democratic Audit of the United Kingdom, https://www.democraticaudit.com/ [accessed 14 November 2021].
21 See: Mark Evans, *Constitution-making and the Labour Party* (London: Palgrave Macmillan, 2004).
22 John Hibbing and Elizabeth Theiss-Morse, *Stealth Democracy* (Cambridge: Cambridge University Press, 2002).
23 For Australia see: Gerry Stoker, Jinjing Li, Max Halupka and Mark Evans, 'Complacent Young Citizens or Cross-generational Solidarity? An Analysis of Australian Attitudes to Democratic Politics', *Australian Journal of Political Science*, 52, 2 (2017), pp. 218–35, p. 230; and Mark Evans, Gerry Stoker and Max Halupka, *How Australian Federal Politicians Would Like to Reform Their Democracy*. For the UK see: Gerry Stoker and Colin Hay, 'Understanding and Challenging Populist Negativity towards Politics: The Perspectives of British Citizens', *Political Studies*, 65, 1 (2017), pp. 4–23, p. 23.

INDEX

Australia
    Citizen's Jury 68
    Covid-19 management 7, 31, 120, 165, 169, 173
    CPI scores 105
    democratic reform 203
    digital innovation 77
    Indigenous Parliament 198
    media performance 143
    NADIA project 79–80
    NPM model 149
    policy officers 122–4, 127, 130
    political culture 42
    public trust 205
    same sex marriage 21
    Tax Office's *My Tax* 77
    technological innovation 73
    Westminster advisory system 123
authoritarian regime 1, 6–7, 30, 111, 164–5, 182
autocracy 7, 46, 180, 182, 191

Blair, Tony 156, 202
Brexit process 15, 21, 47–8, 55–7, 121, 139, 200, 203, 205
budgetary decision-making 53–5, 85
bureaucracy
    citizen treatment 11, 14
    crisis management 168
    expert advice 119, 175
    policy making process 89
    public value management 148, 150–1, 153
    role of IT and digital technology 73

Cambridge Analytica and the Facebook data breach 136
Churchill, Winston 177
citizens
    budgetary decision-making 53–5, 85
    crisis management 168–71
    Decide Madrid (case study) 86
    decision-making process 195–7
    as democratic agents 18–21
    digital media initiatives 71–2
    elected assemblies, role in 100–2
    juries 67–8
    as main democratic agents 18–30
    responsiveness to concerns 181, 195
    role in saving democracy 18–21

Citizens' Assembly (ICA) 59
Civic Culture, The (Almond and Sidney Verba) 193
CLEAR model 103
climate crisis 17, 37, 66–7, 104, 111, 169, 176, 179–80, 182–4, 192
collaborative governance
    best practice 128
    experts' role 127–30
Constitutional Convention (ICC) 59
Conte, Giuseppe 168, 173
Covid-19 72, 81
    citizen behaviour 7, 28
    climate crisis, comparison to 66
    digital intervention, examples 72, 81, 87
    perceptions of political leadership 174
crisis management
    citizens behaviour 168–71
    coping mechanism 177
    Covid-19 163–6
    expert's role 172–5
    government behaviour 167–8
    implementation process 168
    learning experiences 177–8
    quality of democracy during 175–6
    sense of democracy during 2
Crosby, Ned 67

deliberative democracy
    autonomy and equality of participants 69
    citizens' panels 64
    decision-making process 61, 69
    definition 59
    deliberative mapping 64–5
    design and facilitation 69
    engagement methods 69
    European Citizen's Consultation 62–3
    formal public space 69
    four key features 60–1
    participatory governance systems *versus* 59–61
    policy directions 66
    policy, programme and service design 62–3
    principles of engagement 69
    public sector decisions 70
    quality of participation 70
    strategic decision-making 62
    termination of pregnancy, example 60–1
    University of Michigan consensus dialogue 65

Index

democracy. See also specific forms
    areas of failure in long-term policy-making 179–80
    citizens and politicians as main agents 18–30
    definition 117
    European view 29–30
    future trends 179–92
    long term consequences 180–1, 189–92
    Nordhaus model 180–2
    principles of justice 179
    protective power of 193–4
    reform strategy 16, 27–9, 180, 184–9, 201–4
    regular and competitive elections, need for 184
    short-termism 180–4
    variety of reforms option 184–9
democratic governance
    collaborative practice 118–20, 127–9
    combating truth decay 130
    demand-side barriers 122–4
    evidence-based practice 126–7, 131–2
    four main pathways 126
    integrity reform 105–6
    market institutions, interaction with 108–9
    national integrity systems 106–8
    output legitimacy 117–18
    participatory governance systems 129–30
    pathways assessment 130–1
    public attitude 121
    supply-side barriers 122
    types of expertise 118–20
    Wiltshire criteria 125
Denmark
    Danish Board of Technology Foundation (DBTF) 64
    EGDI index 73
    media power 142
    political culture 42
    use of technology 74, 77
design-led digital democracy
    citizen-centred design 74, 82
    civic action 87–8
    co-design 75–6
    communication channels 87
    co-production of programmes and services 81
    design principles 86
    digital innovation 77
    digital party, concept 82–3
    four models 73
    functional technology 86
    gamification 82–3
    intuitive content 87
    Online Forums and Structured Templates 84
    Open Space Technology 84
    participatory governance 71, 84–6
    state-directed governance 72

Digital Era Governance 1 (DEG1) 75, 77
    use of technology 73–4
Digital Era Governance 2 (DEG2) 74
    artificial intelligence 79
    Big Data 79–80
    Digital 2.0 technologies 74
    four promising streams 79
    Robotic process automation (RPA) 79
digital innovation
    Anglophone countries 77
    City Council of Madrid's 'Decide Madrid' 85
    government exemplars 77
digital media 82, 87. See also digital innovation
    citizen-led initiatives 71–2
Digital Native Governance (DNG) 74
direct democracy
    controversies 47–8
    democratic symmetry 57
    localism strategies 49–51, 53
    participatory budgeting 53–5
    policy instrument 46
    prudential criteria 55–7
    right to recall local members 51–2
    voting in referenda 46–7

eBird database 81
Edelman Trust barometer 136, 138
elected assemblies
    ability and diversity issues 91–3
    citizens role of campaigning and scrutiny 100–2
    evaluation of democratic performance 103
    gender equality 91–2
    lack of public confidence 91
    linkage role 99–100
    parliament and citizen, role in 98–9
    policy development 102–3
    reforms 104
    solutions for lack of diversity 95–8
    structural and agency factors 93–5
elites 17–18, 20, 25, 45, 61, 95, 120, 136–7, 147, 150, 166, 170–1, 194, 201–3
evidence-based practice. See also expertise/expert
    strategic and innovative policy system 131
    supply and demand-side barriers 120–4
    Wiltshire criteria 125
expertise/expert
    collaborative role 127–9
    combatting 'truth decay' 130
    crisis management 172–5
    pathways to progress 126, 130–2
    public attitude 121
    role in participatory governance systems 129–30
    types 118–21

Index

France 29
    citizens assemblies 66–7
    Covid-19 66
    digital party 82
    online climate assemblies 88

Germany
    attitude to politics 193
    Covid-19 management 81
    in 1930s and 1940s 18

innovation. *See also* Digital Era Governance 1 (DEG1); Digital Era Governance 2 (DEG2)
    citizen-centric digital innovation 77
    democratic governance 3, 5, 18, 91, 114, 153, 200–1, 203, 205
    digital democracy 2
    experts' role 101, 175
    policy 75
    public engagement 69
integrity reform
    behavioural challenges 111–15
    evaluation 116
    Nolan principles 115
    policy instruments 116
Intergenerational Solidarity Index (ISI) 182
Ireland
    constitutional reform proposals 59
    deliberative mini-publics 66
    pregnancy termination/abortion 59, 61
Italy
    attitude to politics 193
    Covid-19 management 165, 168
    digital party 82
    direct democracy 46
    Five Star Movement 82–3

Johnson, Boris 169, 172–4

knowledge institutions 53, 80, 119, 121–2, 126

liberal democracy 5, 65, 120
    adaptive capacity 194
    media system 133–5, 143
    public service 160
localism 35, 45
    consultative and binding referenda 53
    direct democracy 49–51
    election commitments 51–2

Macron, Emmanuel 66–7
Massively Open Online Social Experiments ('MOOSEs') 81
media
    accountability 143
    business models 137–8
    conservative critics 139–40
    decline of democratic values 136–7
    demand-side interventions 142–3
    democratic role 143–4
    in digital era 137
    Edward Snowden Leaks 135
    general decline in standards 136–7
    governments distrust 136
    power complexities 140
    reader distrust 138–9
    role in liberal democracy 133–5
    supply-side interventions 141–2
    traditional and new 135–6
Mexico
    attitude to politics 42, 193
    democratic performance 2
    participatory governance systems 41–2
Morrison, Scott 169, 173, 182

new public management (NPM) 72–3, 107, 148, 150–1, 154
New Zealand 7
    digital-first service delivery 78
    EGDI index 73
    gamification 83
    Integrated Data Infrastructure 77
    performance management 156
    policy capability 122, 130
    Public Finance Act 1989 157
    public value management 149
    Westminster advisory system 123
Nolan principles 115–16
Nordhaus model 180–1

OECD 176
    on integrity measures 106–8, 112–13

participatory budgeting 53–5
participatory governance systems
    crowdsourcing 205
    deliberative democracy *versus* 59–61
    democratic reforms 36, 129–30
    design-led digital democracy 71, 84–6
    engagement methods 38–42
    expertise/expert 129–30
    ideal practice 41
    key feature 35
    Mexico City example 41
    multi-dimensional problems and solutions 37–8
    public services 157–9
    quality participation 42–3
    role of direct democracy 40
    technological advances, role in 36–7

Index

'top-down' and 'bottom-up' strategies 198
  value of participation 36
  well-being outcomes 157–9
policy interventions
  integrity reforms 116
  long, and short term goal 180–92
  service quality 197–8
political system
  core features 200–1, 203
  corruption, impact on 105
  crisis management 167, 177
  decision-making framework 189
  linkage role 99, 110
  long-term action 179, 182
  partisan loyalties 20–1
  public accountability 93
  quality and strength of inputs 14, 199–201
  representative democracies, challenges 9, 25
  resource distribution 108
  roles of elected assembles 98
  vote counts 28
politicians
  list of characteristics 26
  professionalization 109–11
  role in saving democracy 22–6
post-Covid-19 67, 86, 150, 159, 176, 205
public management 72, 150
public power, ethical dilemmas 108
public services
  authentic practice 153, 160–2
  evaluation criteria 116, 161–2
  forms of mandates 153–5
  idea of stewardship 183, 191, 198
  management toolkit 148–9
  new values and practices 159–60
  NPM reforms 149–51
  participatory governance systems 157–9
  professional and political resistance 151–3
  public involvement in decision-making 152
  social purpose 155
  strategic outcomes 155–7
  trust between government and citizen 147–8
  value creation 159–62
public trust 3, 42, 54, 67, 70, 74, 91, 105, 107, 110, 147
  civil liberties and 202
  during crisis management 176
  in journalists/media 136–7, 142
  policy concerns 183, 193
public value
  authentic commitments 147
  creation 155–6
  long-term thinking 189
  pathways to progress 126

public service experience 147–62
  strategic vision 157

representative democracy. *See also* crisis management
  challenges 92
  direct democracy comparison with 45–6, 51, 53
  dominant conceptions 41
  ethical dilemmas 108, 115
  legitimacy 16
  old power institution 15–16
  parliaments and assemblies 91
  quality 37
  system theory 7–10

Sen, Amartya 193
Singapore
  Covid-19 management 81
  EGDI index 73
  eGov2015 (case study) 78
  use of technology 74, 77
Spain
  digital party 82
  Participa 83
Switzerland 2, 46, 48
  long term policy 188
  political culture 42

Transparency International, *2019 Corruption Perceptions Index* 105
Trudeau, Justin 169
Trump, Donald 15, 46, 93, 105
trust. *See* public trust

UK
  anti-intellectualism 121
  Black and ethnic minority in parliament 92
  Brexit process 55–6
  Charter 88 202–3
  citizens assemblies 62, 103
  Climate Assembly 67
  Covid-19 66
  e-Petitions 101
  'GM Nation' Public Debate 84
  manual workers 91–2
  Outreach and the National Assembly for Wales 100
  Outreach and the Scottish parliament 102
  public trust 205
  Recall of MPs Act 2015 52
  social care reforms 103
UNESCO 133
US government

242

Index

Apps for America 81
Apps for Democracy 81
Big Data for decision making 79–80
citizens' juries 67
Data.gov catalogue 80–1
Foundations for Evidence Based Policymaking Act 80
medical marijuana measures 46–7
National Issues Forums 84

Open Government Data Act 80–1
participatory budgets 62
University of Michigan consensus dialogue 65

Volunteer Science Inc. 81

Wellcome Global Monitor 121
Wiltshire criteria 125
World Values Survey (WVS) 29